Matt Kindt Tyler Jenkins Hilary Jenkins

BLACK BADGE™

Volume One

BOOM! STUDIOS

BLACK BADGE Volume One, May 2019. Published by BOOM! Studios, a division of Boom Entertainment, Inc. Black Badge is ™ & © 2019 Matt Kindt & Tyler Jenkins. Originally published in single magazine form as BLACK BADGE No. 1-4. ™ & © 2018 Matt Kindt & Tyler Jenkins. All rights reserved. BOOM! Studios™ and the BOOM! Studios logo are trademarks of Boom Entertainment, Inc., registered in various countries and categories. All characters, events, and institutions depicted herein are fictional. Any similarity between any of the names, characters, persons, events, and/or institutions in this publication to actual names, characters, and persons, whether living or dead, events, and/or institutions is unintended and purely coincidental. BOOM! Studios does not read or accept unsolicited submissions of ideas, stories, or artwork.

BOOM! Studios, 5670 Wilshire Boulevard, Suite 400, Los Angeles, CA, 90036-5679. Printed in China. First Printing.

ISBN: 978-1-68415-353-4, eISBN: 978-1-64144-336-4

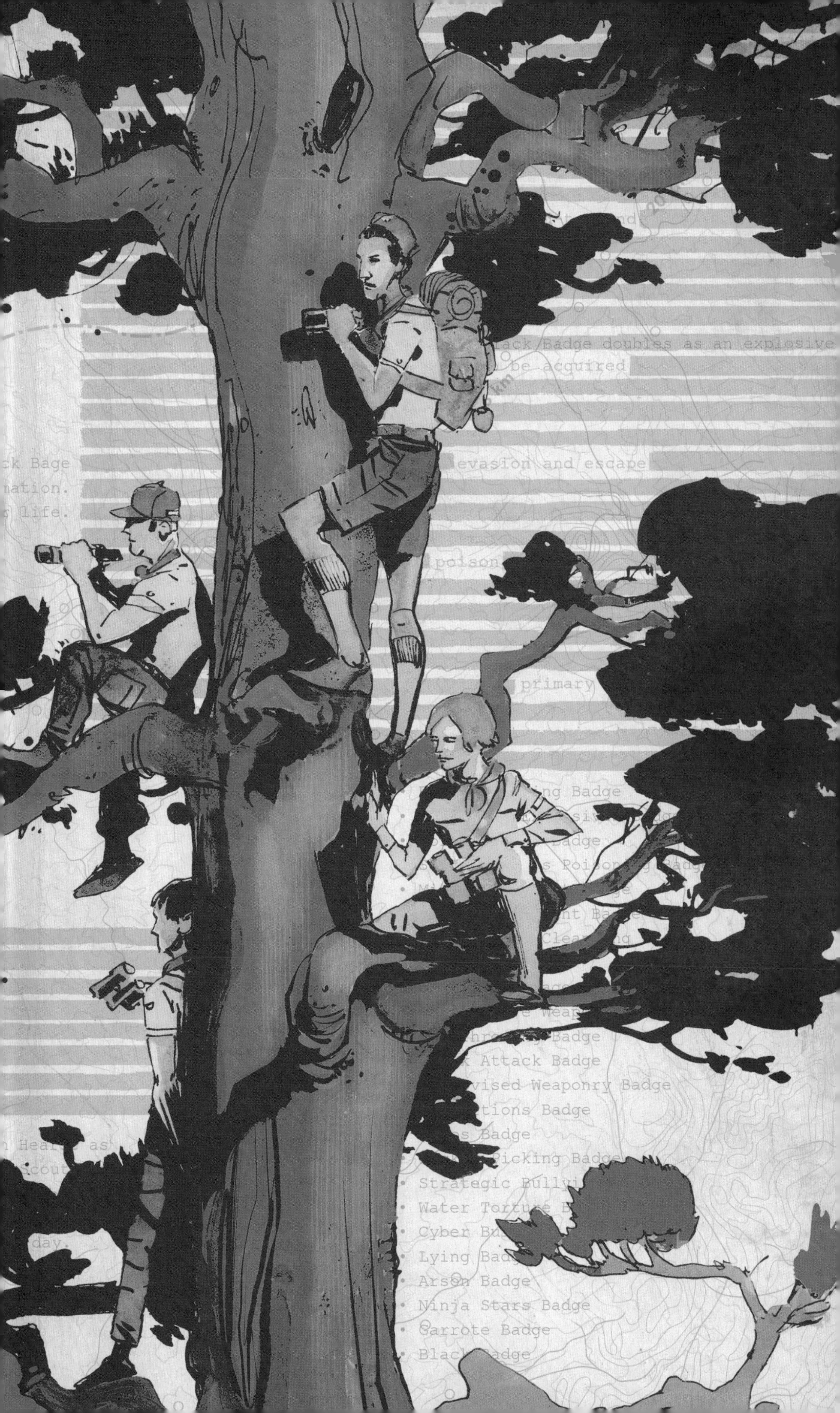

Badge doubles as an explosive
be acquired
evasion and escape
poison
primary
Attack Badge
Weaponry Badge
Strategic
Water
Lying
Arson Badge
Ninja Stars Badge
Garrote Badge

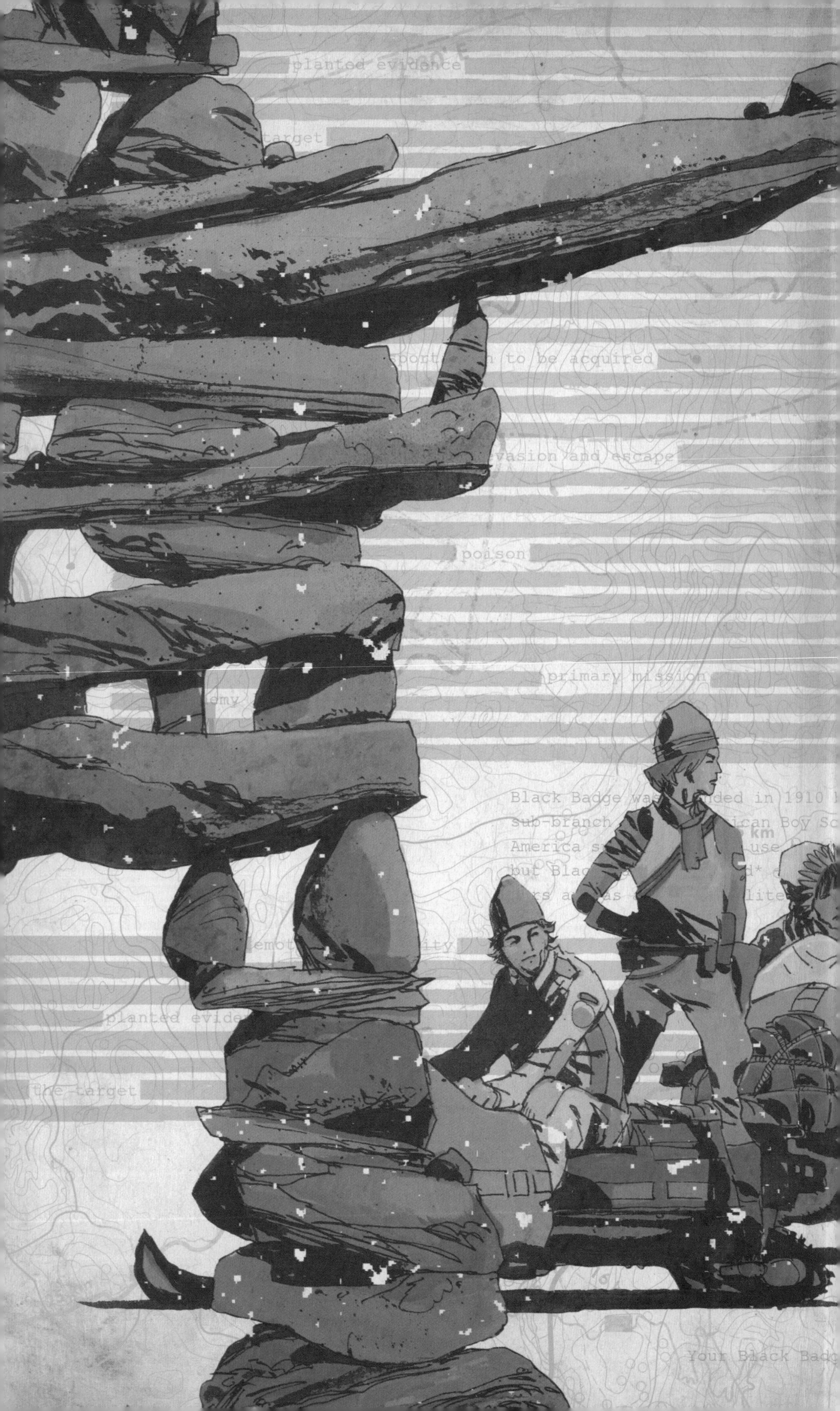
planted evidence
target
to be acquired
vasion and escape
poison
primary mission
Black Badge wa
sub-branch
America
the target

Household Explosives Badge
Forest Fires Badge
Surreptitious Poisoning Badge
d Management Badge
Inducement Badge
ime Scene Cleansing Badge
Wet Work Badge
Weapon Sabotage Badge
Alternative Weaponry Badge
Axe Throwing Badge
Shark Attack Badge
Improvised Weaponry Badge
Demolitions Badge
Traps Badge
Pocket Picking Badge
Strategic Bullying Badge
Water Torture Badge
Cyber Bullying Badge
Lying Badge
Arson Badge
Ninja Stars Badge
Garrote Badge
Black Badge

How you received you Black Bage
is privileged information.
Guard it with your life.

BLACK BADGE™

Created by
Matt Kindt + Tyler Jenkins

Written by
Matt Kindt

Illustrated by
Tyler Jenkins

with Colors by
Hilary Jenkins

Lettered by
Jim Campbell

Cover by
Matt Kindt

Designer
Scott Newman

Editor
Eric Harburn

Special Thanks
Matthew Levine

n Randolph Hearst as
er the Boy Scouts of
e ABS was disbanded

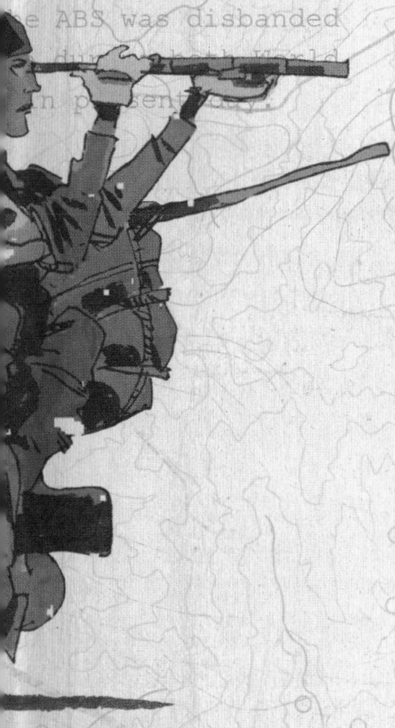

s as an explosive throwing star.

Black Badge was founded in 1910 by William Randolph Hea
sub-branch of the American Boy Scouts. After the Boy Sco
America sued Hearst for use of the name, the ABS was dis
but Black Badge remained* - becoming active during both
Wars and as a sort of elite scouting club in present da

Chapter One

[redacted] emotional stability [redacted] initiation [redacted] North Korea [redacted] extraction [redacted] trespassers will be killed [redacted] evasion and escape [redacted] frying pan [redacted] enemy lines [redacted]

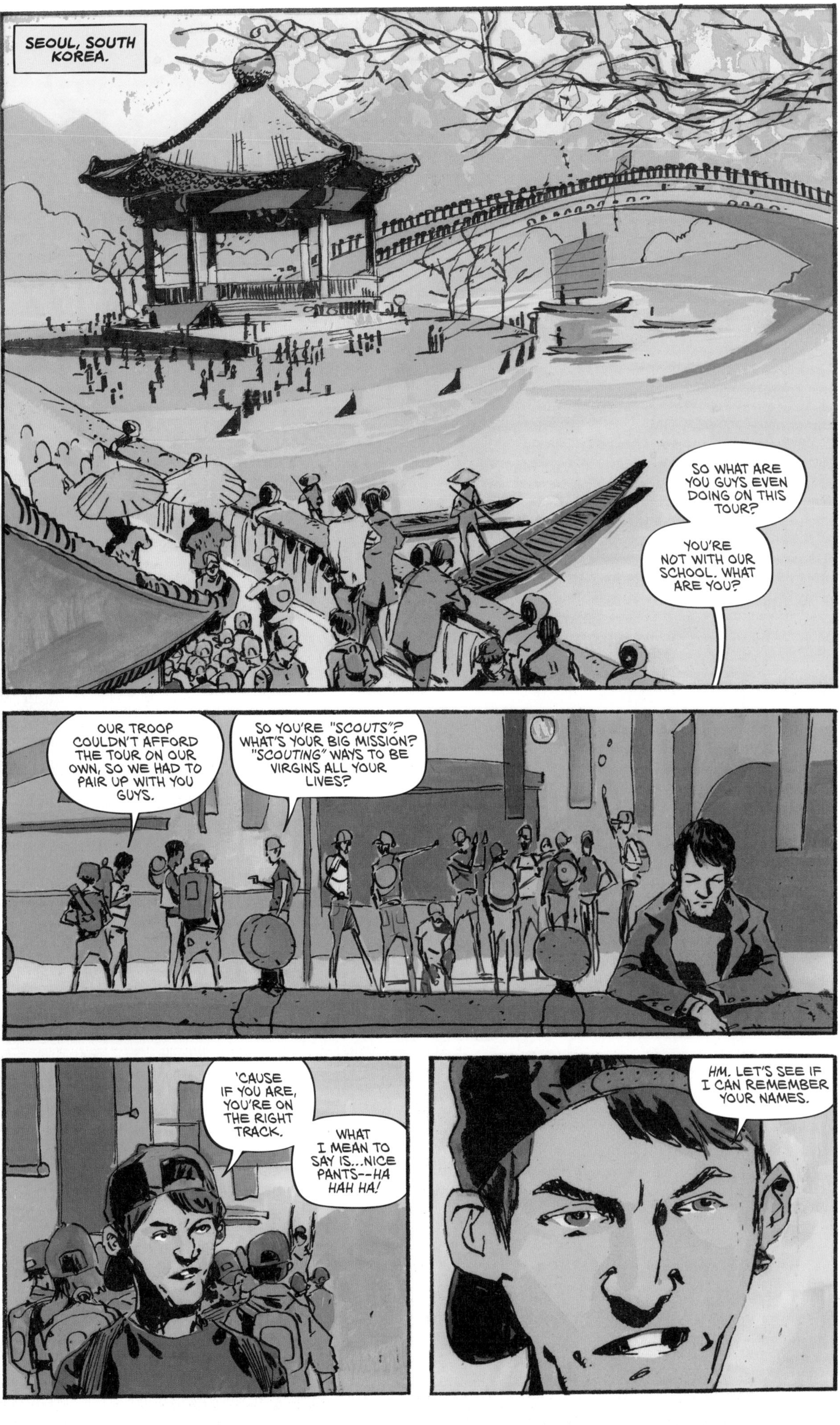

SEOUL, SOUTH KOREA.
SO WHAT ARE YOU GUYS EVEN DOING ON THIS TOUR?
YOU'RE NOT WITH OUR SCHOOL. WHAT ARE YOU?
OUR TROOP COULDN'T AFFORD THE TOUR ON OUR OWN, SO WE HAD TO PAIR UP WITH YOU GUYS.
SO YOU'RE "SCOUTS"? WHAT'S YOUR BIG MISSION? "SCOUTING" WAYS TO BE VIRGINS ALL YOUR LIVES?
'CAUSE IF YOU ARE, YOU'RE ON THE RIGHT TRACK.
WHAT I MEAN TO SAY IS...NICE PANTS--HA HAH HA!
HM. LET'S SEE IF I CAN REMEMBER YOUR NAMES.

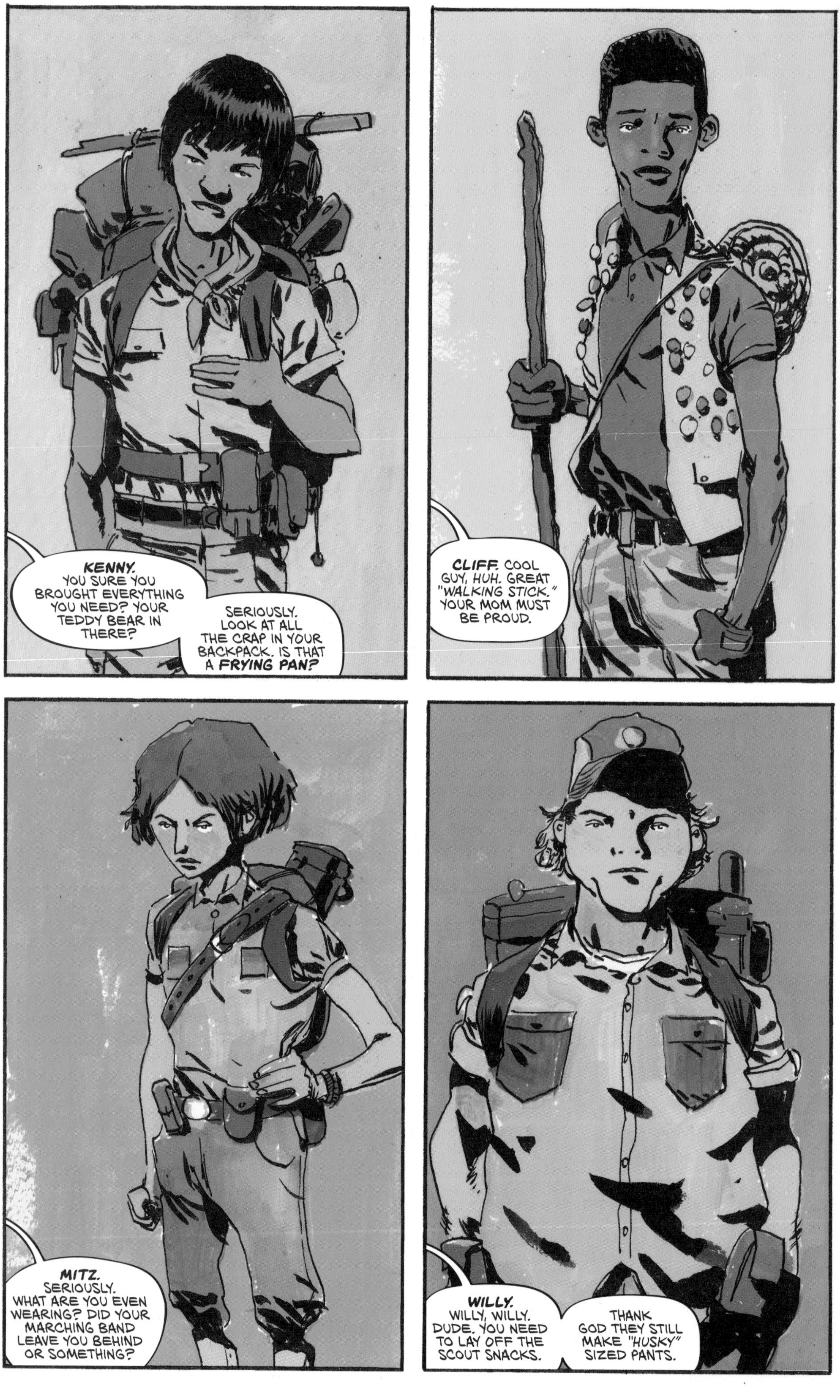
KENNY. YOU SURE YOU BROUGHT EVERYTHING YOU NEED? YOUR TEDDY BEAR IN THERE?
SERIOUSLY. LOOK AT ALL THE CRAP IN YOUR BACKPACK. IS THAT A FRYING PAN?
CLIFF. COOL GUY, HUH. GREAT "WALKING STICK." YOUR MOM MUST BE PROUD.
MITZ. SERIOUSLY. WHAT ARE YOU EVEN WEARING? DID YOUR MARCHING BAND LEAVE YOU BEHIND OR SOMETHING?
WILLY. WILLY, WILLY. DUDE. YOU NEED TO LAY OFF THE SCOUT SNACKS.
THANK GOD THEY STILL MAKE "HUSKY" SIZED PANTS.

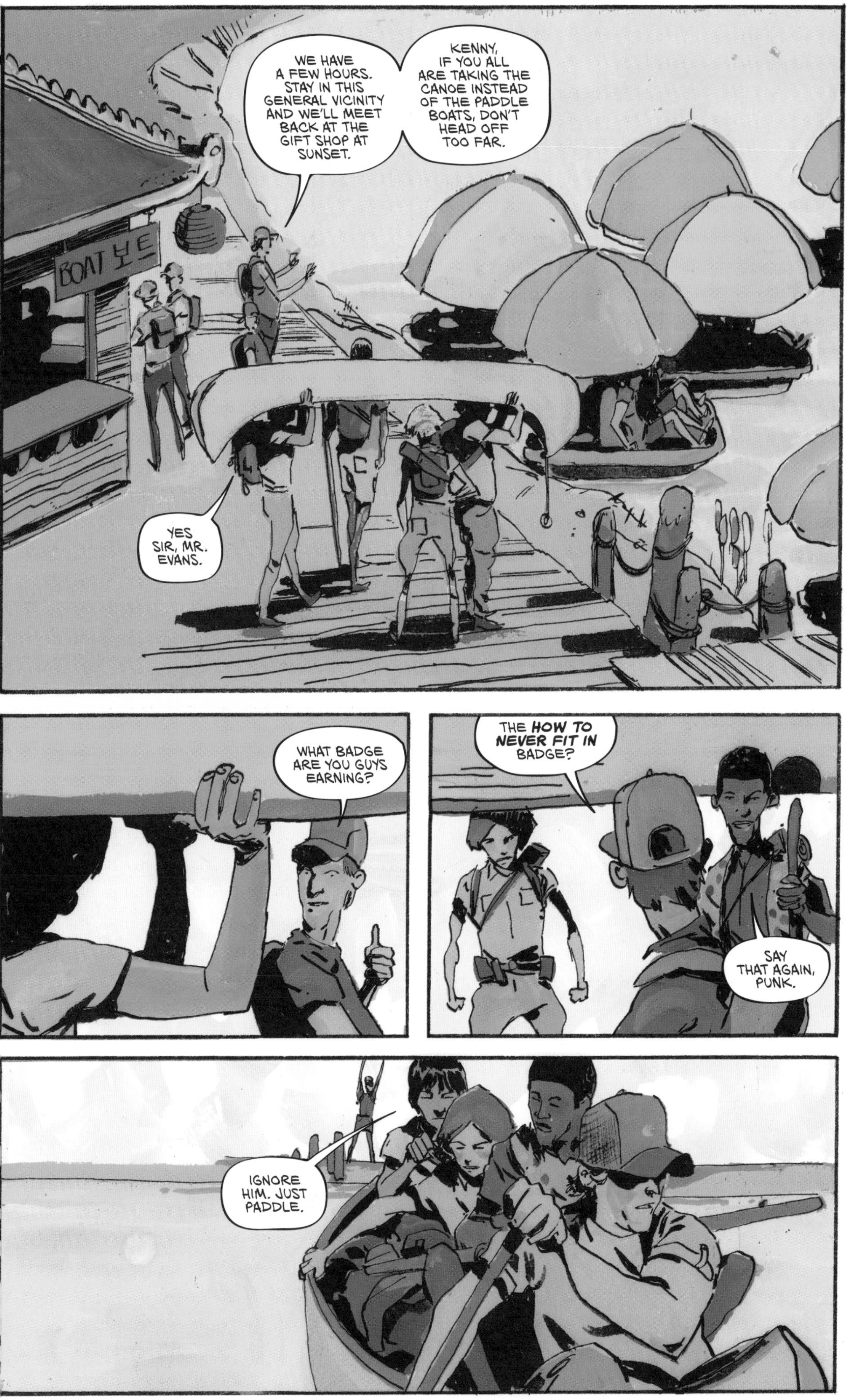
WE HAVE A FEW HOURS. STAY IN THIS GENERAL VICINITY AND WE'LL MEET BACK AT THE GIFT SHOP AT SUNSET.
KENNY, IF YOU ALL ARE TAKING THE CANOE INSTEAD OF THE PADDLE BOATS, DON'T HEAD OFF TOO FAR.
BOAT 보트
YES SIR, MR. EVANS.
WHAT BADGE ARE YOU GUYS EARNING?
THE ***HOW TO NEVER FIT IN*** BADGE?
SAY THAT AGAIN, PUNK.
IGNORE HIM. JUST PADDLE.

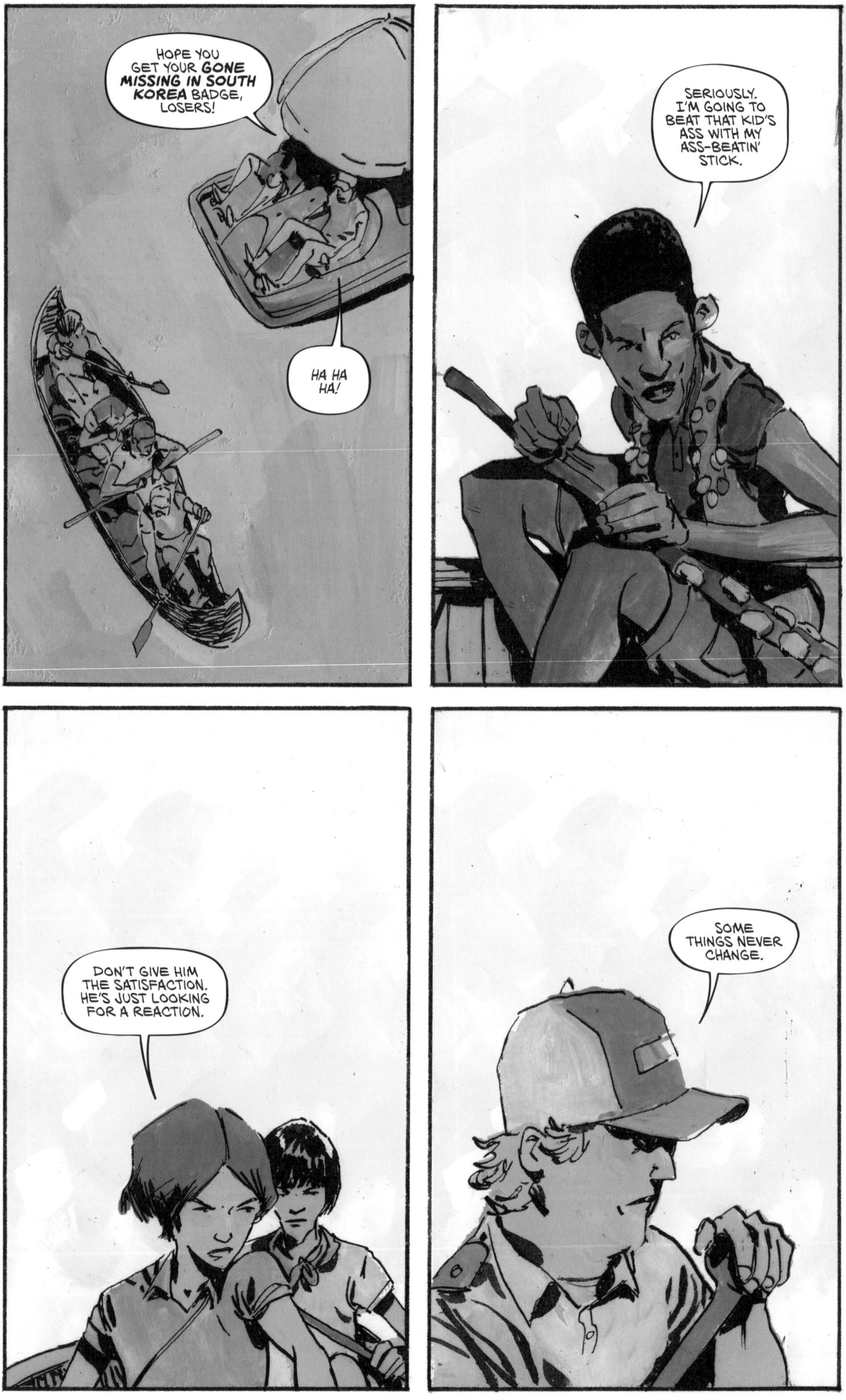
HOPE YOU GET YOUR GONE MISSING IN SOUTH KOREA BADGE, LOSERS!
HA HA HA!
SERIOUSLY. I'M GOING TO BEAT THAT KID'S ASS WITH MY ASS-BEATIN' STICK.
DON'T GIVE HIM THE SATISFACTION. HE'S JUST LOOKING FOR A REACTION.
SOME THINGS NEVER CHANGE.

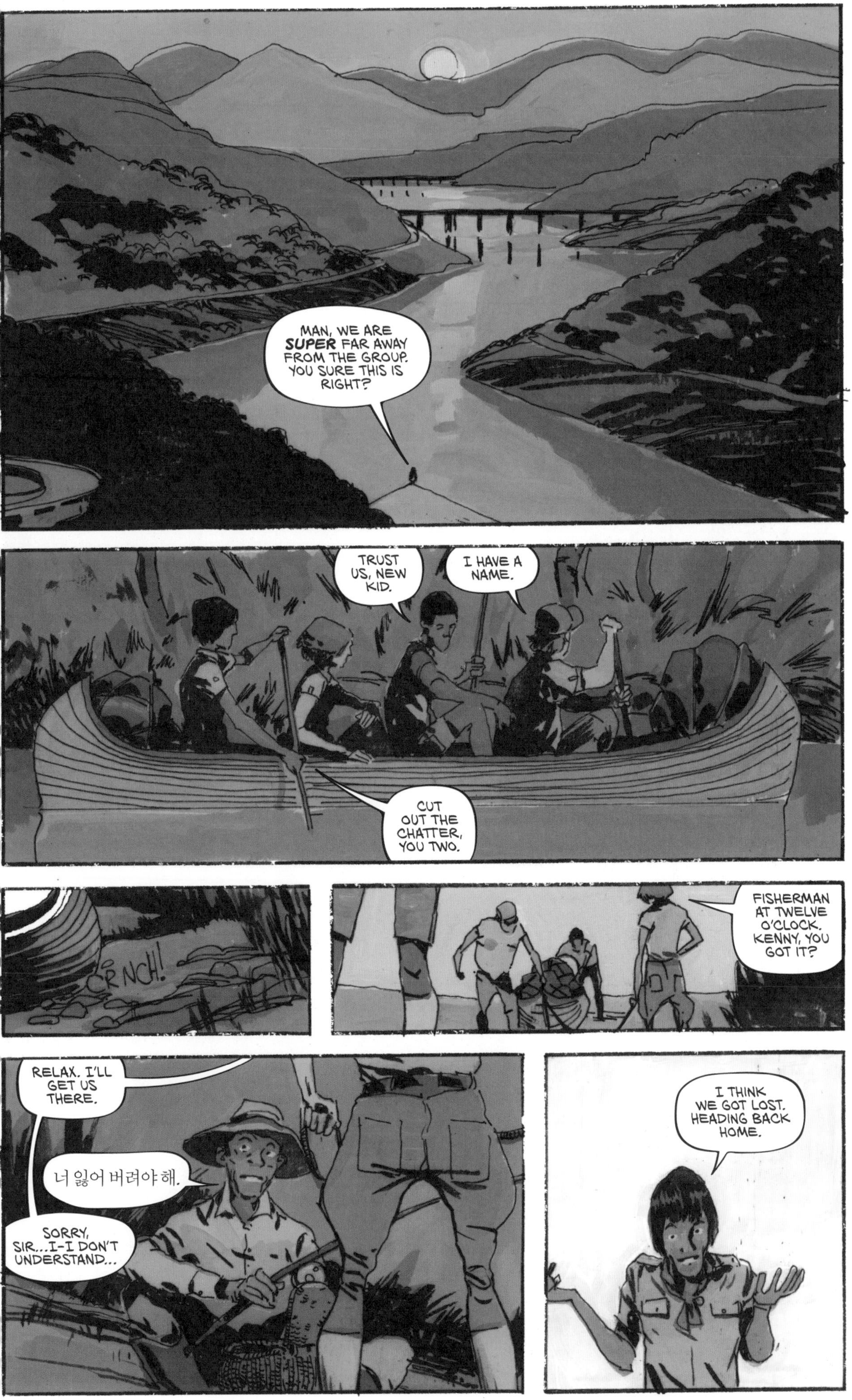
MAN, WE ARE **SUPER** FAR AWAY FROM THE GROUP. YOU SURE THIS IS RIGHT?
TRUST US, NEW KID.
I HAVE A NAME.
CUT OUT THE CHATTER, YOU TWO.
CRNCH!
FISHERMAN AT TWELVE O'CLOCK. KENNY, YOU GOT IT?
RELAX. I'LL GET US THERE.
너 잃어 버려야 해.
SORRY, SIR...I-I DON'T UNDERSTAND...
I THINK WE GOT LOST. HEADING BACK HOME.

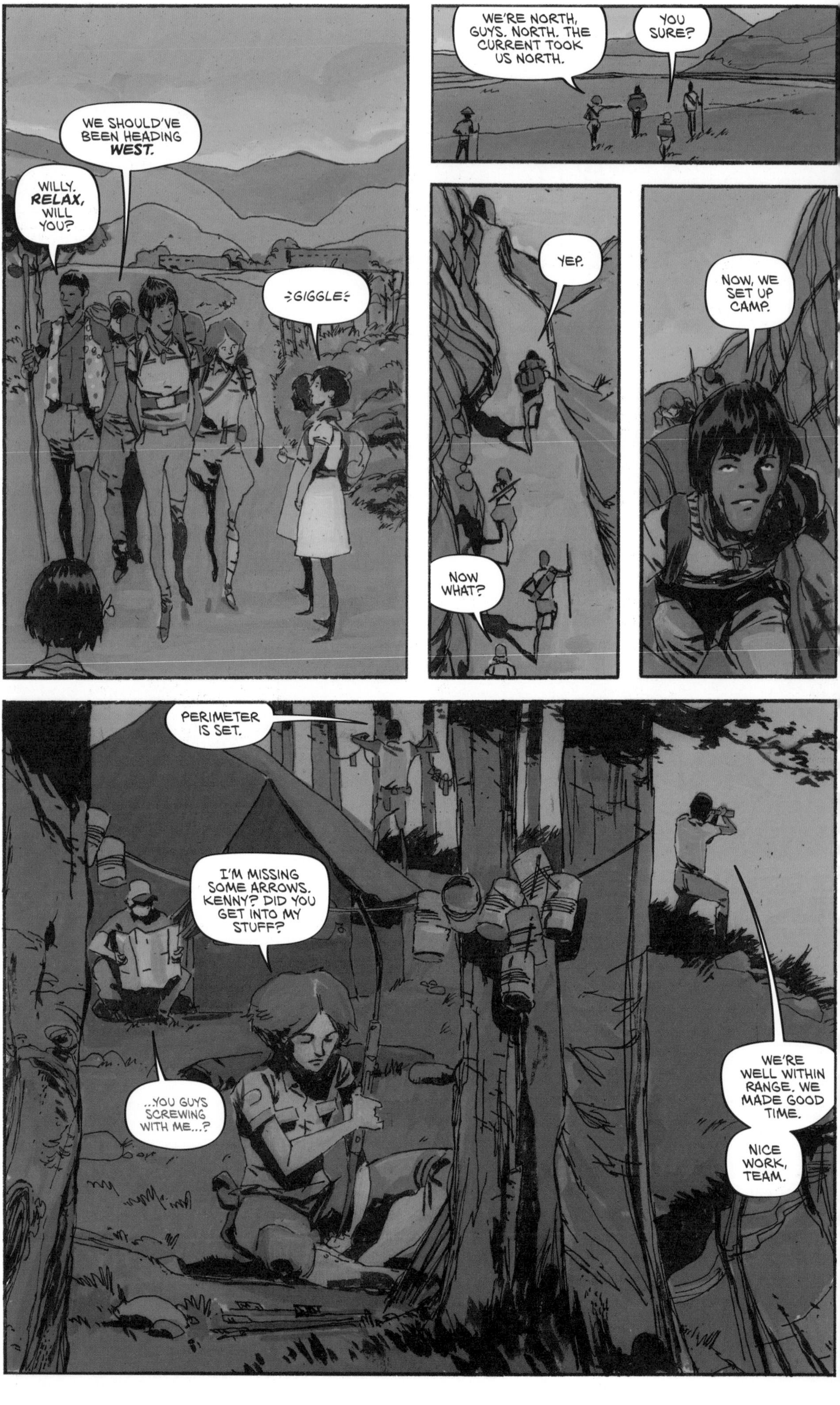

WE SHOULD'VE BEEN HEADING **WEST.**
WILLY. **RELAX,** WILL YOU?
=GIGGLE=
WE'RE NORTH, GUYS. NORTH. THE CURRENT TOOK US NORTH.
YOU SURE?
YEP.
NOW WHAT?
NOW, WE SET UP CAMP.
PERIMETER IS SET.
I'M MISSING SOME ARROWS. KENNY? DID YOU GET INTO MY STUFF?
...YOU GUYS SCREWING WITH ME...?
WE'RE WELL WITHIN RANGE. WE MADE GOOD TIME.
NICE WORK, TEAM.

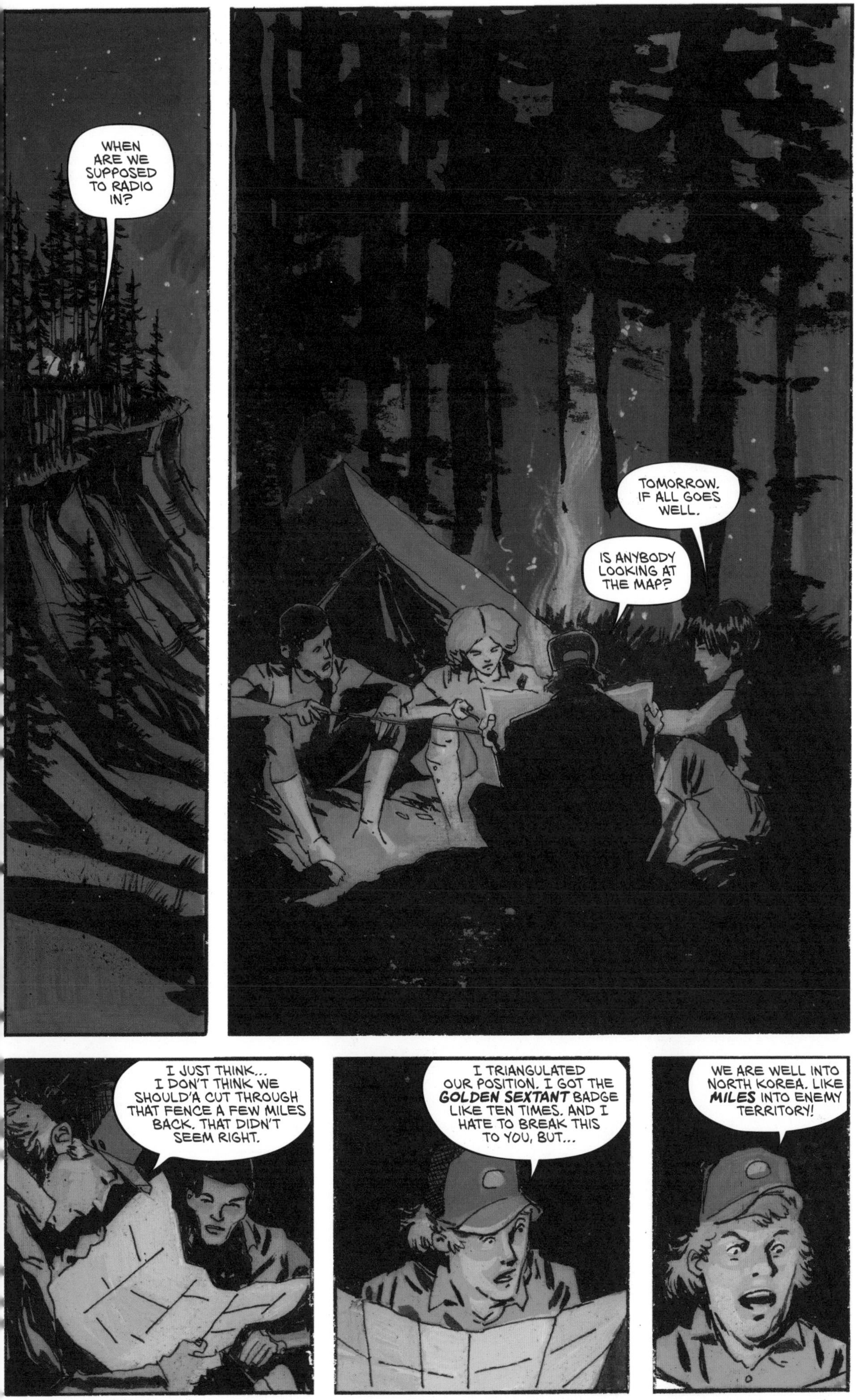
WHEN ARE WE SUPPOSED TO RADIO IN?
TOMORROW. IF ALL GOES WELL.
IS ANYBODY LOOKING AT THE MAP?
I JUST THINK... I DON'T THINK WE SHOULD'A CUT THROUGH THAT FENCE A FEW MILES BACK. THAT DIDN'T SEEM RIGHT.
I TRIANGULATED OUR POSITION. I GOT THE GOLDEN SEXTANT BADGE LIKE TEN TIMES. AND I HATE TO BREAK THIS TO YOU, BUT...
WE ARE WELL INTO NORTH KOREA. LIKE MILES INTO ENEMY TERRITORY!

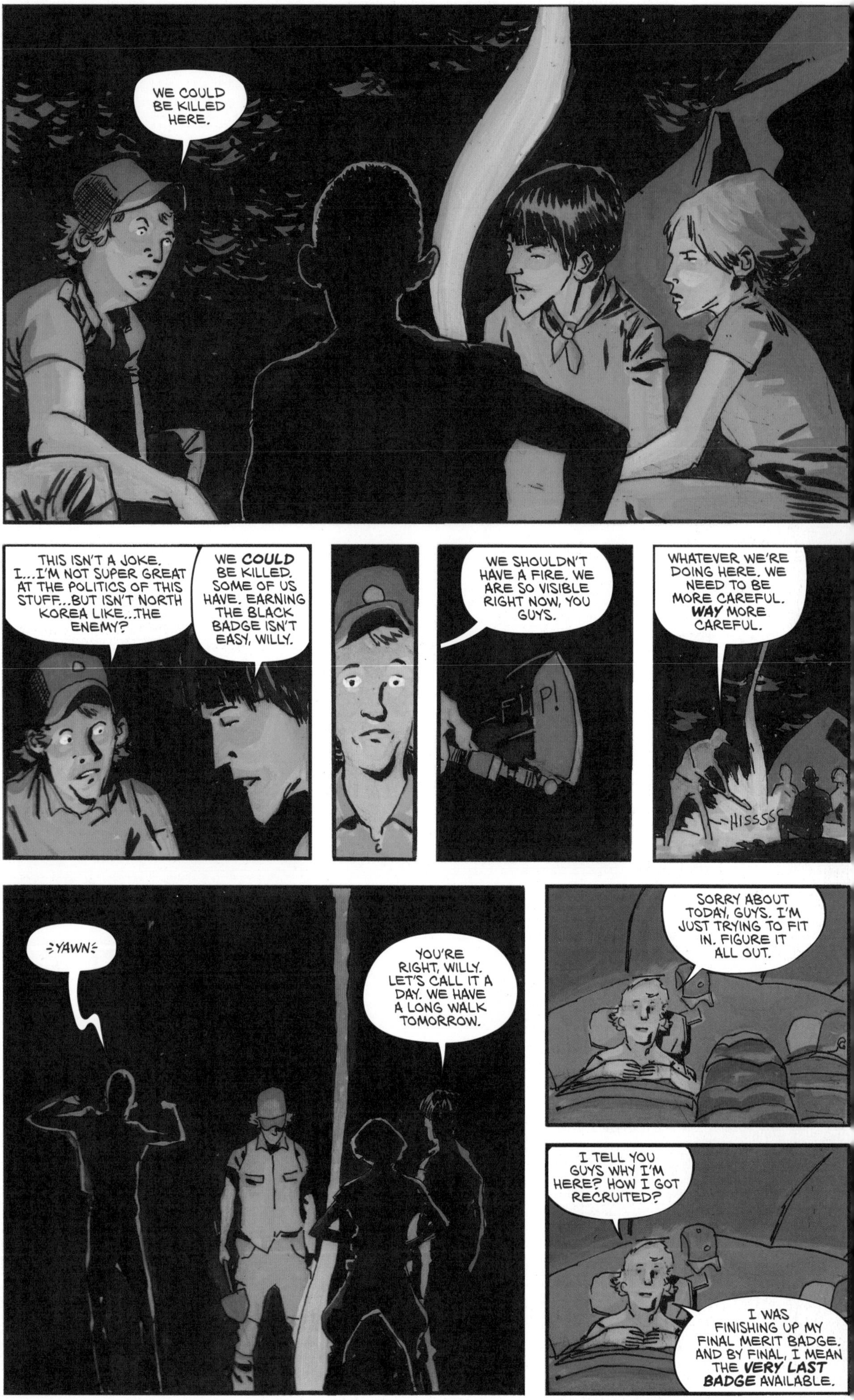
WE COULD BE KILLED HERE.
THIS ISN'T A JOKE. I...I'M NOT SUPER GREAT AT THE POLITICS OF THIS STUFF...BUT ISN'T NORTH KOREA LIKE...THE ENEMY?
WE COULD BE KILLED. SOME OF US HAVE. EARNING THE BLACK BADGE ISN'T EASY, WILLY.
WE SHOULDN'T HAVE A FIRE. WE ARE SO VISIBLE RIGHT NOW, YOU GUYS.
FLIP!
WHATEVER WE'RE DOING HERE. WE NEED TO BE MORE CAREFUL. WAY MORE CAREFUL.
HISSSSS
YAWN
YOU'RE RIGHT, WILLY. LET'S CALL IT A DAY. WE HAVE A LONG WALK TOMORROW.
SORRY ABOUT TODAY, GUYS. I'M JUST TRYING TO FIT IN. FIGURE IT ALL OUT.
I TELL YOU GUYS WHY I'M HERE? HOW I GOT RECRUITED?
I WAS FINISHING UP MY FINAL MERIT BADGE. AND BY FINAL, I MEAN THE VERY LAST BADGE AVAILABLE.

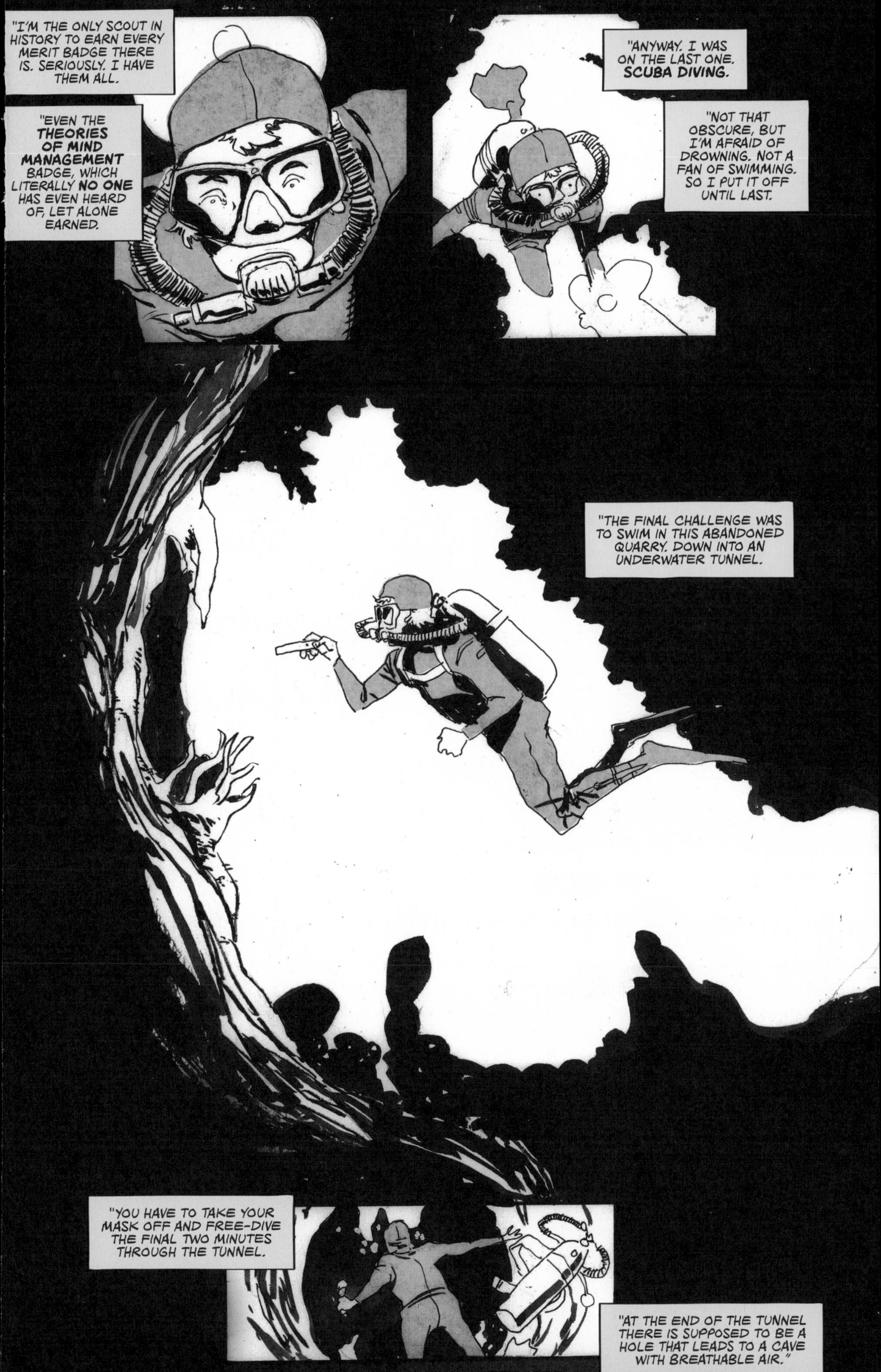
"I'M THE ONLY SCOUT IN HISTORY TO EARN EVERY MERIT BADGE THERE IS. SERIOUSLY. I HAVE THEM ALL.
"EVEN THE **THEORIES OF MIND MANAGEMENT** BADGE, WHICH LITERALLY **NO ONE** HAS EVEN HEARD OF, LET ALONE EARNED.
"ANYWAY. I WAS ON THE LAST ONE. **SCUBA DIVING.**
"NOT THAT OBSCURE, BUT I'M AFRAID OF DROWNING. NOT A FAN OF SWIMMING. SO I PUT IT OFF UNTIL LAST.
"THE FINAL CHALLENGE WAS TO SWIM IN THIS ABANDONED QUARRY. DOWN INTO AN UNDERWATER TUNNEL.
"YOU HAVE TO TAKE YOUR MASK OFF AND FREE-DIVE THE FINAL TWO MINUTES THROUGH THE TUNNEL.
"AT THE END OF THE TUNNEL THERE IS SUPPOSED TO BE A HOLE THAT LEADS TO A CAVE WITH BREATHABLE AIR."

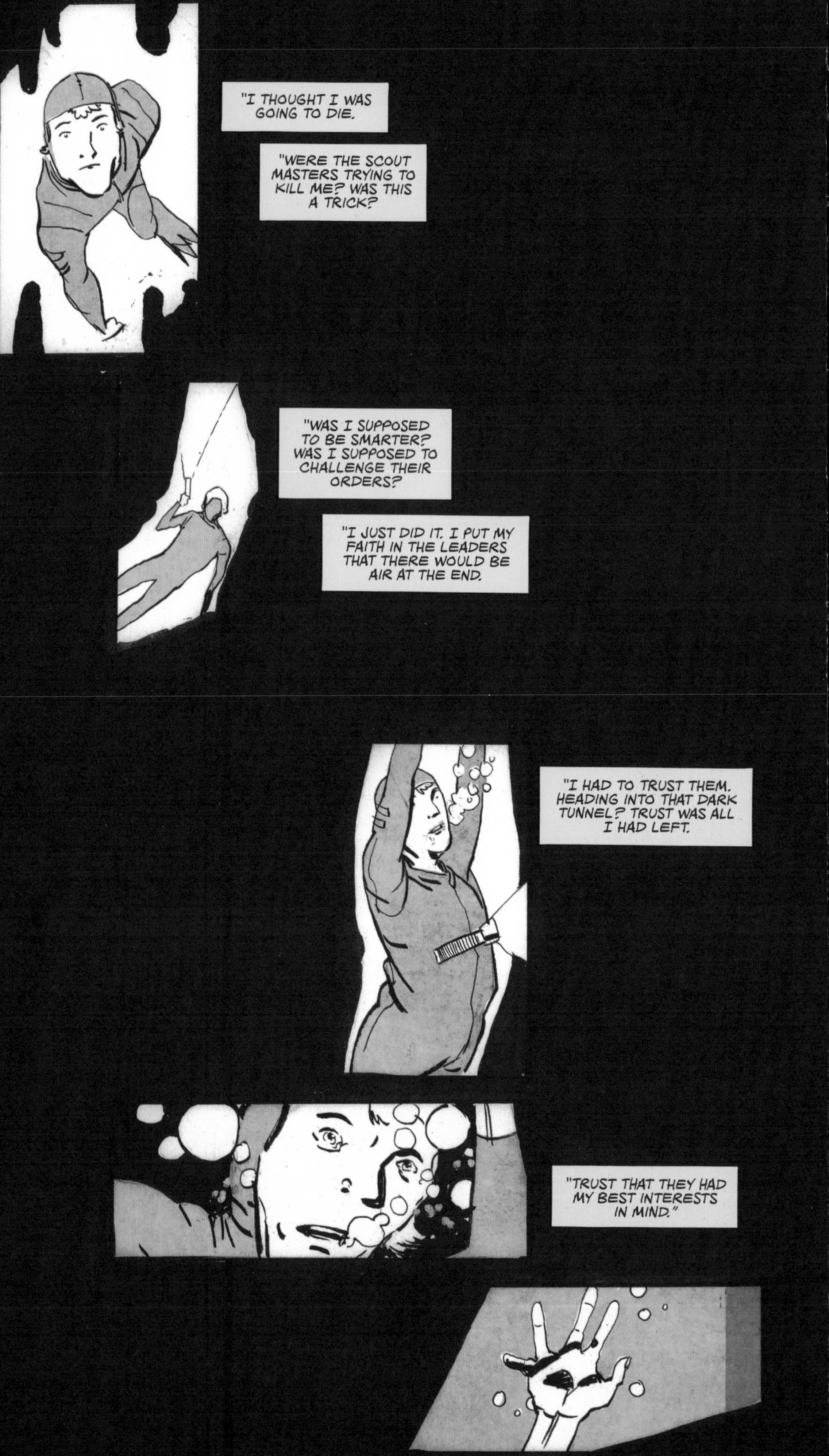
"I THOUGHT I WAS GOING TO DIE.
"WERE THE SCOUT MASTERS TRYING TO KILL ME? WAS THIS A TRICK?
"WAS I SUPPOSED TO BE SMARTER? WAS I SUPPOSED TO CHALLENGE THEIR ORDERS?
"I JUST DID IT. I PUT MY FAITH IN THE LEADERS THAT THERE WOULD BE AIR AT THE END.
"I HAD TO TRUST THEM. HEADING INTO THAT DARK TUNNEL? TRUST WAS ALL I HAD LEFT.
"TRUST THAT THEY HAD MY BEST INTERESTS IN MIND."

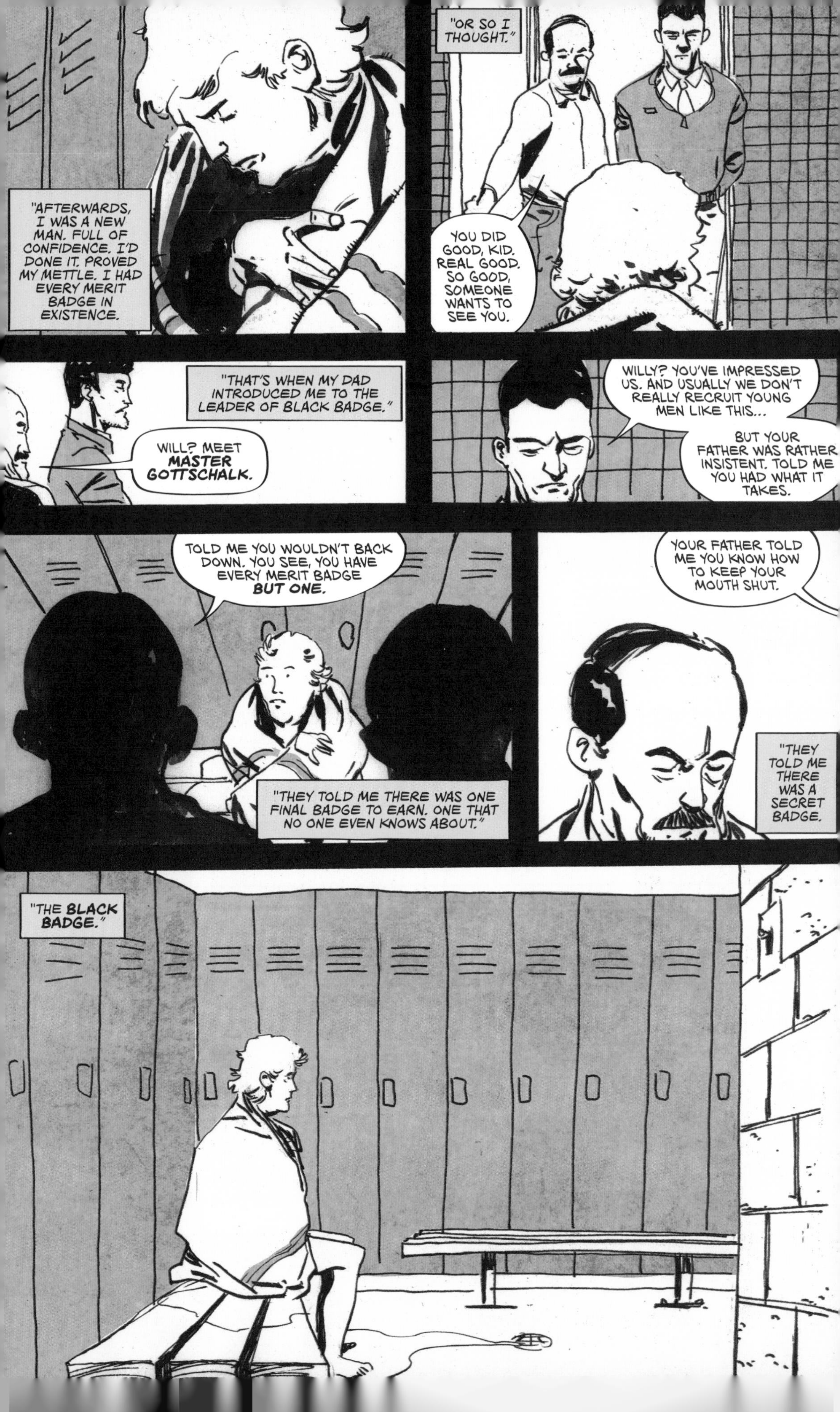
"AFTERWARDS, I WAS A NEW MAN. FULL OF CONFIDENCE. I'D DONE IT. PROVED MY METTLE. I HAD EVERY MERIT BADGE IN EXISTENCE.
"OR SO I THOUGHT."
YOU DID GOOD, KID. REAL GOOD. SO GOOD, SOMEONE WANTS TO SEE YOU.
"THAT'S WHEN MY DAD INTRODUCED ME TO THE LEADER OF BLACK BADGE."
WILL? MEET **MASTER GOTTSCHALK.**
WILLY? YOU'VE IMPRESSED US. AND USUALLY WE DON'T REALLY RECRUIT YOUNG MEN LIKE THIS...
BUT YOUR FATHER WAS RATHER INSISTENT. TOLD ME YOU HAD WHAT IT TAKES.
TOLD ME YOU WOULDN'T BACK DOWN. YOU SEE, YOU HAVE EVERY MERIT BADGE **BUT ONE.**
"THEY TOLD ME THERE WAS ONE FINAL BADGE TO EARN. ONE THAT NO ONE EVEN KNOWS ABOUT."
YOUR FATHER TOLD ME YOU KNOW HOW TO KEEP YOUR MOUTH SHUT.
"THEY TOLD ME THERE WAS A SECRET BADGE.
"THE **BLACK BADGE.**"

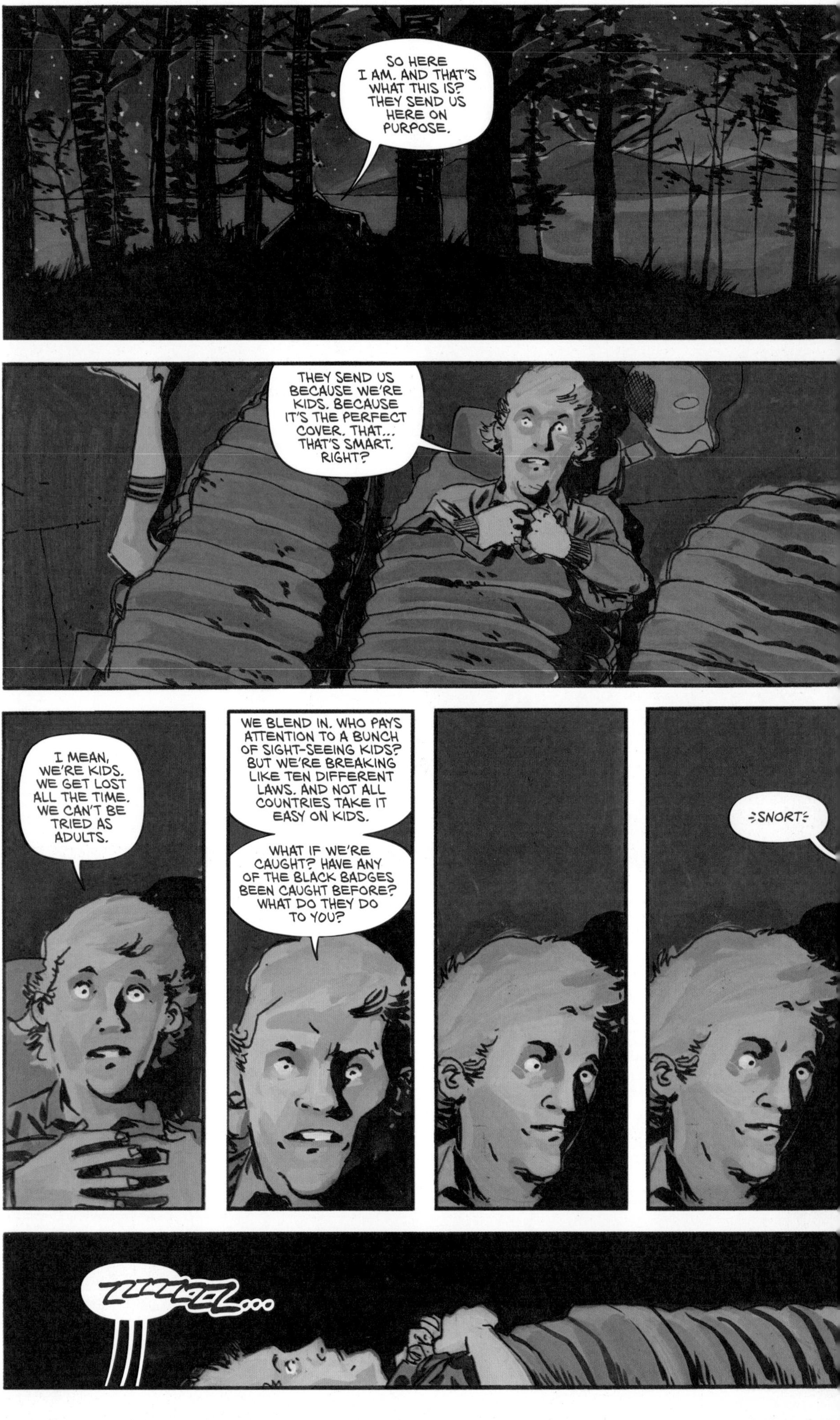

SO HERE I AM. AND THAT'S WHAT THIS IS? THEY SEND US HERE ON PURPOSE.
THEY SEND US BECAUSE WE'RE KIDS. BECAUSE IT'S THE PERFECT COVER. THAT... THAT'S SMART. RIGHT?
I MEAN, WE'RE KIDS. WE GET LOST ALL THE TIME. WE CAN'T BE TRIED AS ADULTS.
WE BLEND IN. WHO PAYS ATTENTION TO A BUNCH OF SIGHT-SEEING KIDS? BUT WE'RE BREAKING LIKE TEN DIFFERENT LAWS. AND NOT ALL COUNTRIES TAKE IT EASY ON KIDS.
WHAT IF WE'RE CAUGHT? HAVE ANY OF THE BLACK BADGES BEEN CAUGHT BEFORE? WHAT DO THEY DO TO YOU?
SNORT
ZZZZZZZ...

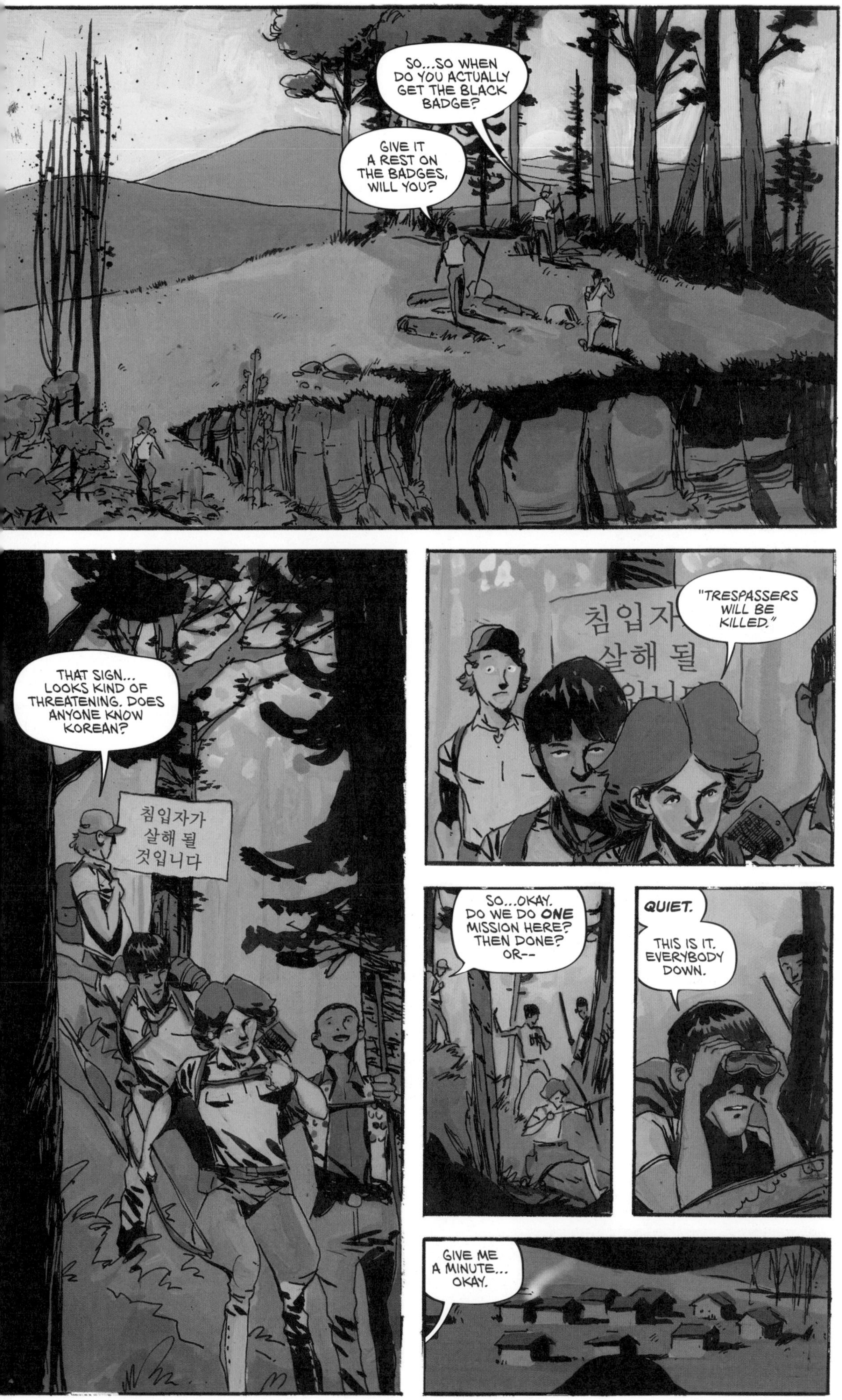
SO...SO WHEN DO YOU ACTUALLY GET THE BLACK BADGE?
GIVE IT A REST ON THE BADGES, WILL YOU?
THAT SIGN... LOOKS KIND OF THREATENING. DOES ANYONE KNOW KOREAN?
침입자가 살해 될 것입니다
"TRESPASSERS WILL BE KILLED."
SO...OKAY. DO WE DO ONE MISSION HERE? THEN DONE? OR--
QUIET.
THIS IS IT. EVERYBODY DOWN.
GIVE ME A MINUTE... OKAY.

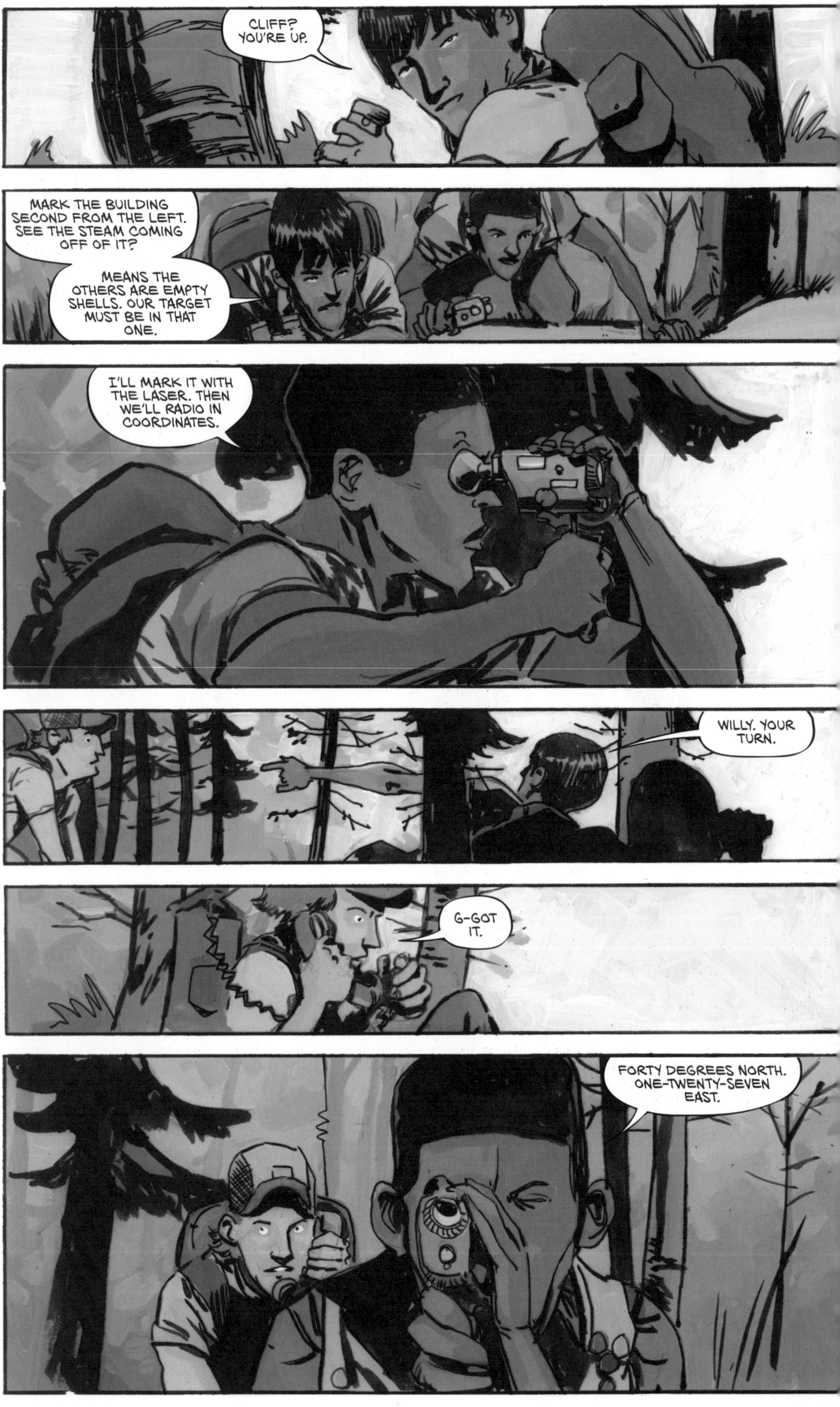
CLIFF? YOU'RE UP.
MARK THE BUILDING SECOND FROM THE LEFT. SEE THE STEAM COMING OFF OF IT?
MEANS THE OTHERS ARE EMPTY SHELLS. OUR TARGET MUST BE IN THAT ONE.
I'LL MARK IT WITH THE LASER. THEN WE'LL RADIO IN COORDINATES.
WILLY. YOUR TURN.
G-GOT IT.
FORTY DEGREES NORTH. ONE-TWENTY-SEVEN EAST.

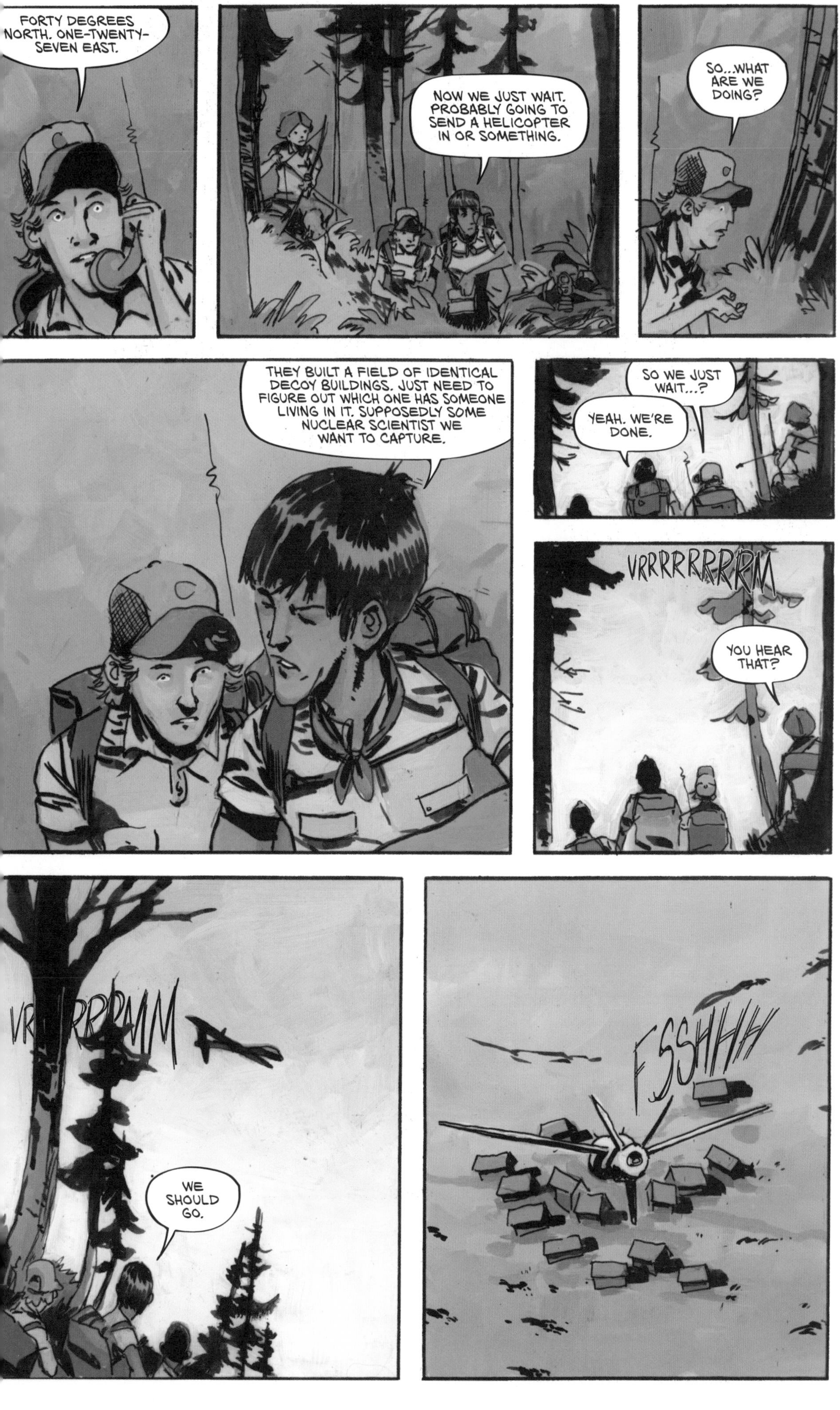
FORTY DEGREES NORTH. ONE-TWENTY-SEVEN EAST.
NOW WE JUST WAIT. PROBABLY GOING TO SEND A HELICOPTER IN OR SOMETHING.
SO...WHAT ARE WE DOING?
THEY BUILT A FIELD OF IDENTICAL DECOY BUILDINGS. JUST NEED TO FIGURE OUT WHICH ONE HAS SOMEONE LIVING IN IT. SUPPOSEDLY SOME NUCLEAR SCIENTIST WE WANT TO CAPTURE.
SO WE JUST WAIT...?
YEAH. WE'RE DONE.
VRRRRRRRRM
YOU HEAR THAT?
VRRRRRMM
WE SHOULD GO.
FSSHHH

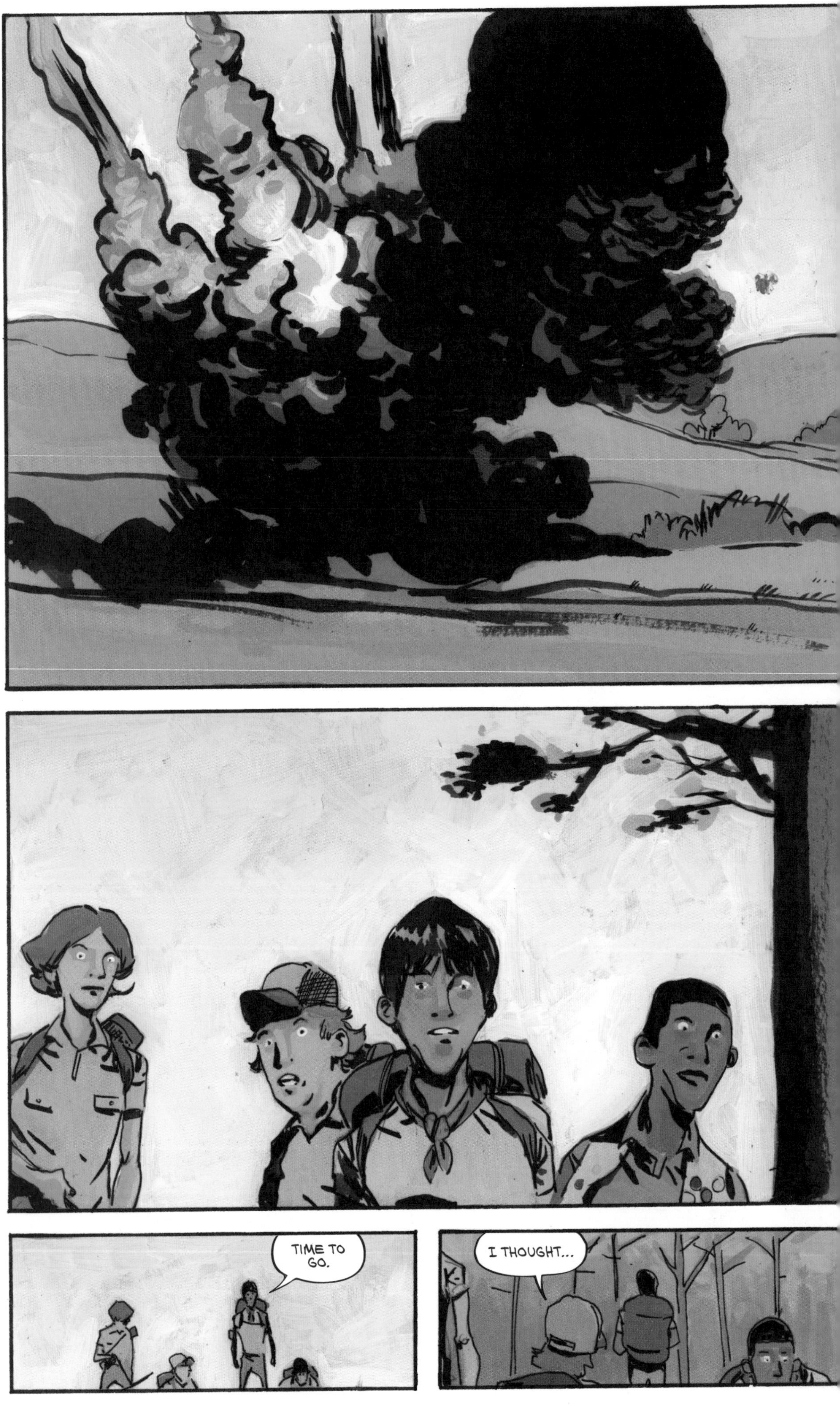
TIME TO GO.
I THOUGHT...

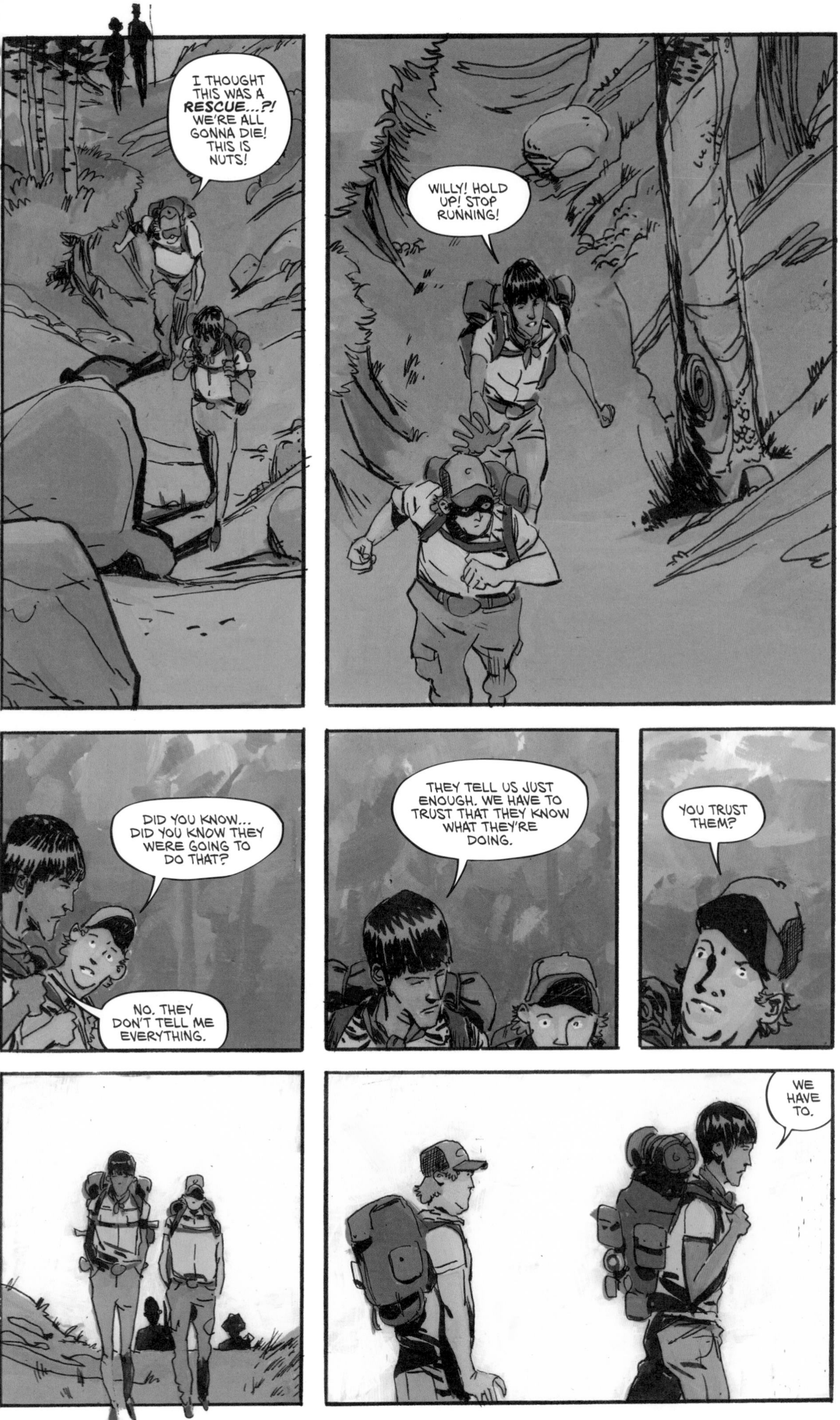
I THOUGHT THIS WAS A **RESCUE...?!** WE'RE ALL GONNA DIE! THIS IS NUTS!
WILLY! HOLD UP! STOP RUNNING!
DID YOU KNOW... DID YOU KNOW THEY WERE GOING TO DO THAT?
NO. THEY DON'T TELL ME EVERYTHING.
THEY TELL US JUST ENOUGH. WE HAVE TO TRUST THAT THEY KNOW WHAT THEY'RE DOING.
YOU TRUST THEM?
WE HAVE TO.

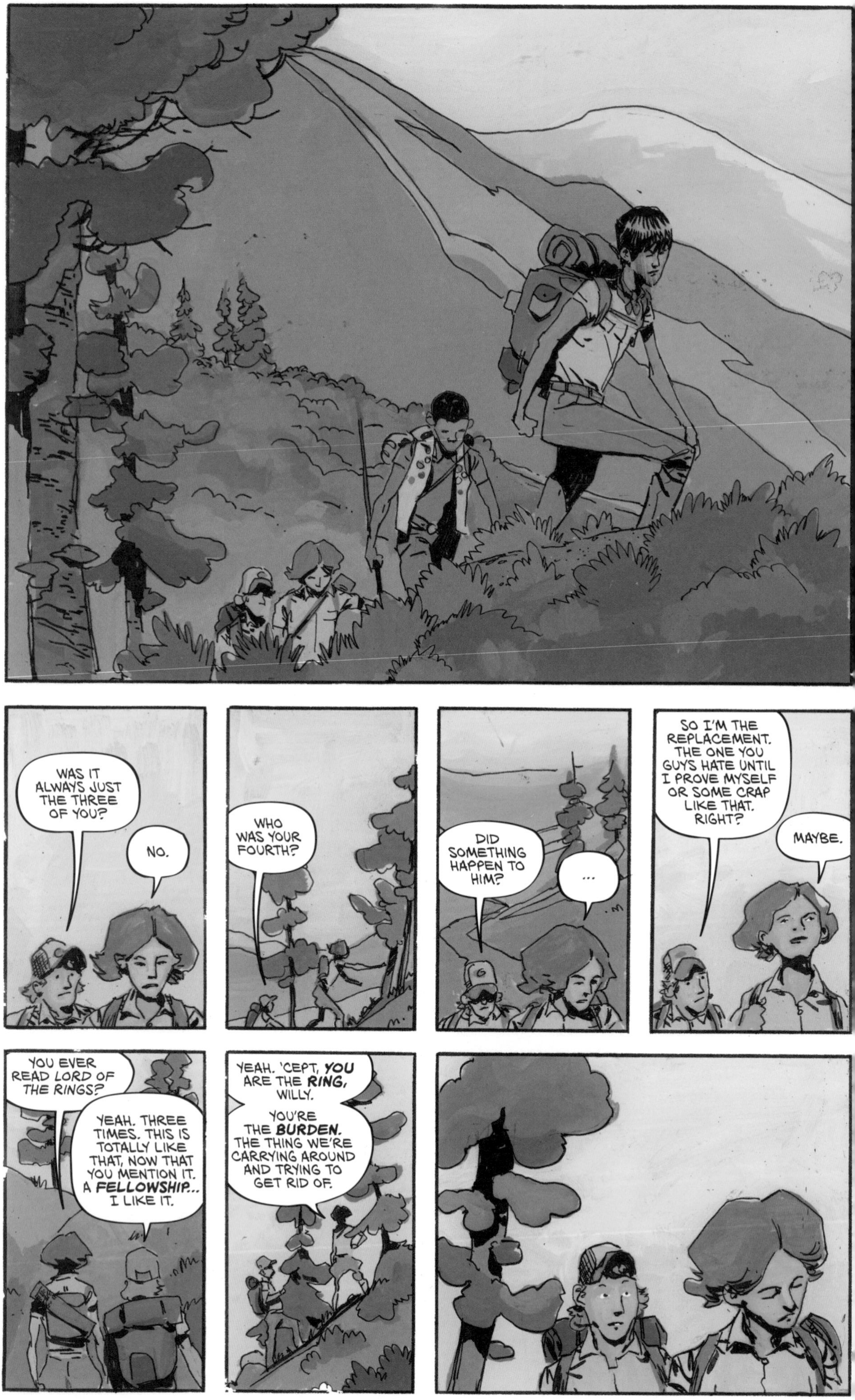
WAS IT ALWAYS JUST THE THREE OF YOU?
NO.
WHO WAS YOUR FOURTH?
DID SOMETHING HAPPEN TO HIM?
...
SO I'M THE REPLACEMENT. THE ONE YOU GUYS HATE UNTIL I PROVE MYSELF OR SOME CRAP LIKE THAT. RIGHT?
MAYBE.
YOU EVER READ LORD OF THE RINGS?
YEAH. THREE TIMES. THIS IS TOTALLY LIKE THAT, NOW THAT YOU MENTION IT. A FELLOWSHIP... I LIKE IT.
YEAH. 'CEPT, YOU ARE THE RING, WILLY.
YOU'RE THE BURDEN. THE THING WE'RE CARRYING AROUND AND TRYING TO GET RID OF.

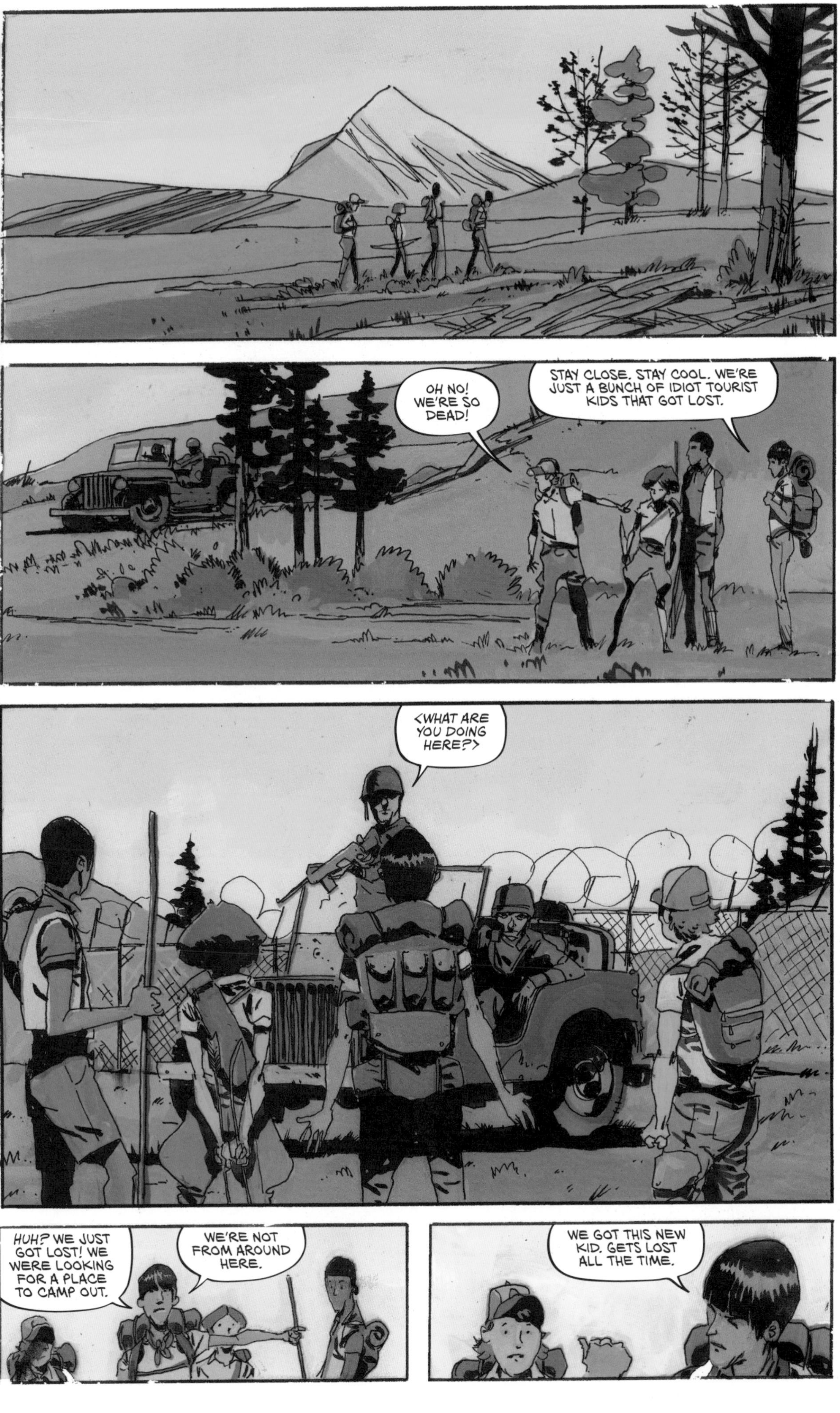
OH NO! WE'RE SO DEAD!
STAY CLOSE. STAY COOL. WE'RE JUST A BUNCH OF IDIOT TOURIST KIDS THAT GOT LOST.
<WHAT ARE YOU DOING HERE?>
HUH? WE JUST GOT LOST! WE WERE LOOKING FOR A PLACE TO CAMP OUT.
WE'RE NOT FROM AROUND HERE.
WE GOT THIS NEW KID. GETS LOST ALL THE TIME.

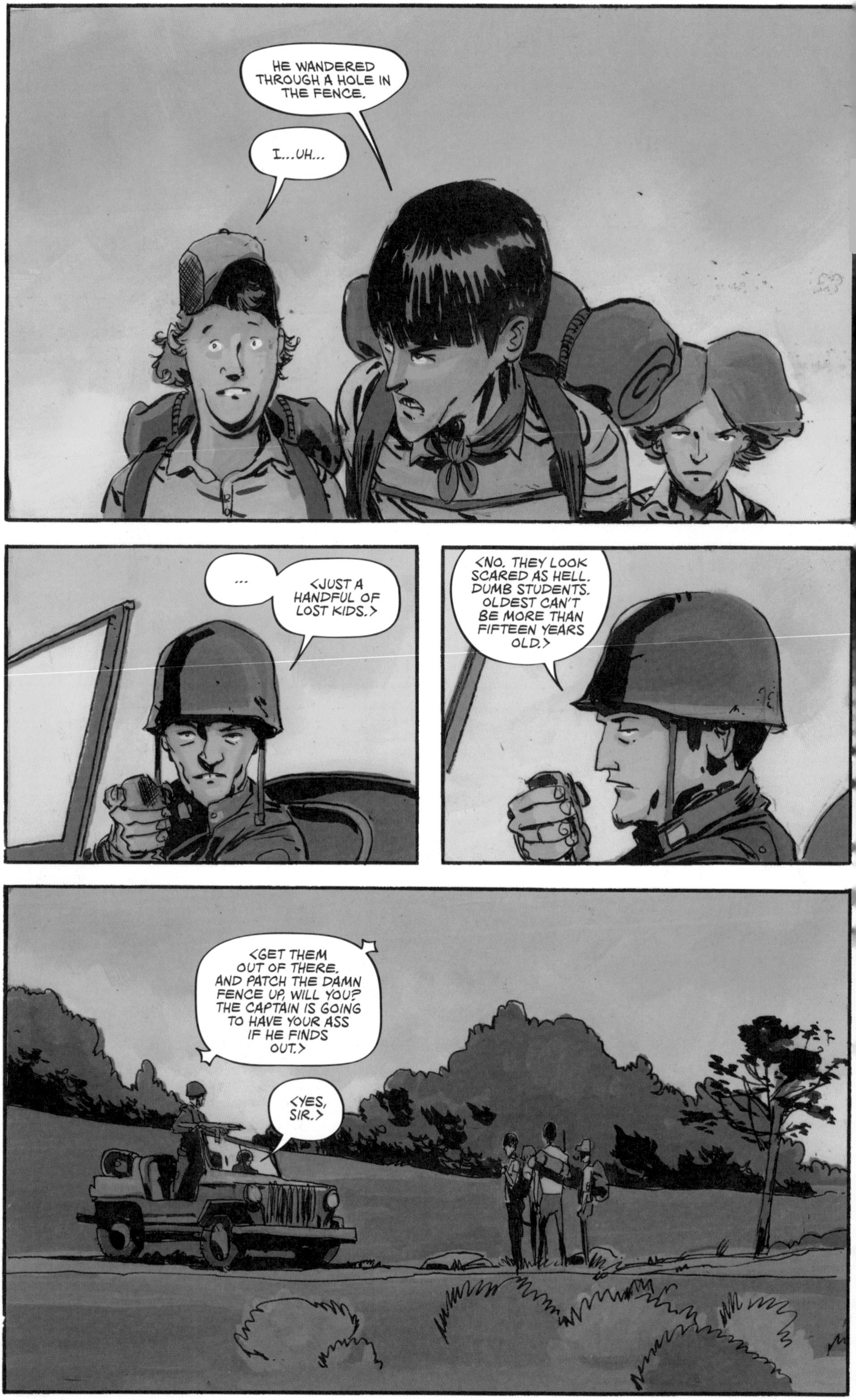
HE WANDERED THROUGH A HOLE IN THE FENCE.
I...UH...
...
<JUST A HANDFUL OF LOST KIDS.>
<NO. THEY LOOK SCARED AS HELL. DUMB STUDENTS. OLDEST CAN'T BE MORE THAN FIFTEEN YEARS OLD.>
<GET THEM OUT OF THERE. AND PATCH THE DAMN FENCE UP, WILL YOU? THE CAPTAIN IS GOING TO HAVE YOUR ASS IF HE FINDS OUT.>
<YES, SIR.>

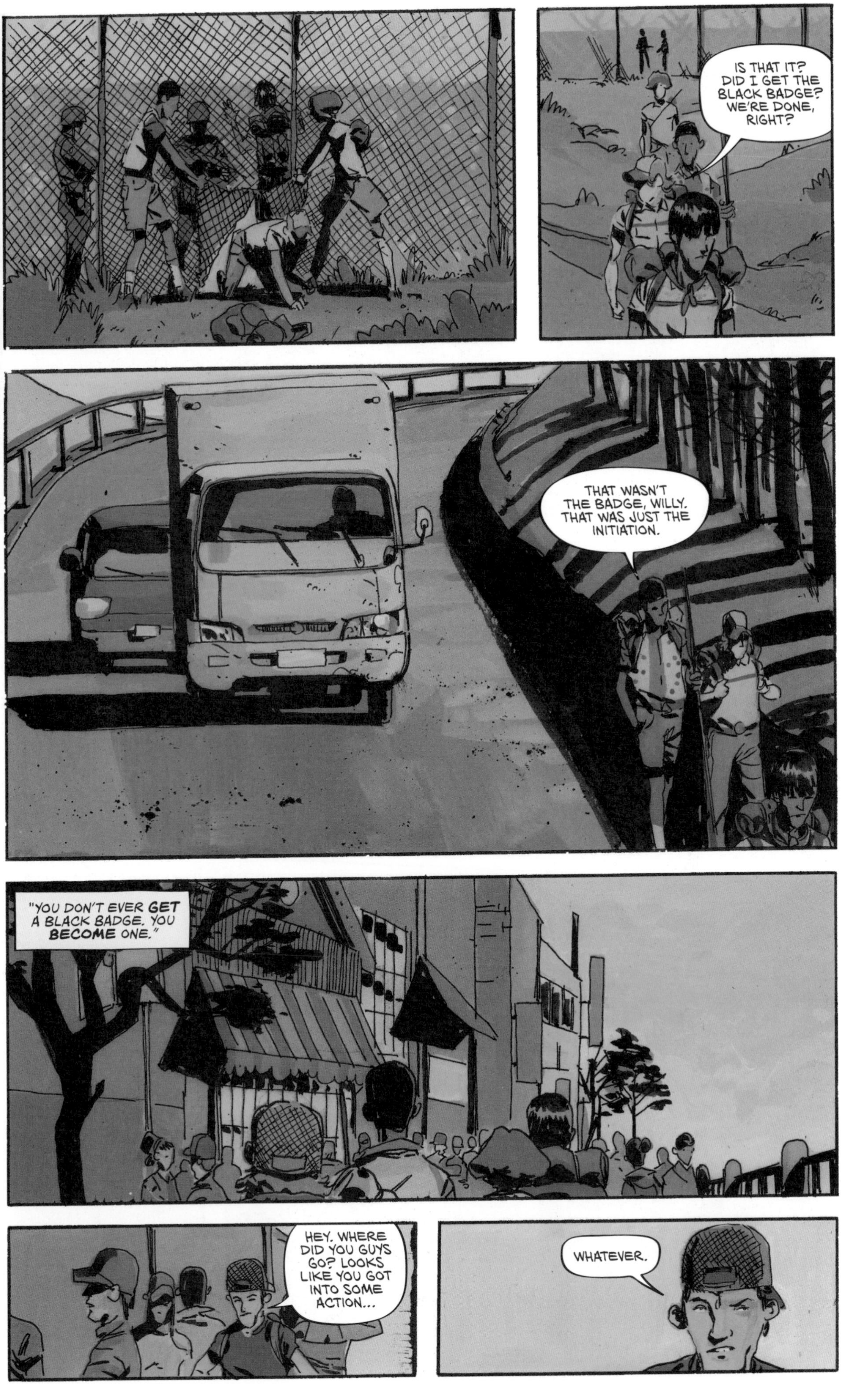
IS THAT IT? DID I GET THE BLACK BADGE? WE'RE DONE, RIGHT?
THAT WASN'T THE BADGE, WILLY. THAT WAS JUST THE INITIATION.
"YOU DON'T EVER **GET** A BLACK BADGE. YOU **BECOME** ONE."
HEY. WHERE DID YOU GUYS GO? LOOKS LIKE YOU GOT INTO SOME ACTION...
WHATEVER.

NOW WHAT?

WE JUST WAIT HERE UNTIL THE EXTRACTION BUS ARRIVES.

WAS THERE...WAS THERE A GUY IN THAT BUILDING THAT BLEW UP? THAT *WE* BLEW UP?

I DON'T KNOW. PROBABLY.

SO WE... WE KIND OF KILLED THAT GUY.

NO. WE JUST CALLED IN THE LOCATION. WE DIDN'T DO THAT. THEY DIDN'T EVEN TELL US WHAT WAS GOING TO HAPPEN.

THEY TOLD US IT WAS AN EXTRACTION, RIGHT, KENNY?

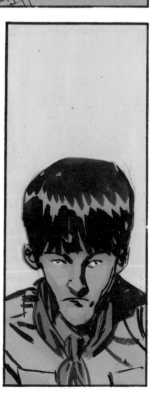

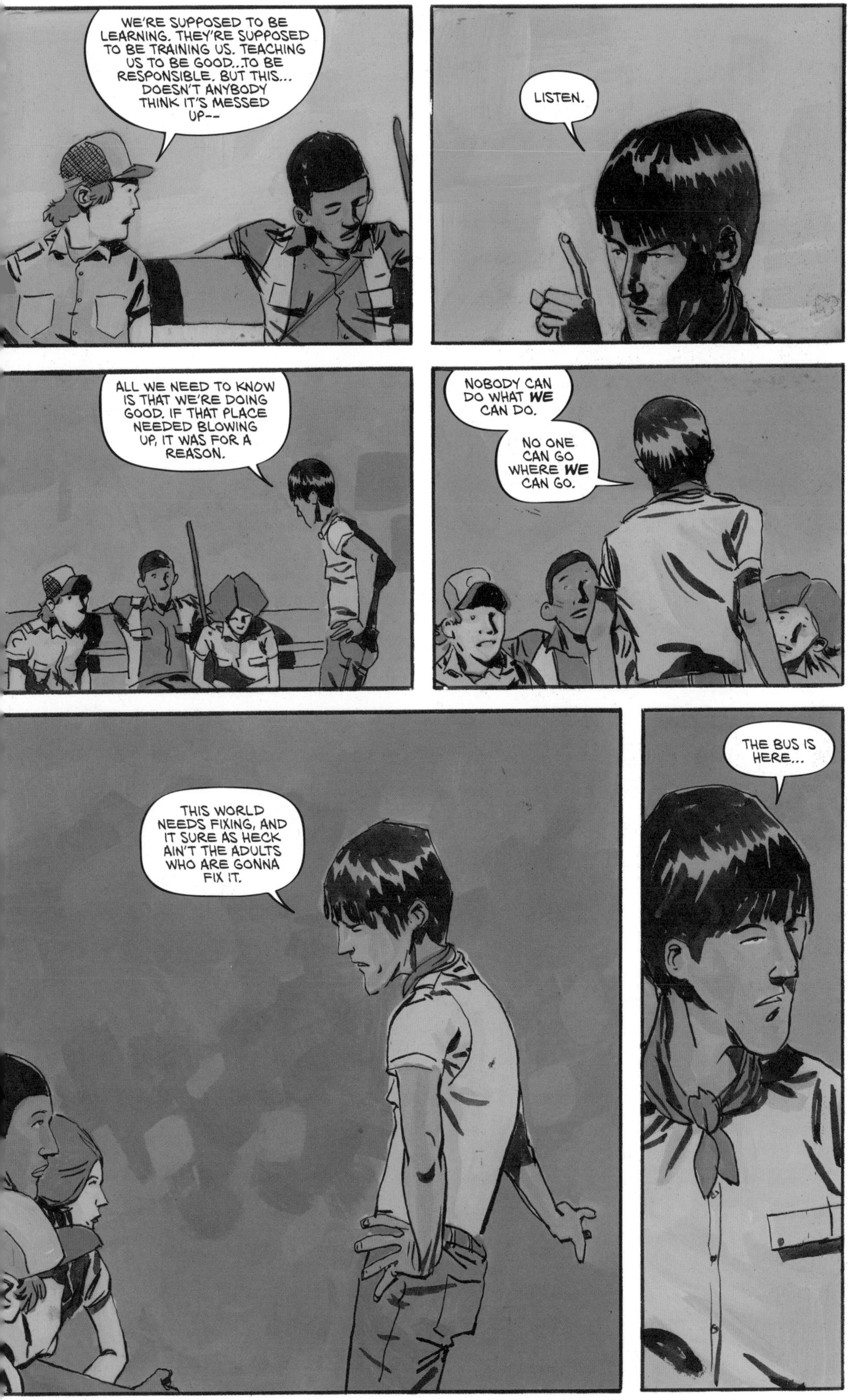
WE'RE SUPPOSED TO BE LEARNING. THEY'RE SUPPOSED TO BE TRAINING US. TEACHING US TO BE GOOD...TO BE RESPONSIBLE. BUT THIS... DOESN'T ANYBODY THINK IT'S MESSED UP--
LISTEN.
ALL WE NEED TO KNOW IS THAT WE'RE DOING GOOD. IF THAT PLACE NEEDED BLOWING UP, IT WAS FOR A REASON.
NOBODY CAN DO WHAT **WE** CAN DO.
NO ONE CAN GO WHERE **WE** CAN GO.
THIS WORLD NEEDS FIXING, AND IT SURE AS HECK AIN'T THE ADULTS WHO ARE GONNA FIX IT.
THE BUS IS HERE...

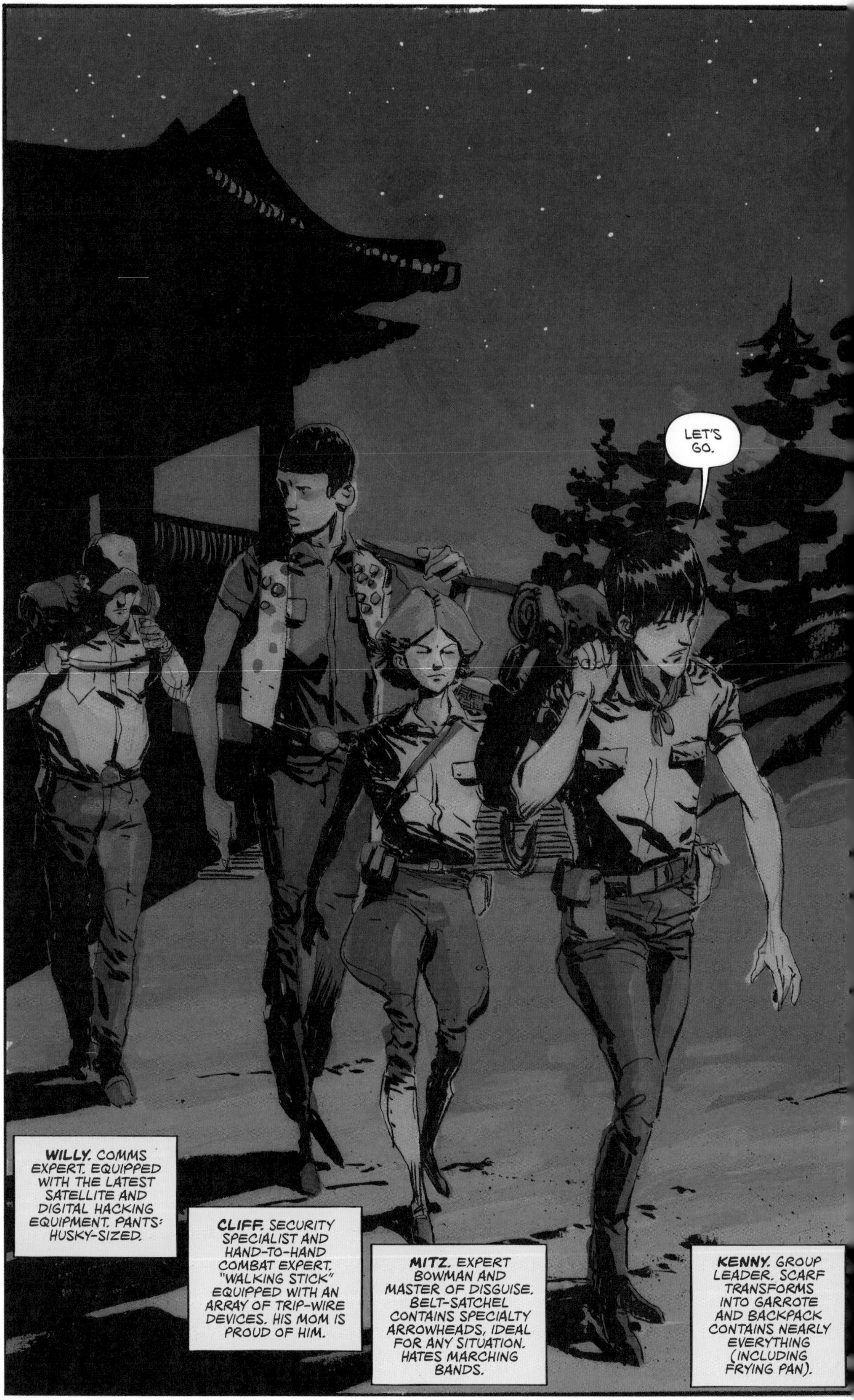
LET'S GO.
WILLY. COMMS EXPERT. EQUIPPED WITH THE LATEST SATELLITE AND DIGITAL HACKING EQUIPMENT. PANTS: HUSKY-SIZED.
CLIFF. SECURITY SPECIALIST AND HAND-TO-HAND COMBAT EXPERT. "WALKING STICK" EQUIPPED WITH AN ARRAY OF TRIP-WIRE DEVICES. HIS MOM IS PROUD OF HIM.
MITZ. EXPERT BOWMAN AND MASTER OF DISGUISE. BELT-SATCHEL CONTAINS SPECIALTY ARROWHEADS, IDEAL FOR ANY SITUATION. HATES MARCHING BANDS.
KENNY. GROUP LEADER. SCARF TRANSFORMS INTO GARROTE AND BACKPACK CONTAINS NEARLY EVERYTHING (INCLUDING FRYING PAN).

"Scout" used to mean the one on watch for the rest.
We have widened the word a little."
— Boy Scouts Handbook, 1911

Garrote hidden in headband.
C-4 disguised as honor badge.
Throwing knives behind sash.
Black Badge doubles as explosive throwing star.
Pocket lined with solidified sarin gas.

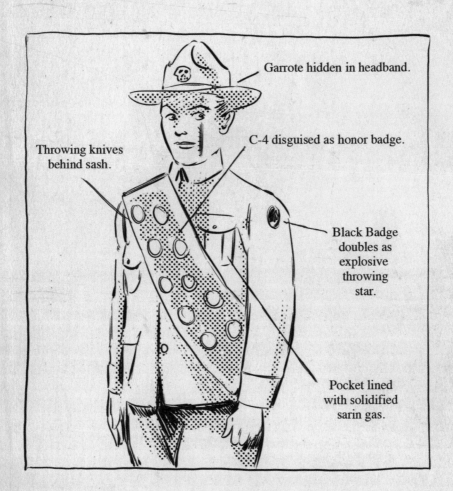

"How you received your Black Badge is
priveleged information. Guard it with your life."
— Black Badge Handbook

Black Badge was founded in 1910 by William Randolph Hea
sub-branch of the American Boy Scouts. After the Boy Sco
America sued Hearst for use of the name, the ABS was dis
but Black Badge remained* - becoming active during both
Wars and as a sort of elite scouting club in present da

Chapter Two

[redacted] sedative arrowhead [redacted] controlled detonation [redacted] Siberia [redacted] ulterior motive [redacted] assessment [redacted]
Young Canadian Mounties [redacted] fluent in Russian [redacted]

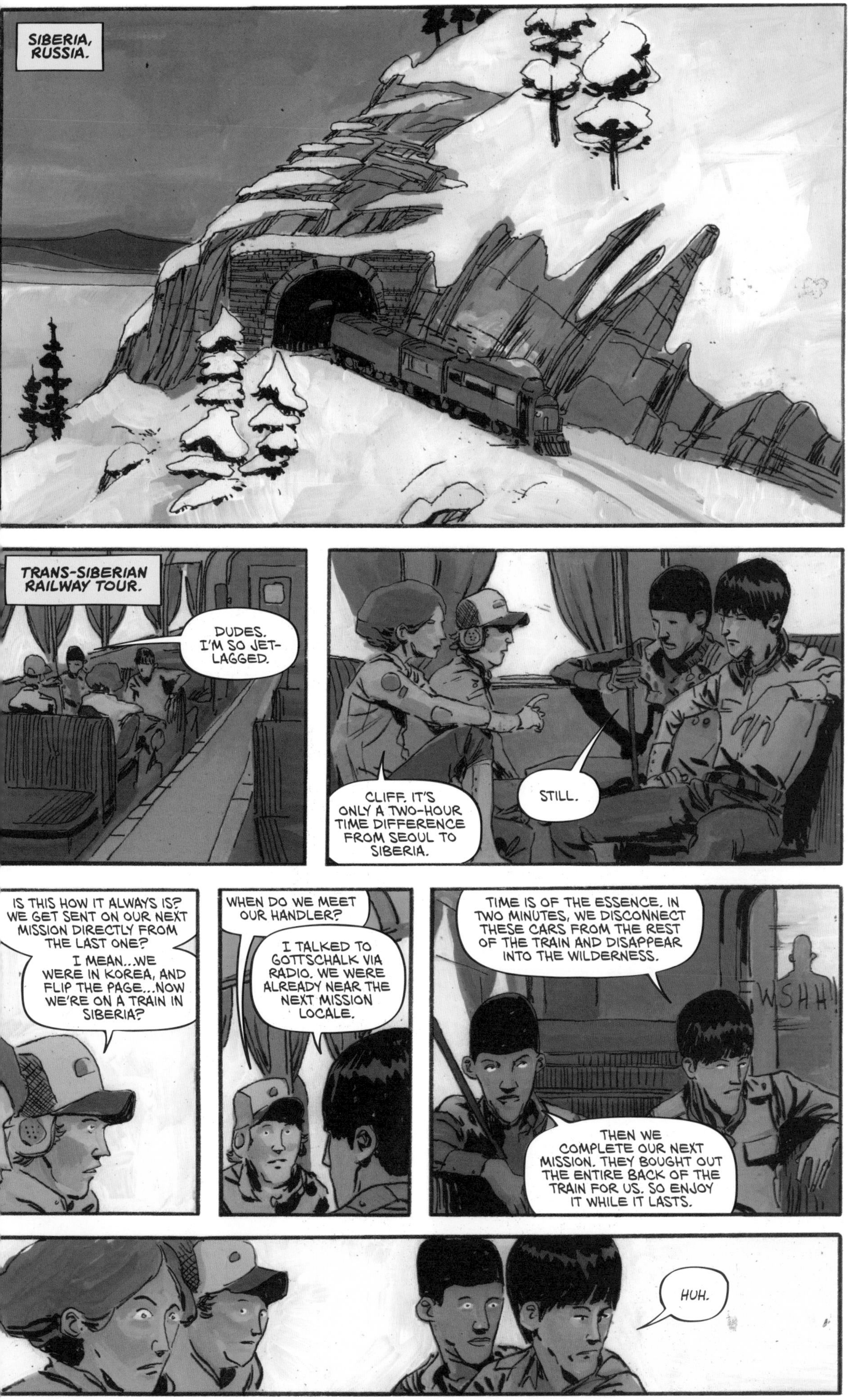
SIBERIA, RUSSIA.
TRANS-SIBERIAN RAILWAY TOUR.
DUDES. I'M SO JET-LAGGED.
CLIFF. IT'S ONLY A TWO-HOUR TIME DIFFERENCE FROM SEOUL TO SIBERIA.
STILL.
IS THIS HOW IT ALWAYS IS? WE GET SENT ON OUR NEXT MISSION DIRECTLY FROM THE LAST ONE?
I MEAN...WE WERE IN KOREA, AND FLIP THE PAGE...NOW WE'RE ON A TRAIN IN SIBERIA?
WHEN DO WE MEET OUR HANDLER?
I TALKED TO GOTTSCHALK VIA RADIO. WE WERE ALREADY NEAR THE NEXT MISSION LOCALE.
TIME IS OF THE ESSENCE. IN TWO MINUTES, WE DISCONNECT THESE CARS FROM THE REST OF THE TRAIN AND DISAPPEAR INTO THE WILDERNESS.
FWSHH!!
THEN WE COMPLETE OUR NEXT MISSION. THEY BOUGHT OUT THE ENTIRE BACK OF THE TRAIN FOR US. SO ENJOY IT WHILE IT LASTS.
HUH.

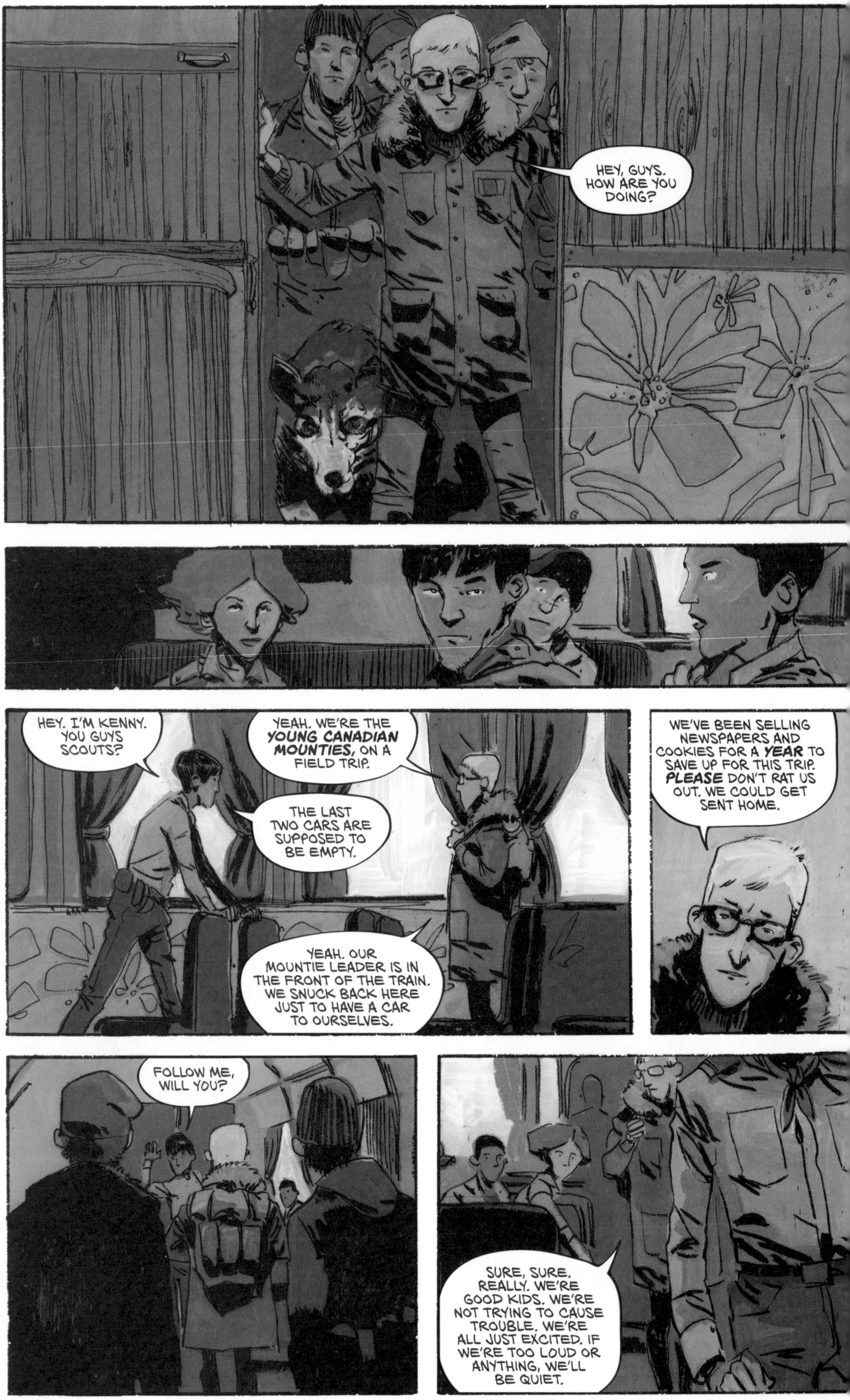
HEY, GUYS. HOW ARE YOU DOING?
HEY. I'M KENNY. YOU GUYS SCOUTS?
YEAH. WE'RE THE *YOUNG CANADIAN MOUNTIES*, ON A FIELD TRIP.
THE LAST TWO CARS ARE SUPPOSED TO BE EMPTY.
YEAH. OUR MOUNTIE LEADER IS IN THE FRONT OF THE TRAIN. WE SNUCK BACK HERE JUST TO HAVE A CAR TO OURSELVES.
WE'VE BEEN SELLING NEWSPAPERS AND COOKIES FOR A **YEAR** TO SAVE UP FOR THIS TRIP. ***PLEASE*** DON'T RAT US OUT. WE COULD GET SENT HOME.
FOLLOW ME, WILL YOU?
SURE, SURE. REALLY. WE'RE GOOD KIDS. WE'RE NOT TRYING TO CAUSE TROUBLE. WE'RE ALL JUST EXCITED. IF WE'RE TOO LOUD OR ANYTHING, WE'LL BE QUIET.

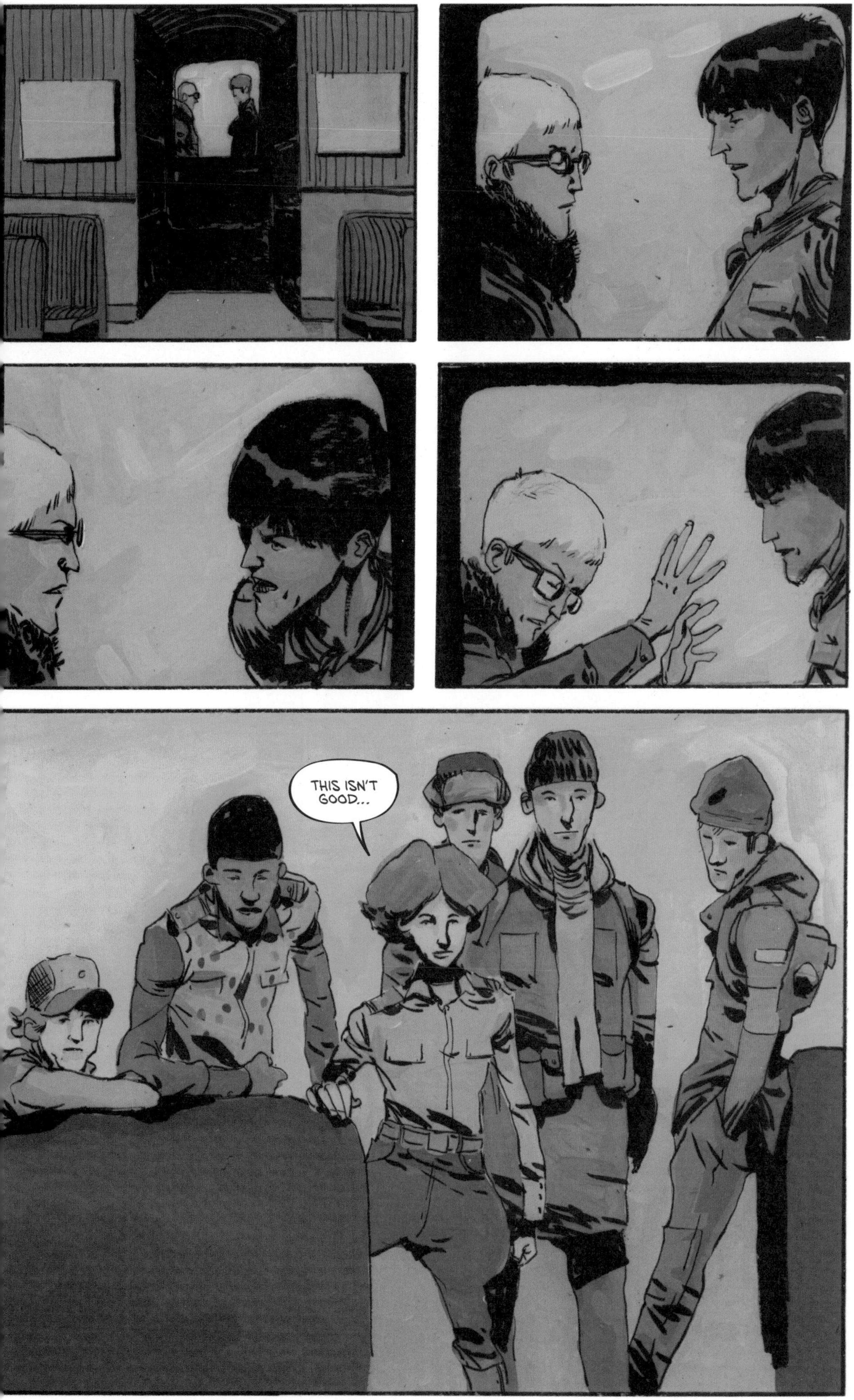
THIS ISN'T GOOD...

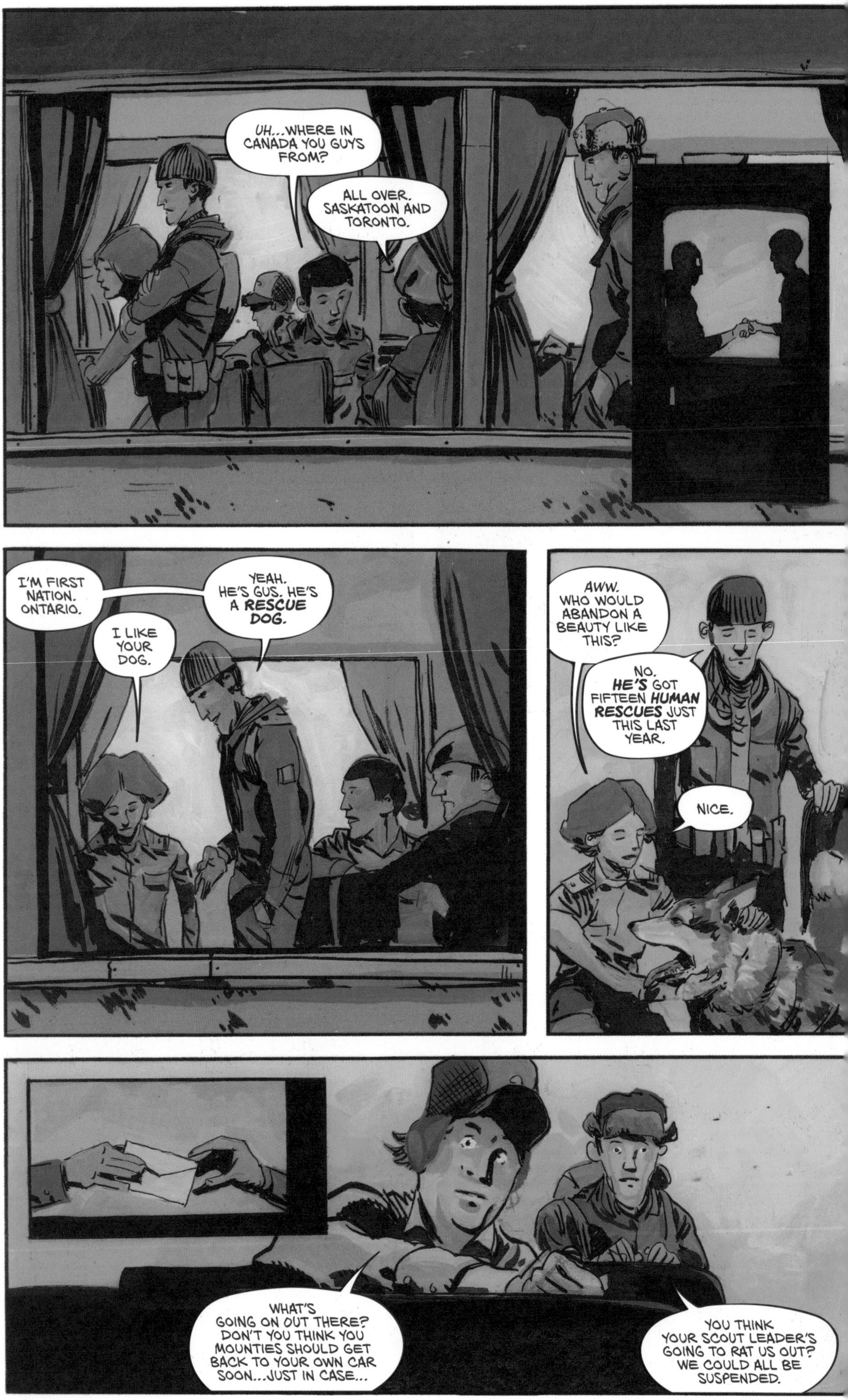
UH...WHERE IN CANADA YOU GUYS FROM?
ALL OVER. SASKATOON AND TORONTO.
I'M FIRST NATION. ONTARIO.
YEAH. HE'S GUS. HE'S A **RESCUE DOG.**
I LIKE YOUR DOG.
AWW. WHO WOULD ABANDON A BEAUTY LIKE THIS?
NO. **HE'S** GOT FIFTEEN **HUMAN RESCUES** JUST THIS LAST YEAR.
NICE.
WHAT'S GOING ON OUT THERE? DON'T YOU THINK YOU MOUNTIES SHOULD GET BACK TO YOUR OWN CAR SOON...JUST IN CASE...
YOU THINK YOUR SCOUT LEADER'S GOING TO RAT US OUT? WE COULD ALL BE SUSPENDED.

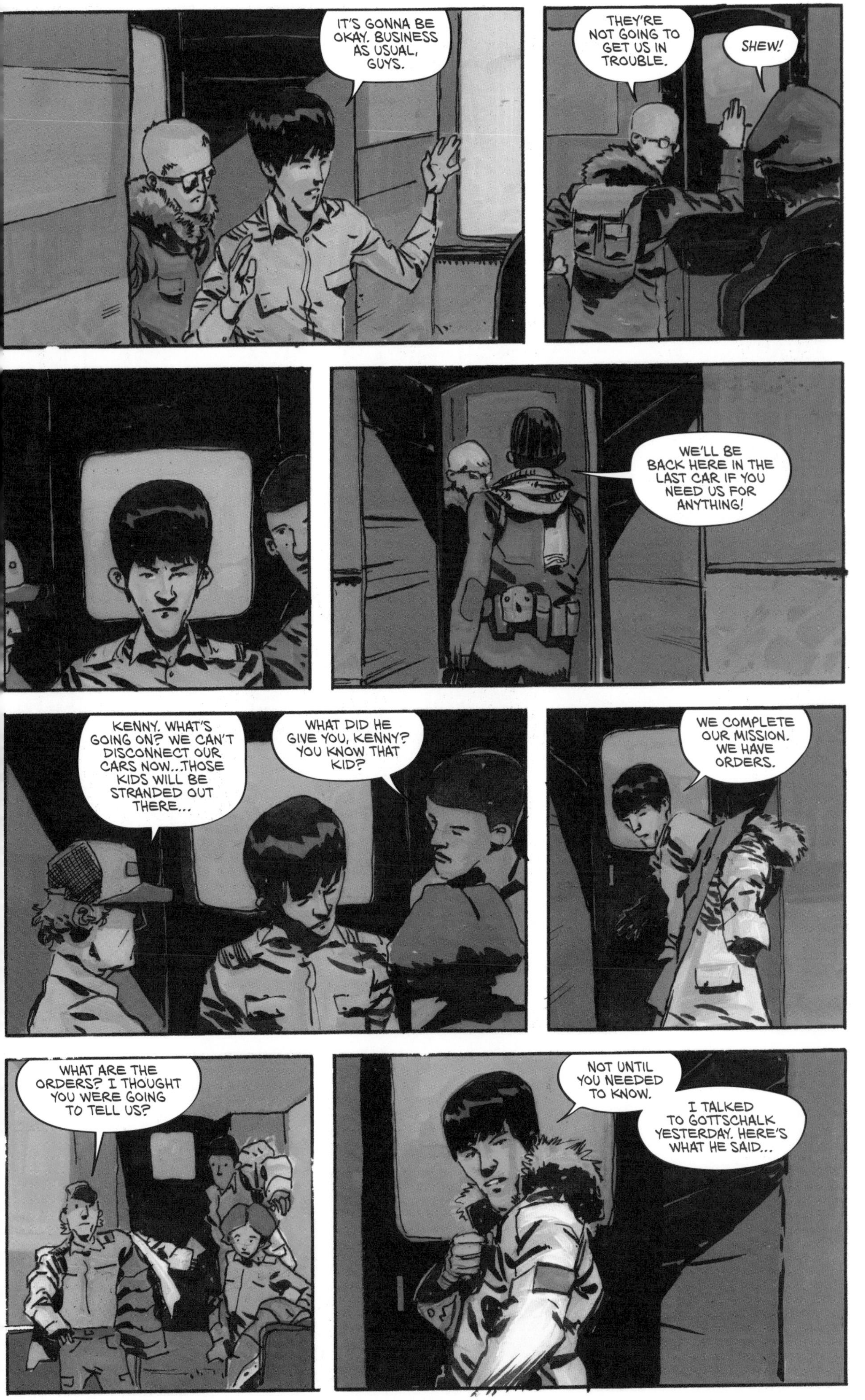
IT'S GONNA BE OKAY. BUSINESS AS USUAL, GUYS.
THEY'RE NOT GOING TO GET US IN TROUBLE.
SHEW!
WE'LL BE BACK HERE IN THE LAST CAR IF YOU NEED US FOR ANYTHING!
KENNY. WHAT'S GOING ON? WE CAN'T DISCONNECT OUR CARS NOW...THOSE KIDS WILL BE STRANDED OUT THERE...
WHAT DID HE GIVE YOU, KENNY? YOU KNOW THAT KID?
WE COMPLETE OUR MISSION. WE HAVE ORDERS.
WHAT ARE THE ORDERS? I THOUGHT YOU WERE GOING TO TELL US?
NOT UNTIL YOU NEEDED TO KNOW.
I TALKED TO GOTTSCHALK YESTERDAY. HERE'S WHAT HE SAID...

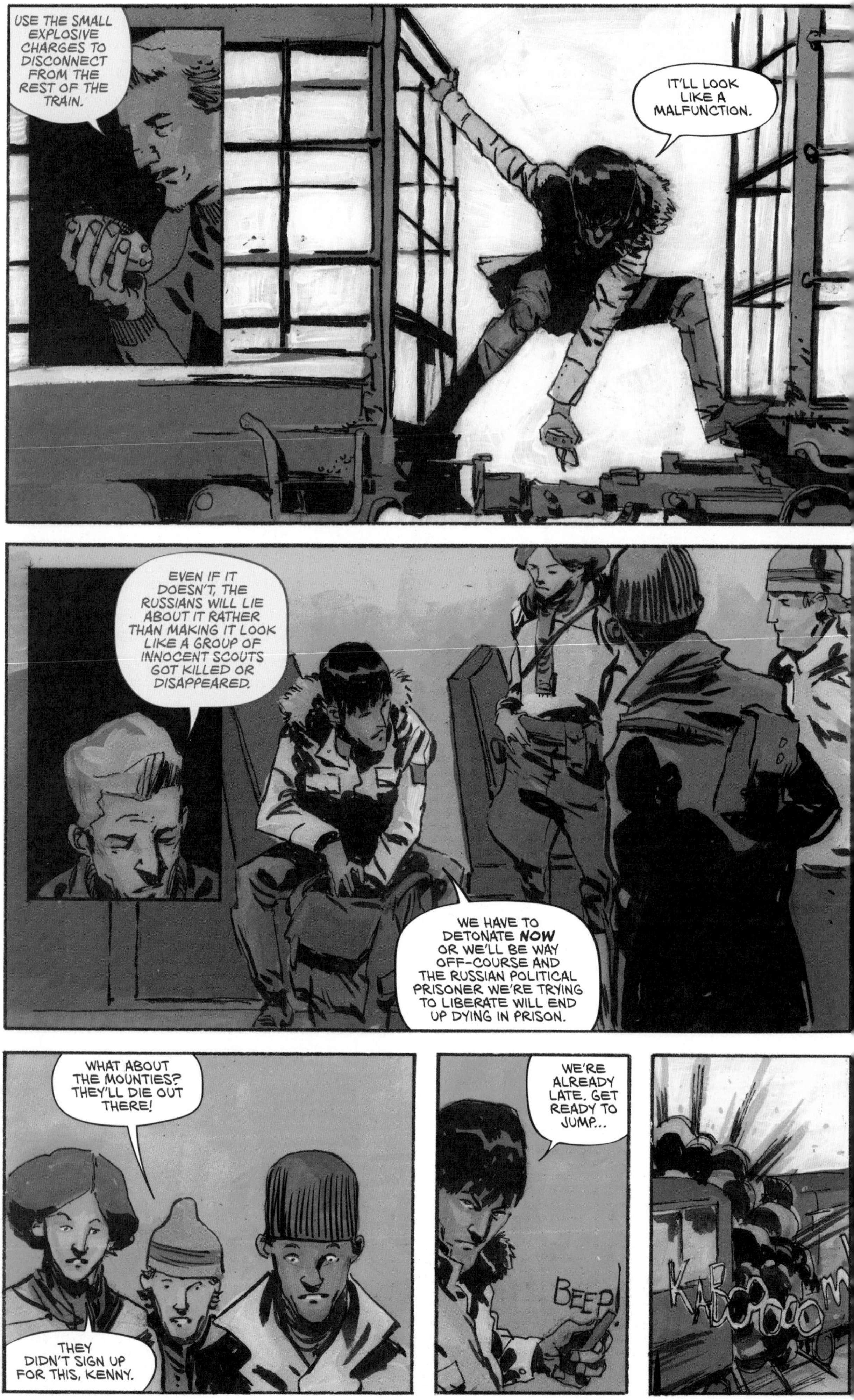
USE THE SMALL EXPLOSIVE CHARGES TO DISCONNECT FROM THE REST OF THE TRAIN.
IT'LL LOOK LIKE A MALFUNCTION.
EVEN IF IT DOESN'T, THE RUSSIANS WILL LIE ABOUT IT RATHER THAN MAKING IT LOOK LIKE A GROUP OF INNOCENT SCOUTS GOT KILLED OR DISAPPEARED.
WE HAVE TO DETONATE **NOW** OR WE'LL BE WAY OFF-COURSE AND THE RUSSIAN POLITICAL PRISONER WE'RE TRYING TO LIBERATE WILL END UP DYING IN PRISON.
WHAT ABOUT THE MOUNTIES? THEY'LL DIE OUT THERE!
THEY DIDN'T SIGN UP FOR THIS, KENNY.
WE'RE ALREADY LATE. GET READY TO JUMP...
BEEP!

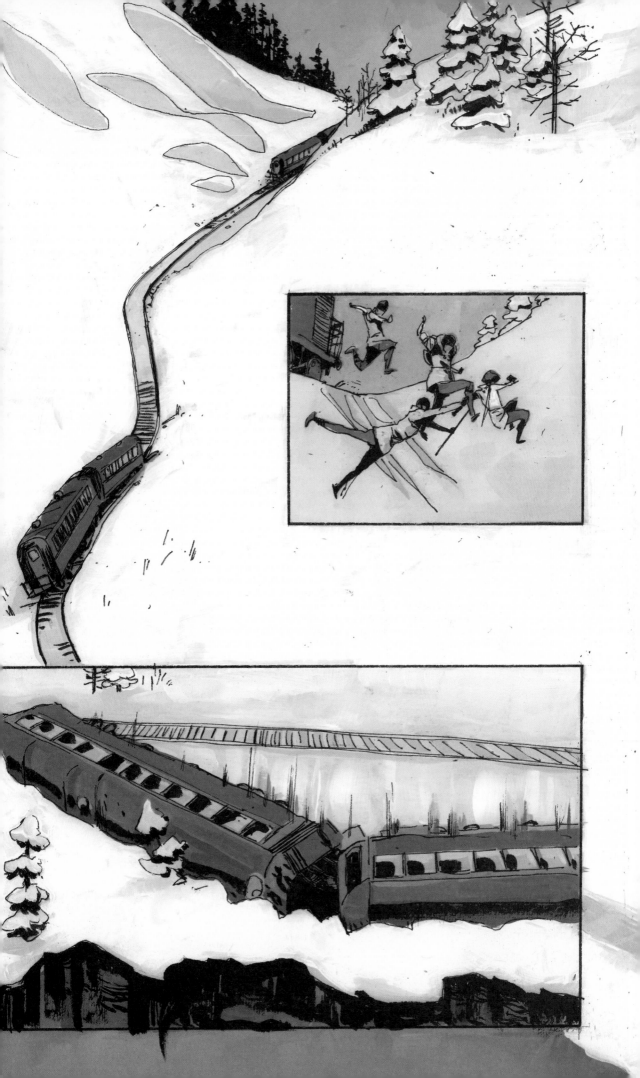

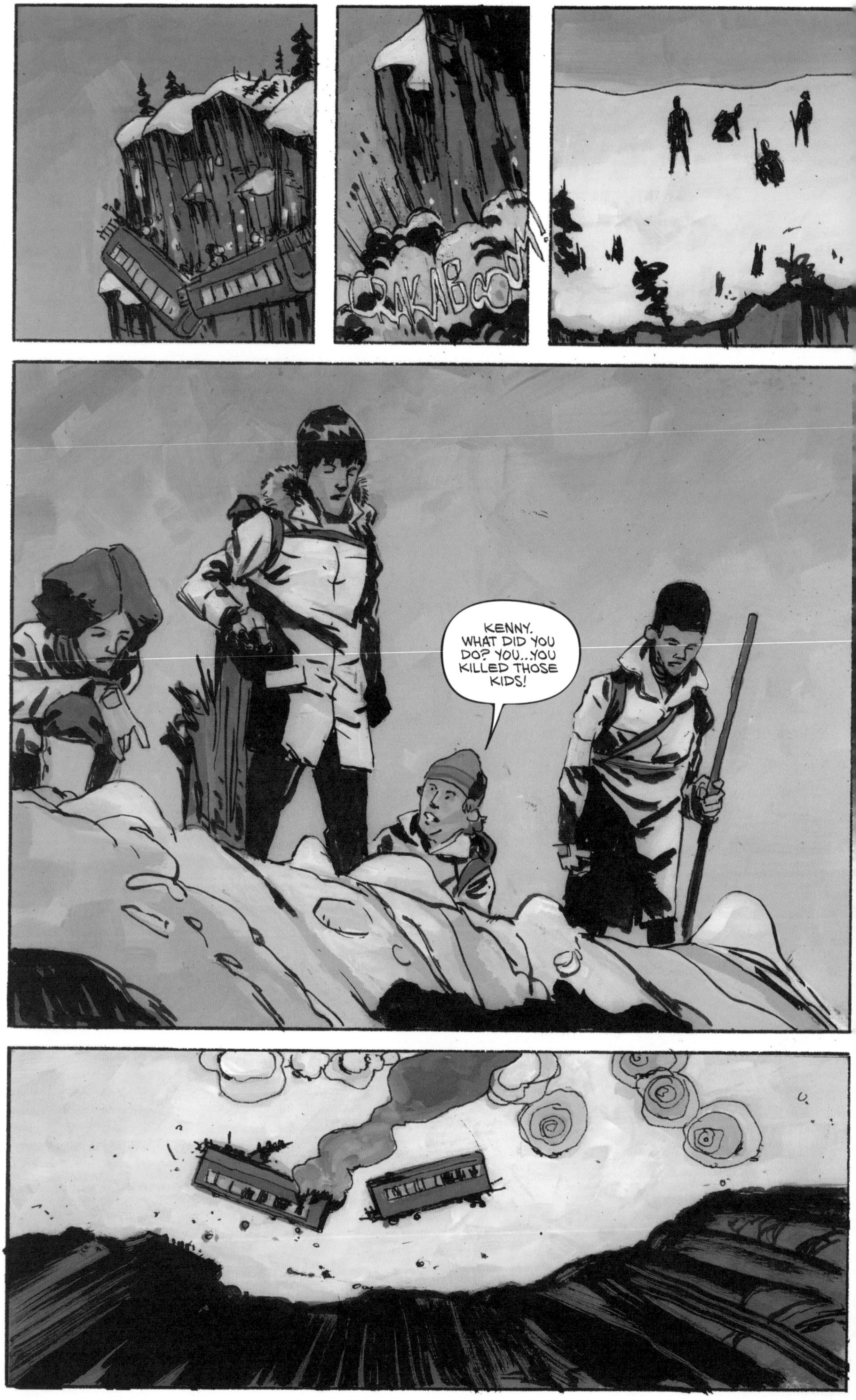
CRAKABOOOM!
KENNY. WHAT DID YOU DO? YOU...YOU KILLED THOSE KIDS!

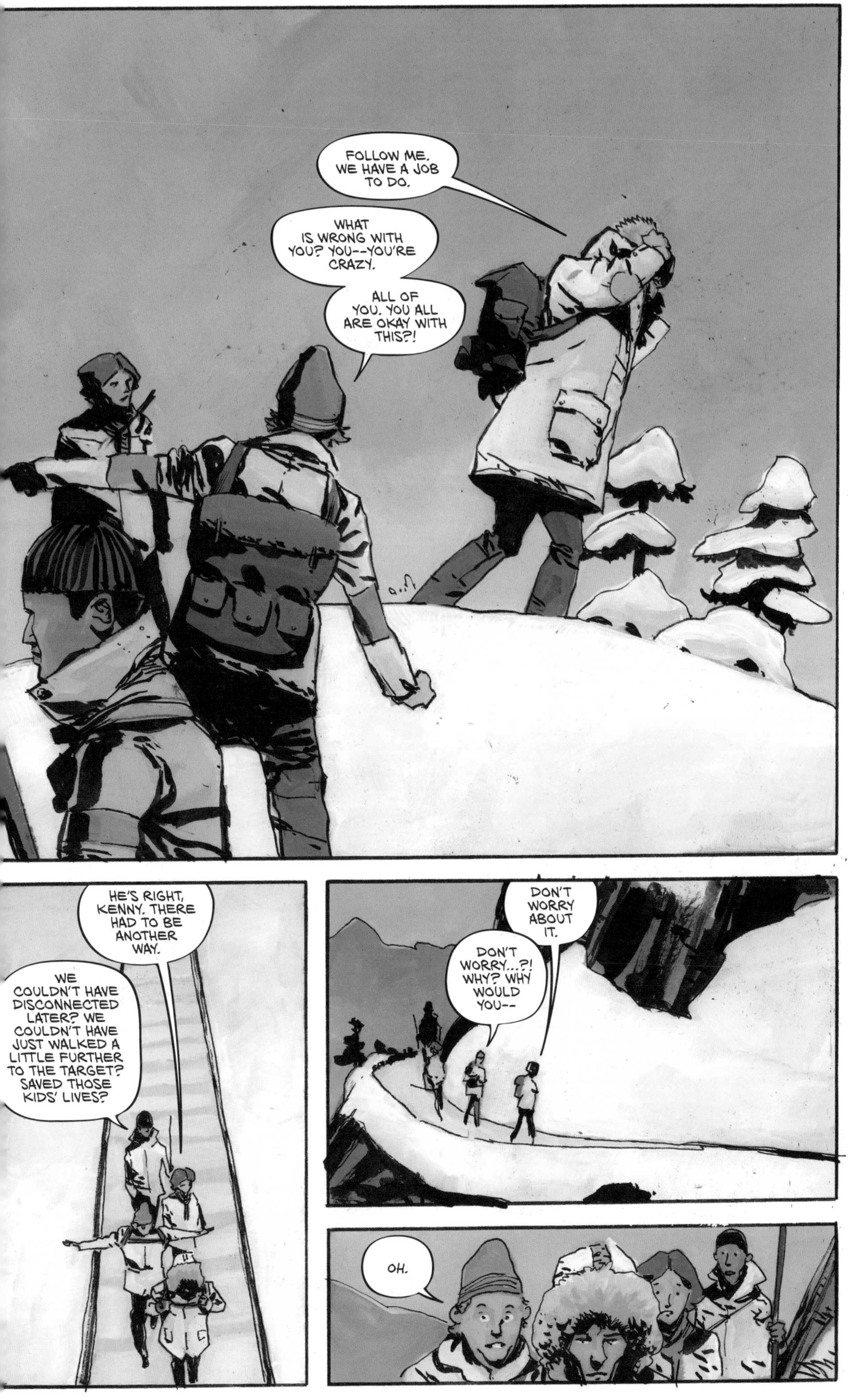
FOLLOW ME. WE HAVE A JOB TO DO.
WHAT IS WRONG WITH YOU? YOU--YOU'RE CRAZY.
ALL OF YOU. YOU ALL ARE OKAY WITH THIS?!
HE'S RIGHT, KENNY. THERE HAD TO BE ANOTHER WAY.
WE COULDN'T HAVE DISCONNECTED LATER? WE COULDN'T HAVE JUST WALKED A LITTLE FURTHER TO THE TARGET? SAVED THOSE KIDS' LIVES?
DON'T WORRY ABOUT IT.
DON'T WORRY...?! WHY? WHY WOULD YOU--
OH.

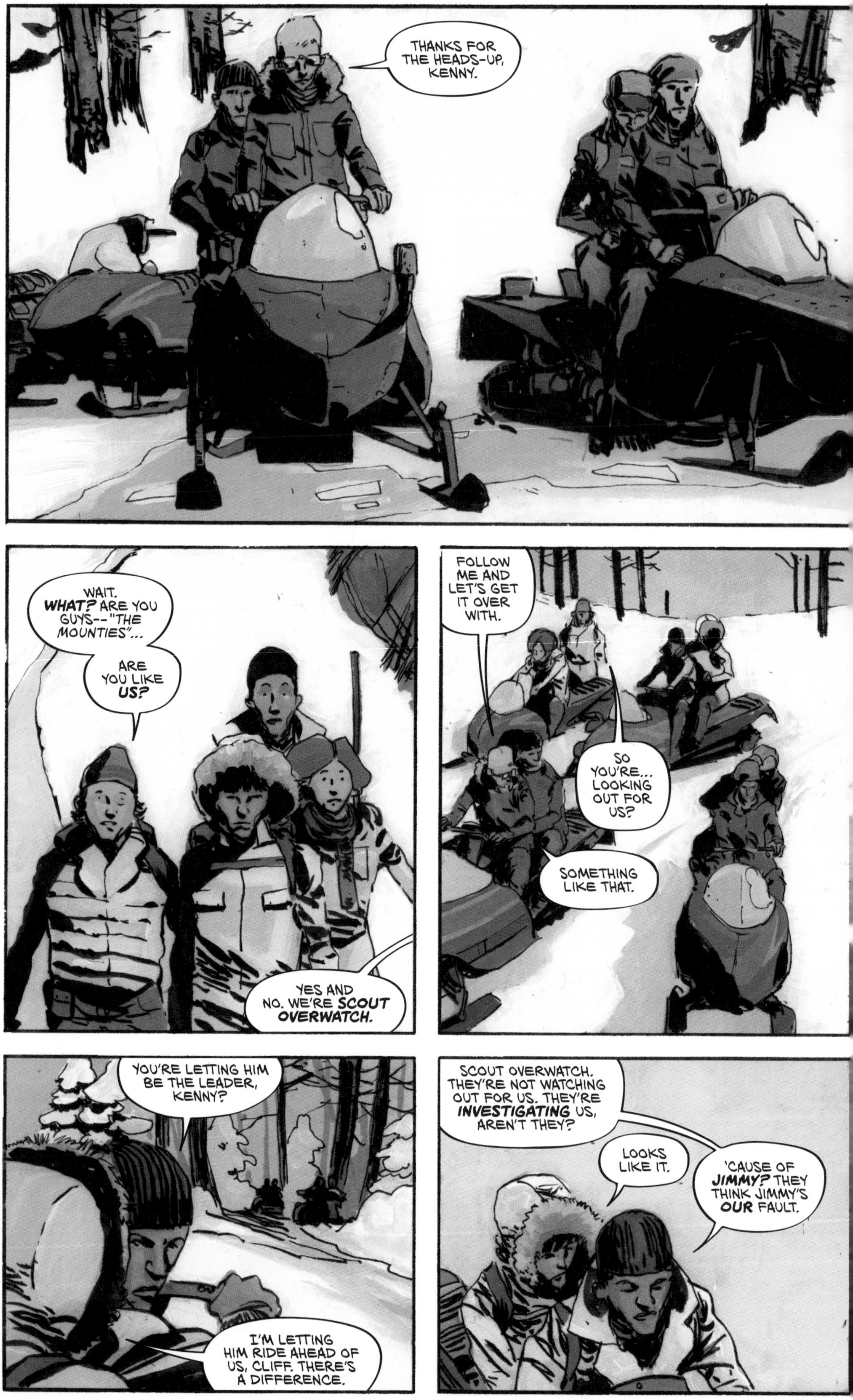
THANKS FOR THE HEADS-UP, KENNY.
WAIT. WHAT? ARE YOU GUYS-- "THE MOUNTIES"...
ARE YOU LIKE US?
YES AND NO. WE'RE SCOUT OVERWATCH.
FOLLOW ME AND LET'S GET IT OVER WITH.
SO YOU'RE... LOOKING OUT FOR US?
SOMETHING LIKE THAT.
YOU'RE LETTING HIM BE THE LEADER, KENNY?
I'M LETTING HIM RIDE AHEAD OF US, CLIFF. THERE'S A DIFFERENCE.
SCOUT OVERWATCH. THEY'RE NOT WATCHING OUT FOR US. THEY'RE INVESTIGATING US, AREN'T THEY?
LOOKS LIKE IT.
'CAUSE OF JIMMY? THEY THINK JIMMY'S OUR FAULT.

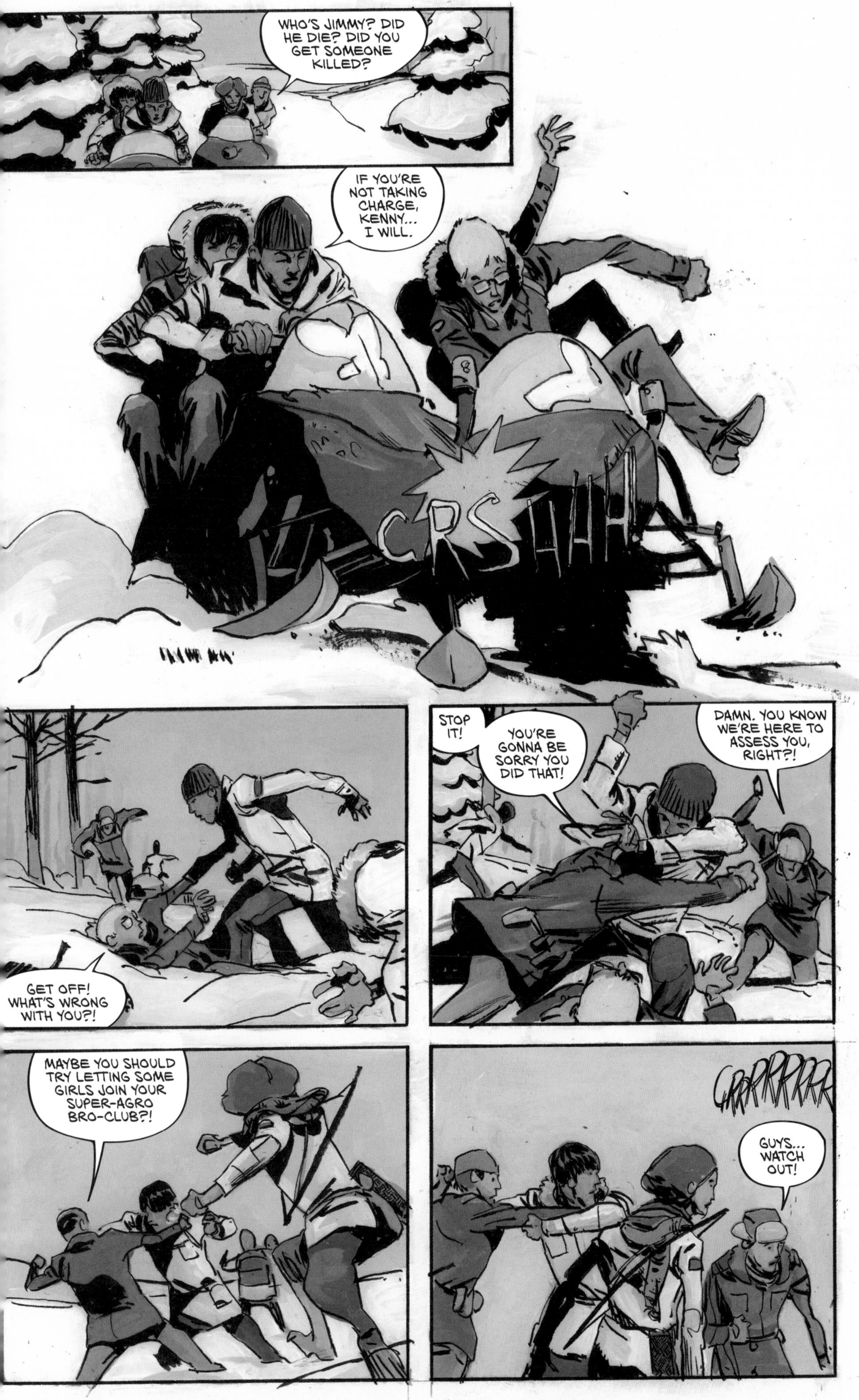
WHO'S JIMMY? DID HE DIE? DID YOU GET SOMEONE KILLED?
IF YOU'RE NOT TAKING CHARGE, KENNY... I WILL.
CRSHAAH
GET OFF! WHAT'S WRONG WITH YOU?!
STOP IT!
YOU'RE GONNA BE SORRY YOU DID THAT!
DAMN. YOU KNOW WE'RE HERE TO ASSESS YOU, RIGHT?!
MAYBE YOU SHOULD TRY LETTING SOME GIRLS JOIN YOUR SUPER-AGRO BRO-CLUB?!
GRRRRRRRR
GUYS... WATCH OUT!

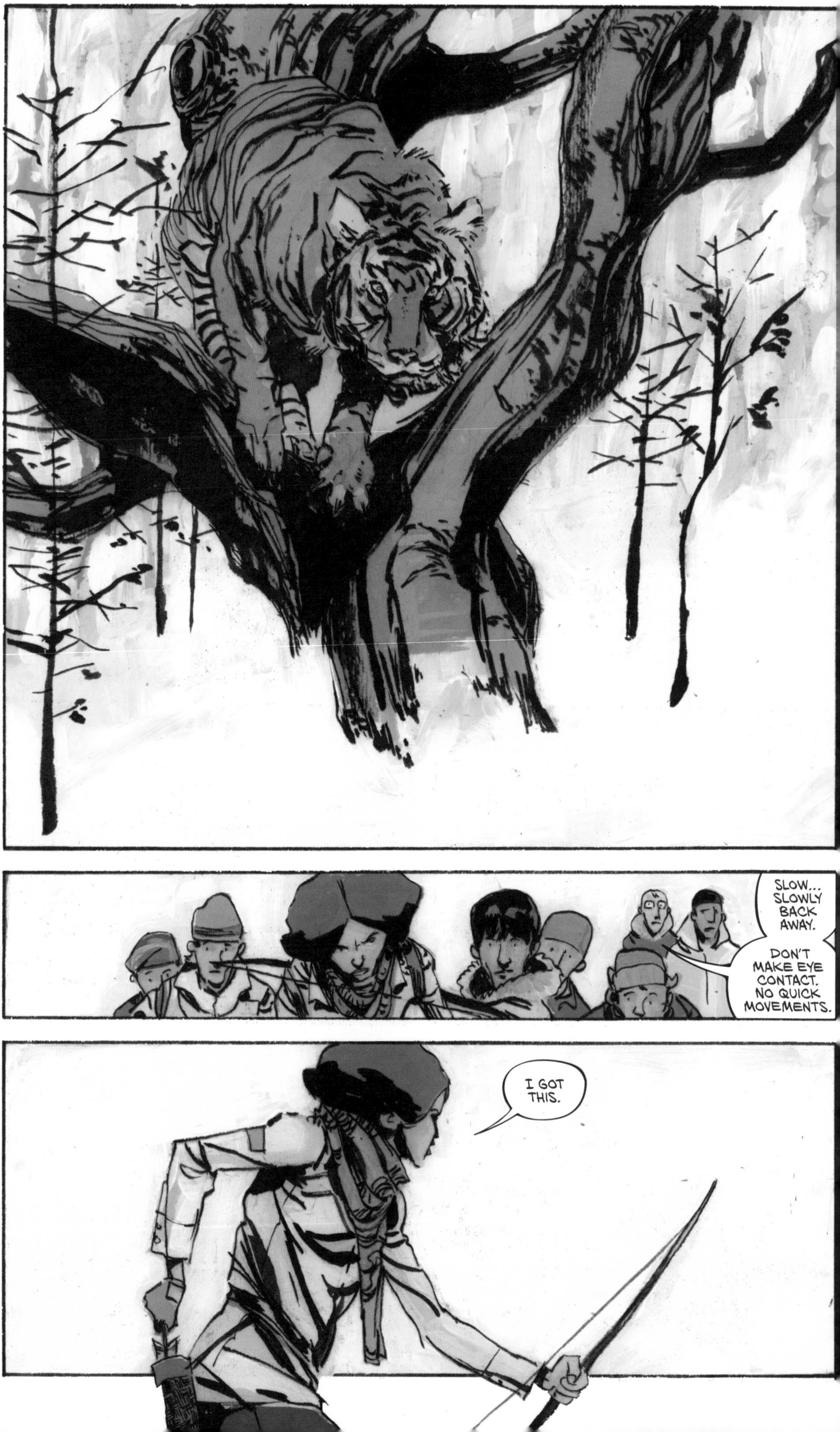
SLOW... SLOWLY BACK AWAY.
DON'T MAKE EYE CONTACT. NO QUICK MOVEMENTS.
I GOT THIS.

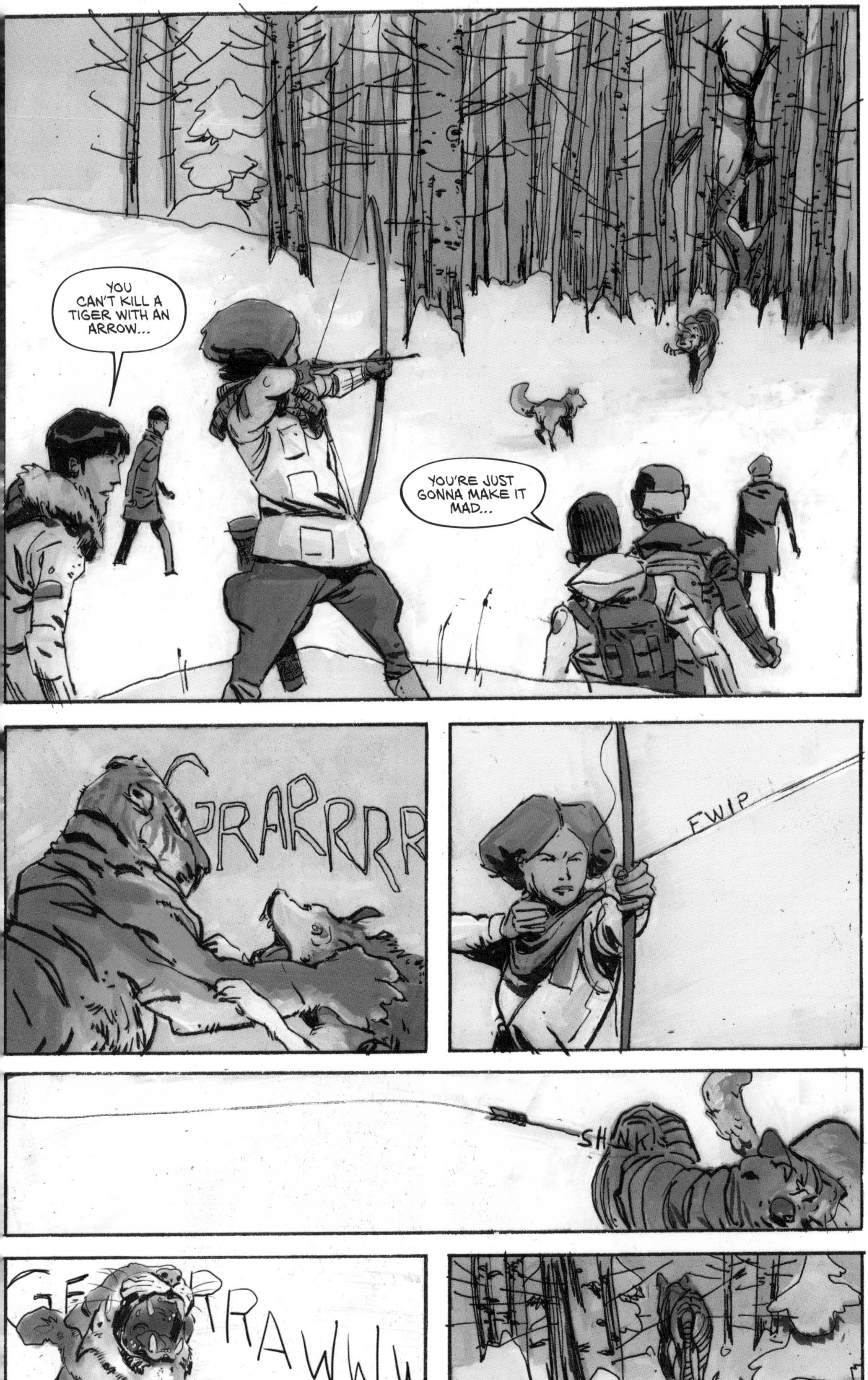
YOU CAN'T KILL A TIGER WITH AN ARROW...
YOU'RE JUST GONNA MAKE IT MAD...
GRARRRR
FWIP
SHNK!
RAWWW

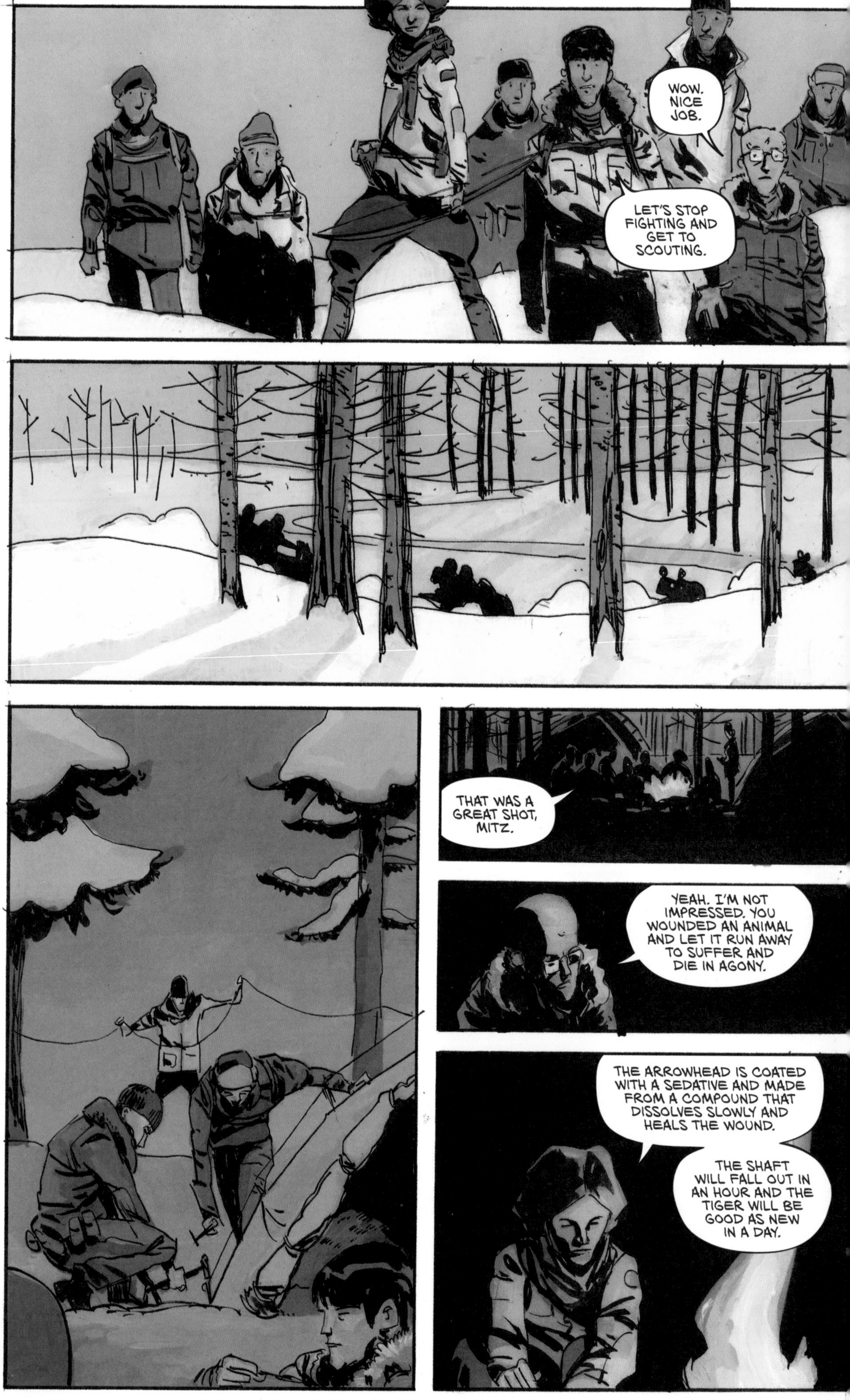
WOW. NICE JOB.
LET'S STOP FIGHTING AND GET TO SCOUTING.
THAT WAS A GREAT SHOT, MITZ.
YEAH. I'M NOT IMPRESSED. YOU WOUNDED AN ANIMAL AND LET IT RUN AWAY TO SUFFER AND DIE IN AGONY.
THE ARROWHEAD IS COATED WITH A SEDATIVE AND MADE FROM A COMPOUND THAT DISSOLVES SLOWLY AND HEALS THE WOUND.
THE SHAFT WILL FALL OUT IN AN HOUR AND THE TIGER WILL BE GOOD AS NEW IN A DAY.

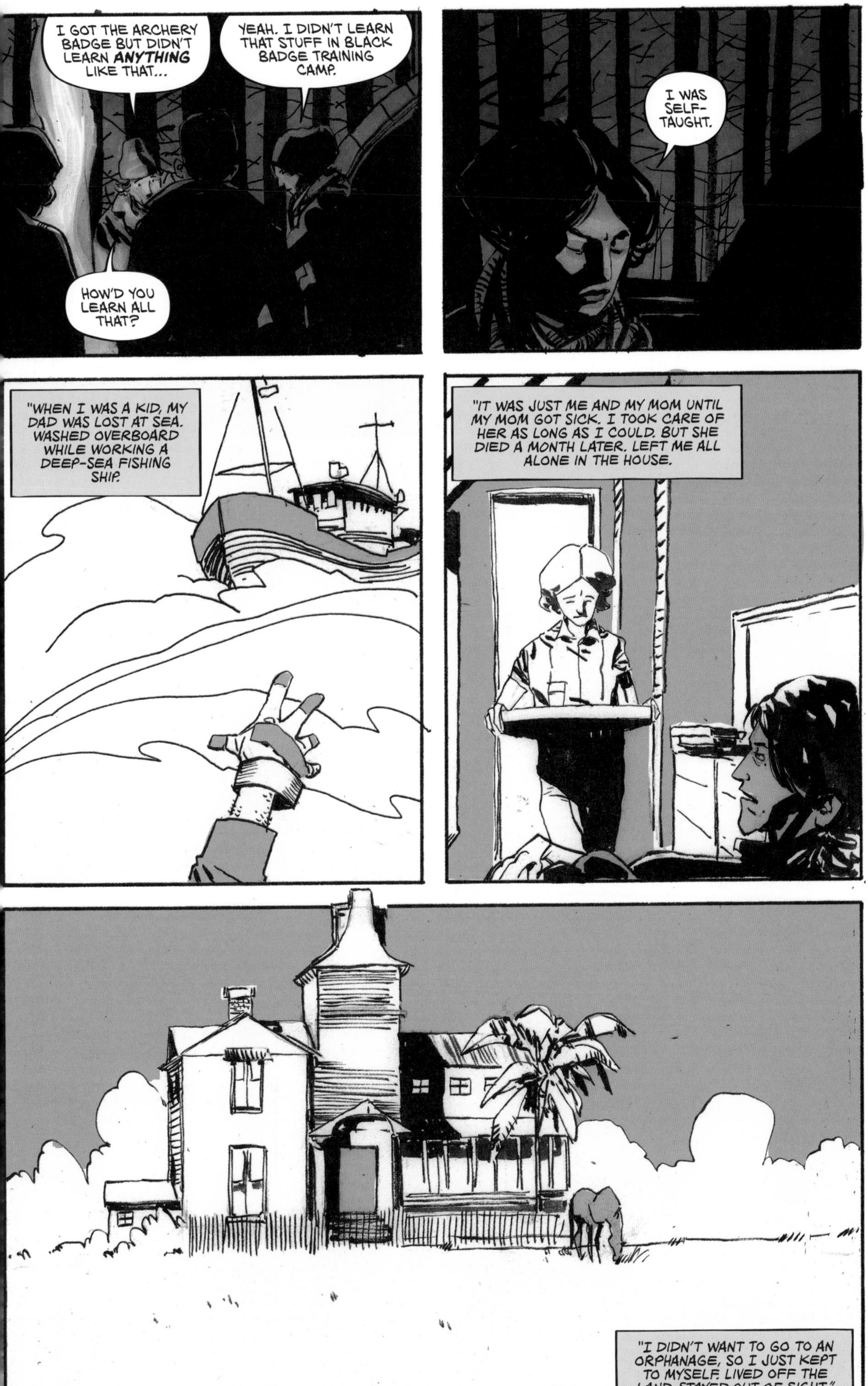

I GOT THE ARCHERY BADGE BUT DIDN'T LEARN **ANYTHING** LIKE THAT...
YEAH. I DIDN'T LEARN THAT STUFF IN BLACK BADGE TRAINING CAMP.
HOW'D YOU LEARN ALL THAT?
I WAS SELF-TAUGHT.
"WHEN I WAS A KID, MY DAD WAS LOST AT SEA. WASHED OVERBOARD WHILE WORKING A DEEP-SEA FISHING SHIP.
"IT WAS JUST ME AND MY MOM UNTIL MY MOM GOT SICK. I TOOK CARE OF HER AS LONG AS I COULD. BUT SHE DIED A MONTH LATER. LEFT ME ALL ALONE IN THE HOUSE.
"I DIDN'T WANT TO GO TO AN ORPHANAGE, SO I JUST KEPT TO MYSELF. LIVED OFF THE LAND. STAYED OUT OF SIGHT."

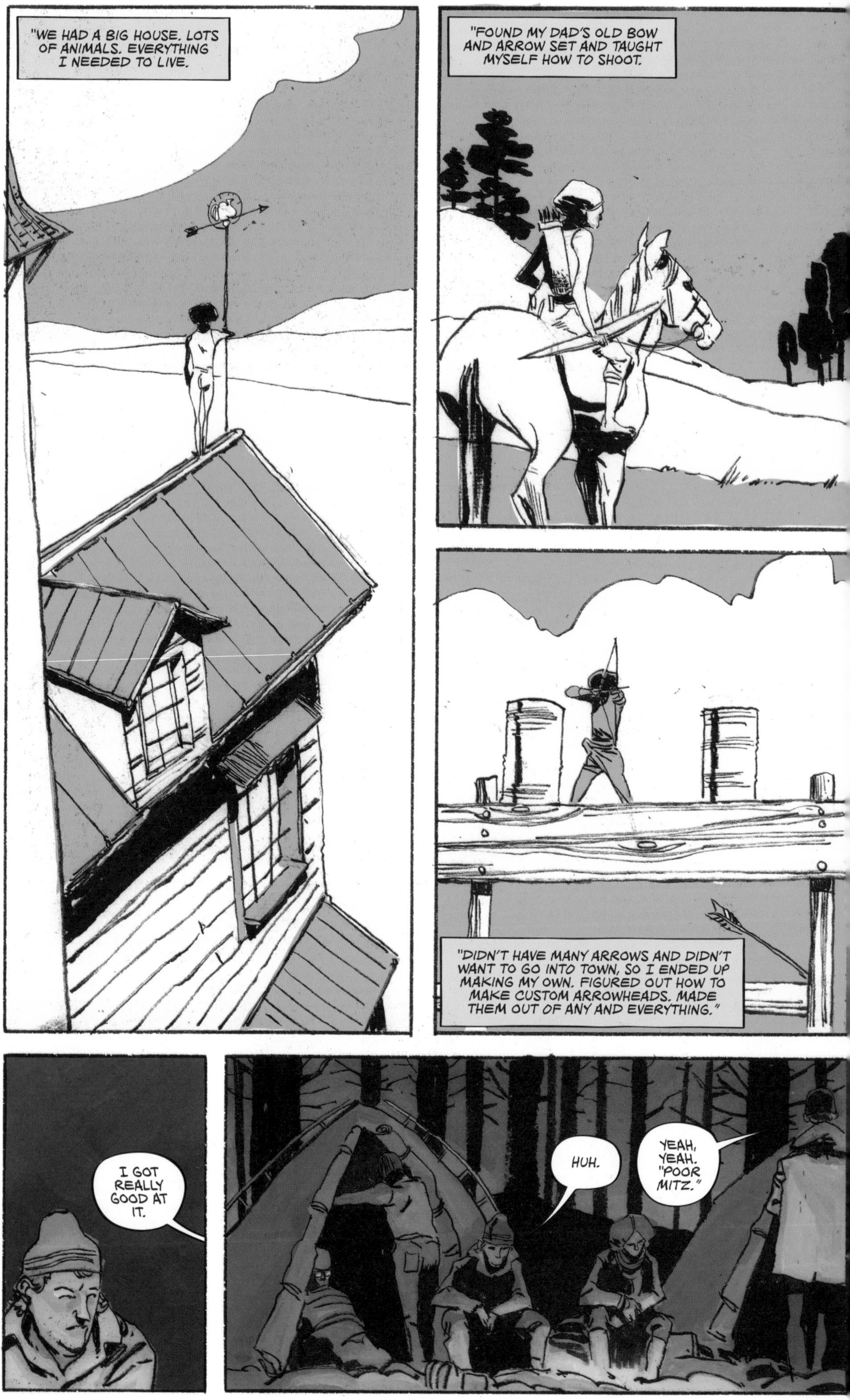
"WE HAD A BIG HOUSE. LOTS OF ANIMALS. EVERYTHING I NEEDED TO LIVE.
"FOUND MY DAD'S OLD BOW AND ARROW SET AND TAUGHT MYSELF HOW TO SHOOT.
"DIDN'T HAVE MANY ARROWS AND DIDN'T WANT TO GO INTO TOWN, SO I ENDED UP MAKING MY OWN. FIGURED OUT HOW TO MAKE CUSTOM ARROWHEADS. MADE THEM OUT OF ANY AND EVERYTHING."
I GOT REALLY GOOD AT IT.
HUH.
YEAH, YEAH. "POOR MITZ."

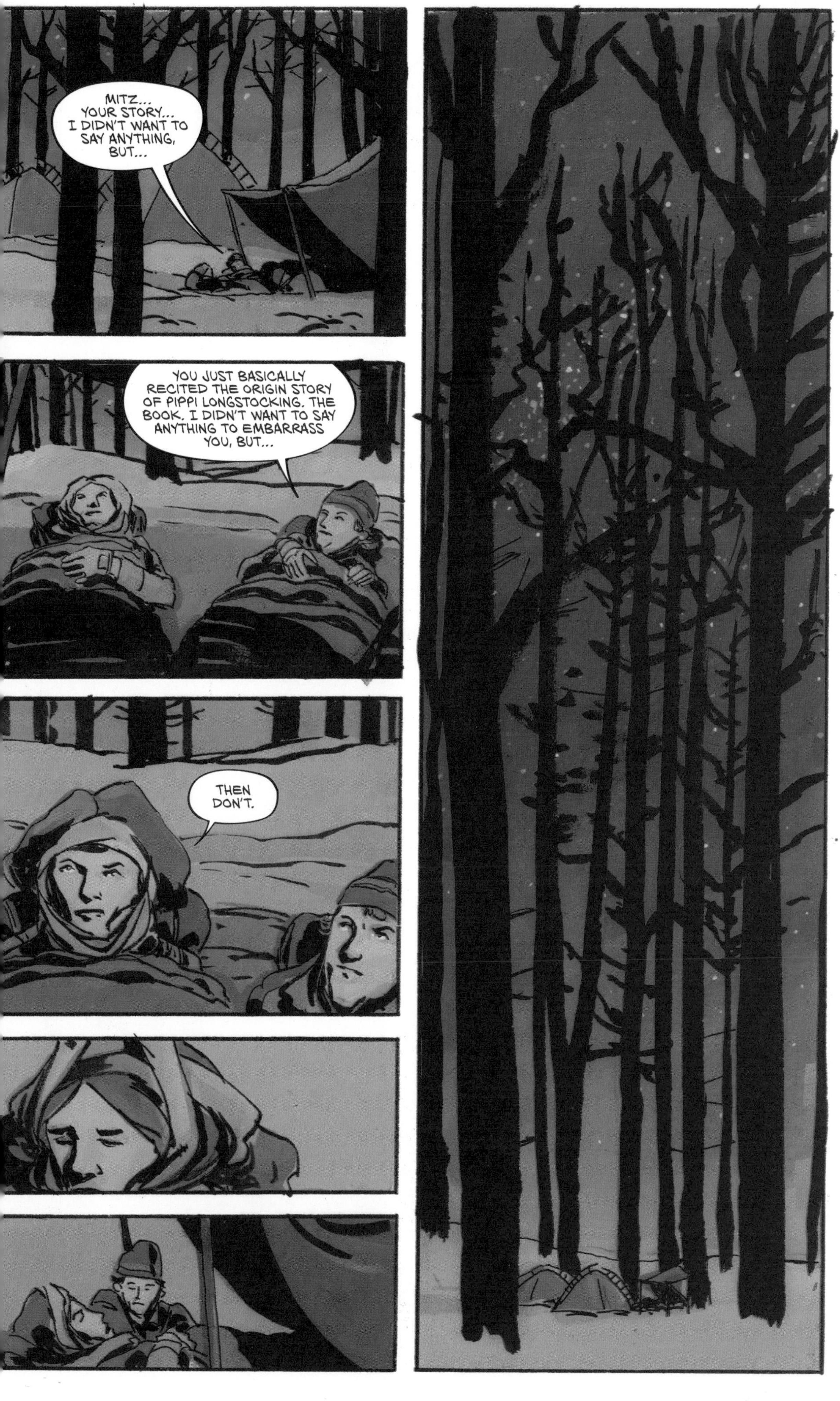

MITZ... YOUR STORY... I DIDN'T WANT TO SAY ANYTHING, BUT...
YOU JUST BASICALLY RECITED THE ORIGIN STORY OF PIPPI LONGSTOCKING. THE BOOK. I DIDN'T WANT TO SAY ANYTHING TO EMBARRASS YOU, BUT...
THEN DON'T.

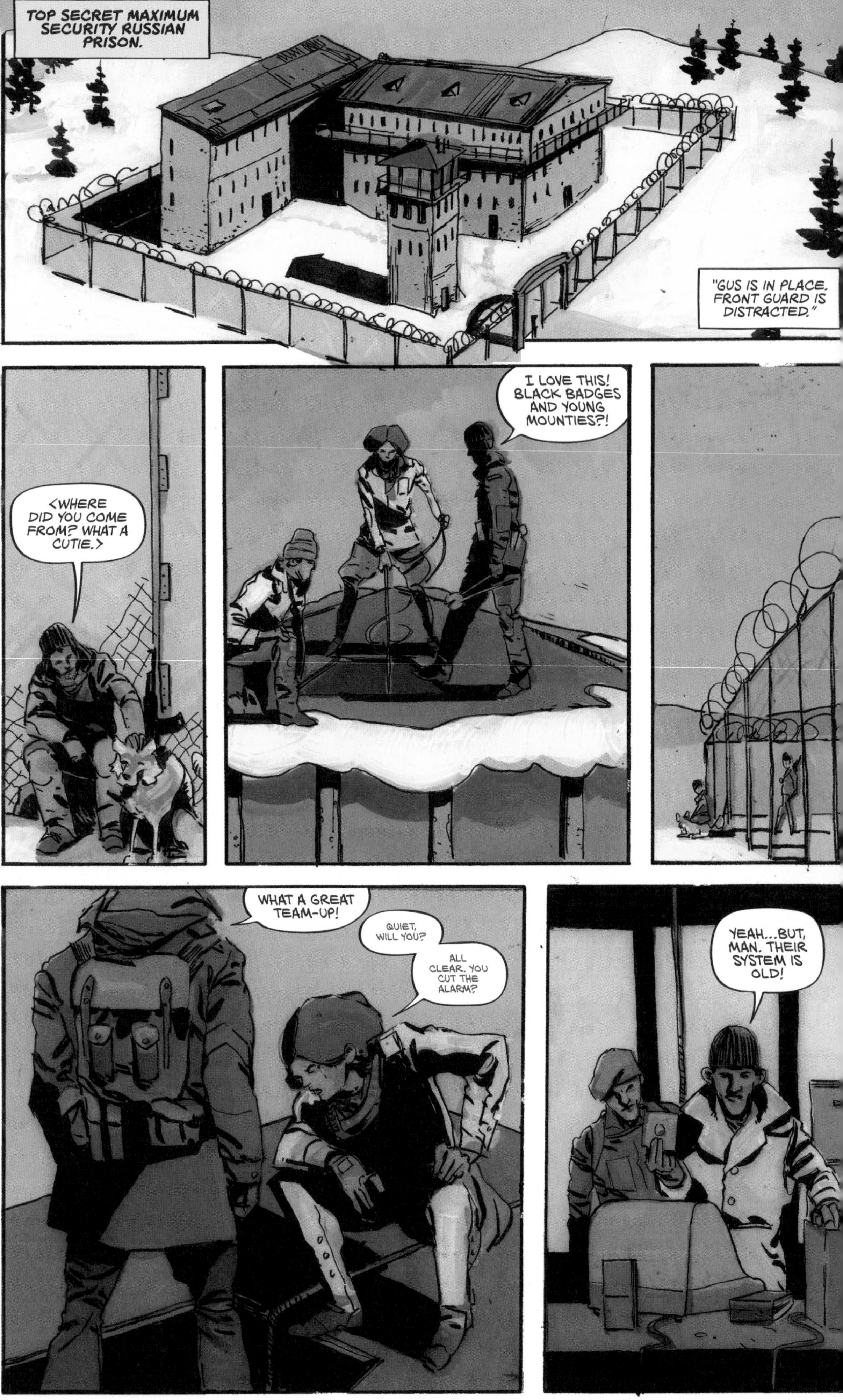
TOP SECRET MAXIMUM SECURITY RUSSIAN PRISON.
"GUS IS IN PLACE. FRONT GUARD IS DISTRACTED."
<WHERE DID YOU COME FROM? WHAT A CUTIE.>
I LOVE THIS! BLACK BADGES AND YOUNG MOUNTIES?!
WHAT A GREAT TEAM-UP!
QUIET, WILL YOU?
ALL CLEAR. YOU CUT THE ALARM?
YEAH...BUT, MAN. THEIR SYSTEM IS OLD!

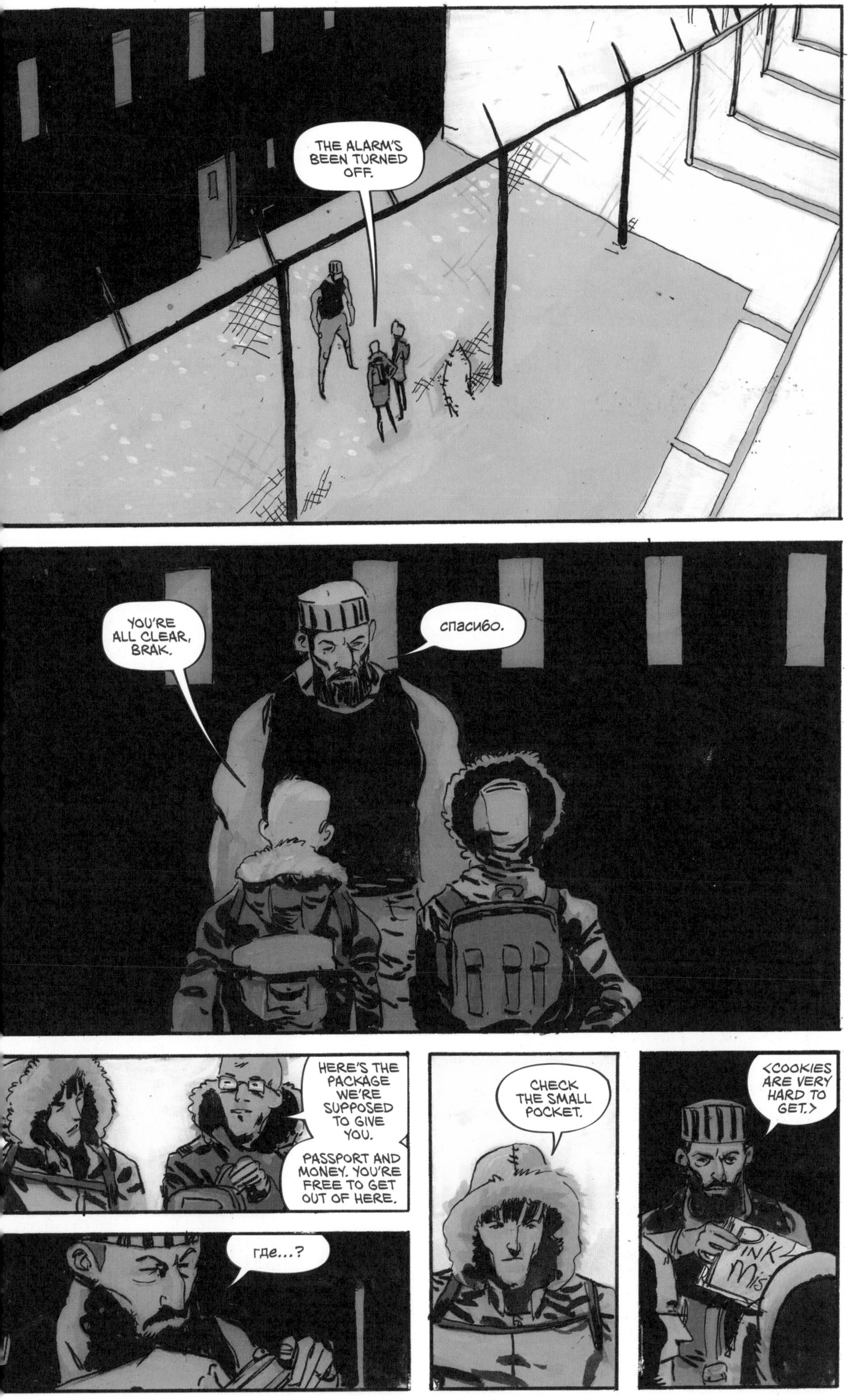
THE ALARM'S BEEN TURNED OFF.
YOU'RE ALL CLEAR, BRAK.
спасибо.
HERE'S THE PACKAGE WE'RE SUPPOSED TO GIVE YOU.
PASSPORT AND MONEY. YOU'RE FREE TO GET OUT OF HERE.
где...?
CHECK THE SMALL POCKET.
<COOKIES ARE VERY HARD TO GET.>

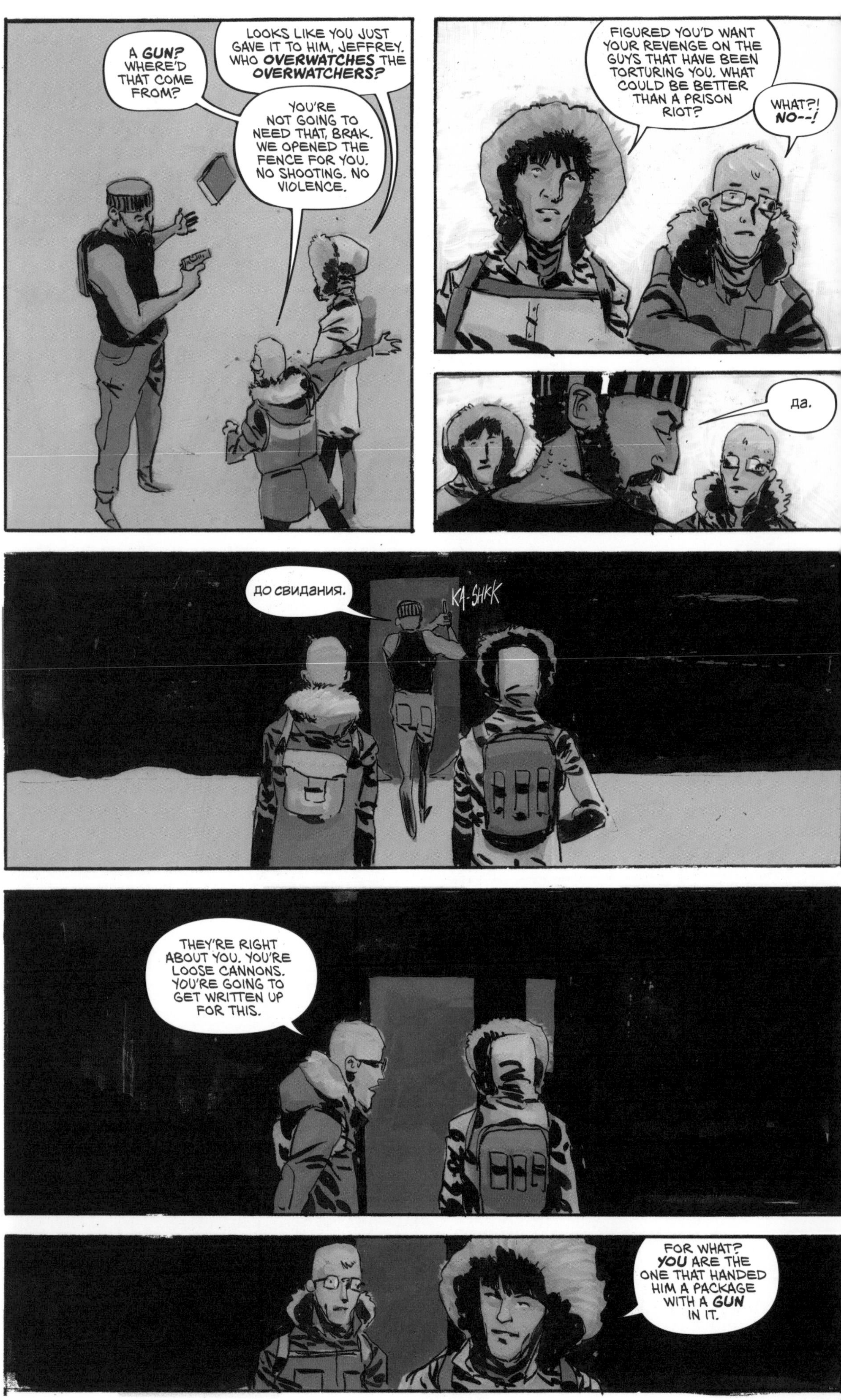
A GUN? WHERE'D THAT COME FROM?
LOOKS LIKE YOU JUST GAVE IT TO HIM, JEFFREY. WHO OVERWATCHES THE OVERWATCHERS?
YOU'RE NOT GOING TO NEED THAT, BRAK. WE OPENED THE FENCE FOR YOU. NO SHOOTING. NO VIOLENCE.
FIGURED YOU'D WANT YOUR REVENGE ON THE GUYS THAT HAVE BEEN TORTURING YOU. WHAT COULD BE BETTER THAN A PRISON RIOT?
WHAT?! NO--!
Да.
До свидания.
KA-SHKK
THEY'RE RIGHT ABOUT YOU. YOU'RE LOOSE CANNONS. YOU'RE GOING TO GET WRITTEN UP FOR THIS.
FOR WHAT? YOU ARE THE ONE THAT HANDED HIM A PACKAGE WITH A GUN IN IT.

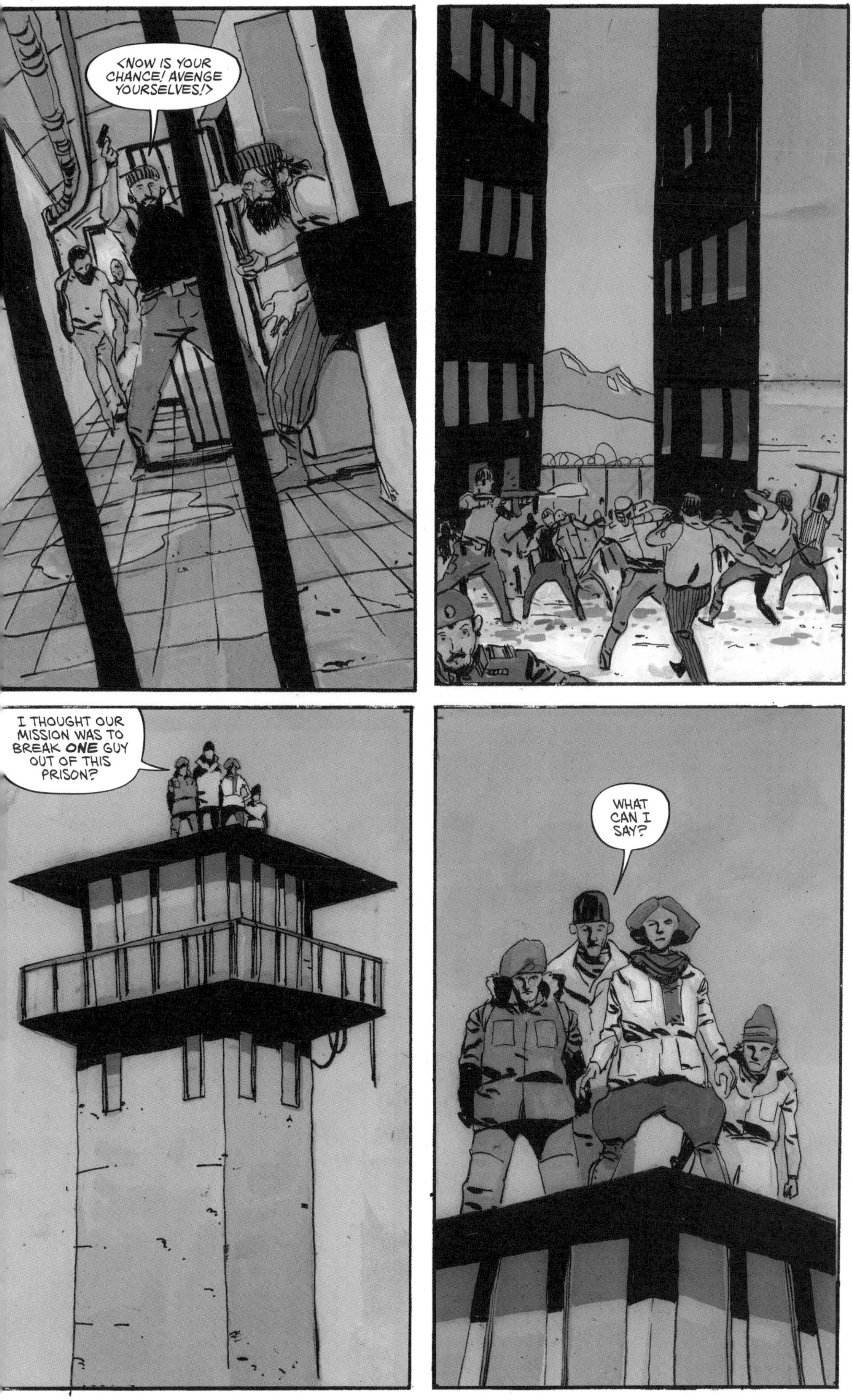
<NOW IS YOUR CHANCE! AVENGE YOURSELVES!>
I THOUGHT OUR MISSION WAS TO BREAK **ONE** GUY OUT OF THIS PRISON?
WHAT CAN I SAY?

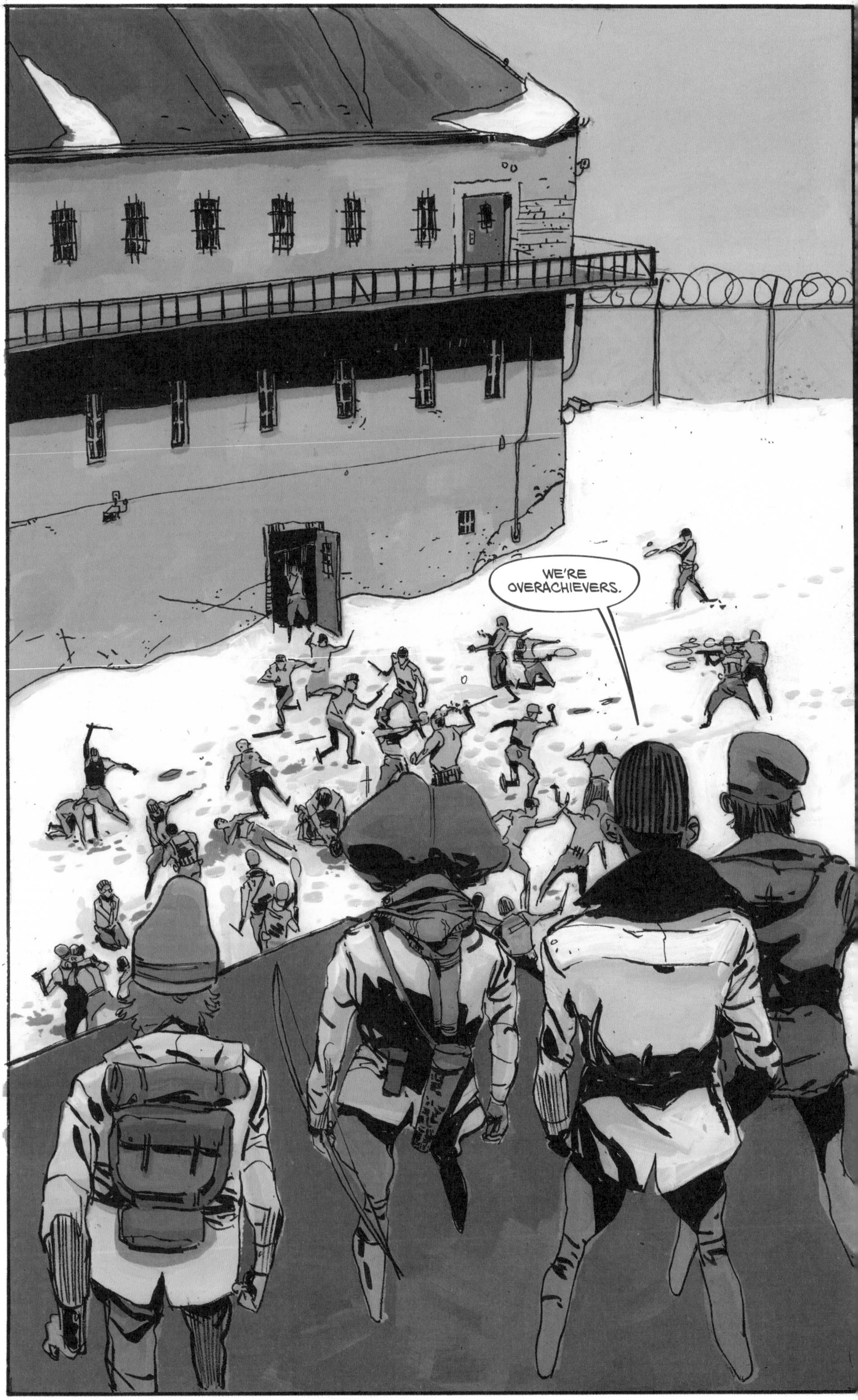
WE'RE OVERACHIEVERS.

VISUAL AID FOR
IMPROVISED WEAPONS

Figure 1. Simple Garrote

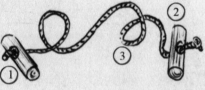

1: Double Overhand Stopper Knot

2: Two pieces of 1-inch dowel

3: Two feet of heavy duty rope or wire.

Black Badge was founded in 1910 by William Randolph Hea
sub-branch of the American Boy Scouts. After the Boy Sco
America sued Hearst for use of the name, the ABS was dis
but Black Badge remained* - becoming active during both
Wars and as a sort of elite scouting club in present d

Chapter Three

[redacted] Camp Wayword [redacted] escort mission [redacted]

Codename: Hook Hand [redacted] traitor [redacted] diversionary tactics [redacted] Where is Jimmy? [redacted]

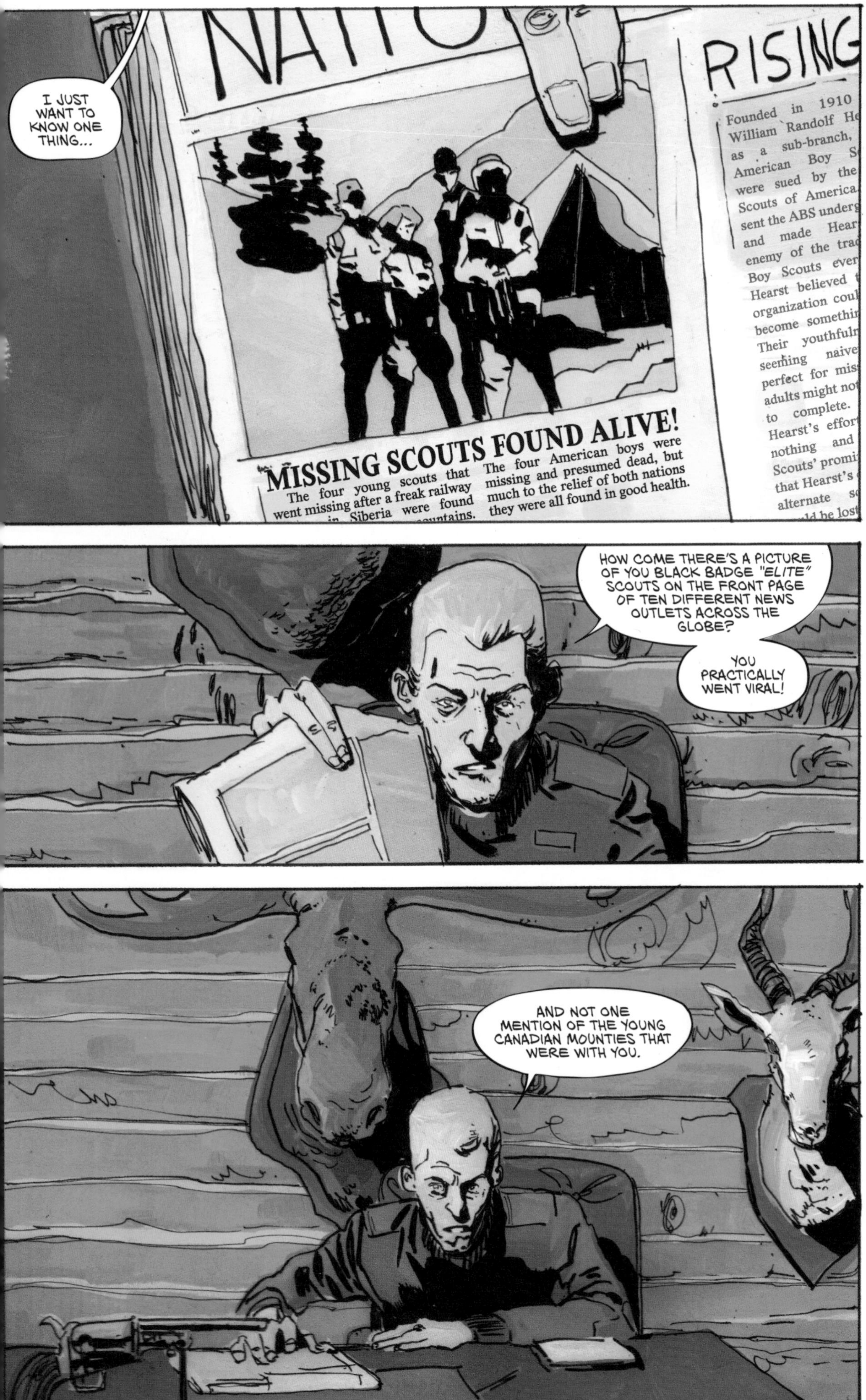
I JUST WANT TO KNOW ONE THING...
RISING
Founded in 1910
William Randolf He
as a sub-branch,
American Boy S
were sued by the
Scouts of America.
sent the ABS underg
and made Hears
enemy of the trad
Boy Scouts ever
Hearst believed t
organization coul
become somethin
Their youthfuln
seeming naive
perfect for miss
adults might not
to complete.
Hearst's effor
nothing and
Scouts' promi
that Hearst's
alternate s
MISSING SCOUTS FOUND ALIVE!
The four young scouts that went missing after a freak railway in Siberia were found
The four American boys were missing and presumed dead, but much to the relief of both nations they were all found in good health.
HOW COME THERE'S A PICTURE OF YOU BLACK BADGE "ELITE" SCOUTS ON THE FRONT PAGE OF TEN DIFFERENT NEWS OUTLETS ACROSS THE GLOBE?
YOU PRACTICALLY WENT VIRAL!
AND NOT ONE MENTION OF THE YOUNG CANADIAN MOUNTIES THAT WERE WITH YOU.

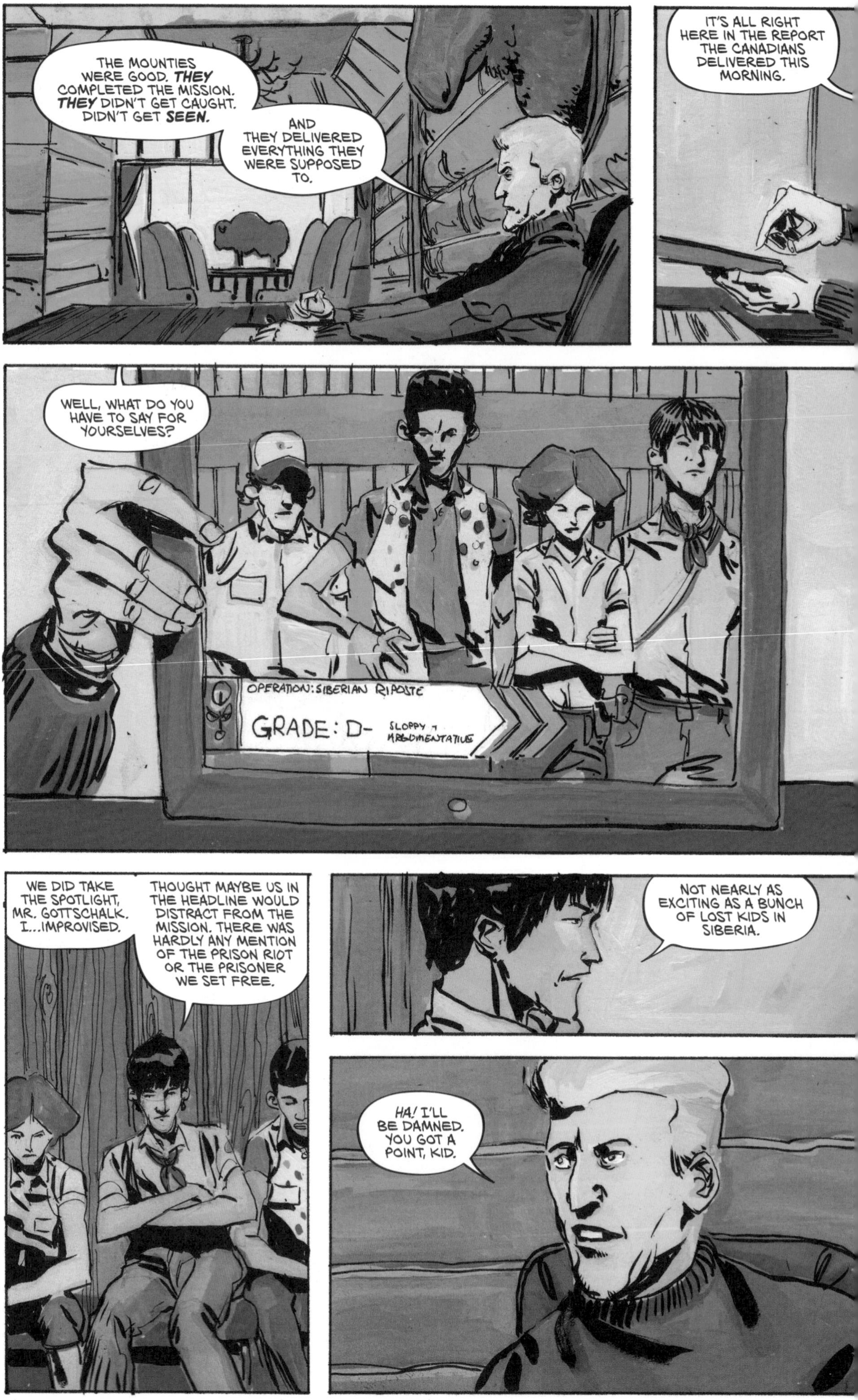

THE MOUNTIES WERE GOOD. **THEY** COMPLETED THE MISSION. **THEY** DIDN'T GET CAUGHT. DIDN'T GET **SEEN.**
AND THEY DELIVERED EVERYTHING THEY WERE SUPPOSED TO.
IT'S ALL RIGHT HERE IN THE REPORT THE CANADIANS DELIVERED THIS MORNING.
WELL, WHAT DO YOU HAVE TO SAY FOR YOURSELVES?
OPERATION: SIBERIAN RIPOSTE
GRADE: D-
SLOPPY + ARGUMENTATIVE
WE DID TAKE THE SPOTLIGHT, MR. GOTTSCHALK. I...IMPROVISED.
THOUGHT MAYBE US IN THE HEADLINE WOULD DISTRACT FROM THE MISSION. THERE WAS HARDLY ANY MENTION OF THE PRISON RIOT OR THE PRISONER WE SET FREE.
NOT NEARLY AS EXCITING AS A BUNCH OF LOST KIDS IN SIBERIA.
HA! I'LL BE DAMNED. YOU GOT A POINT, KID.

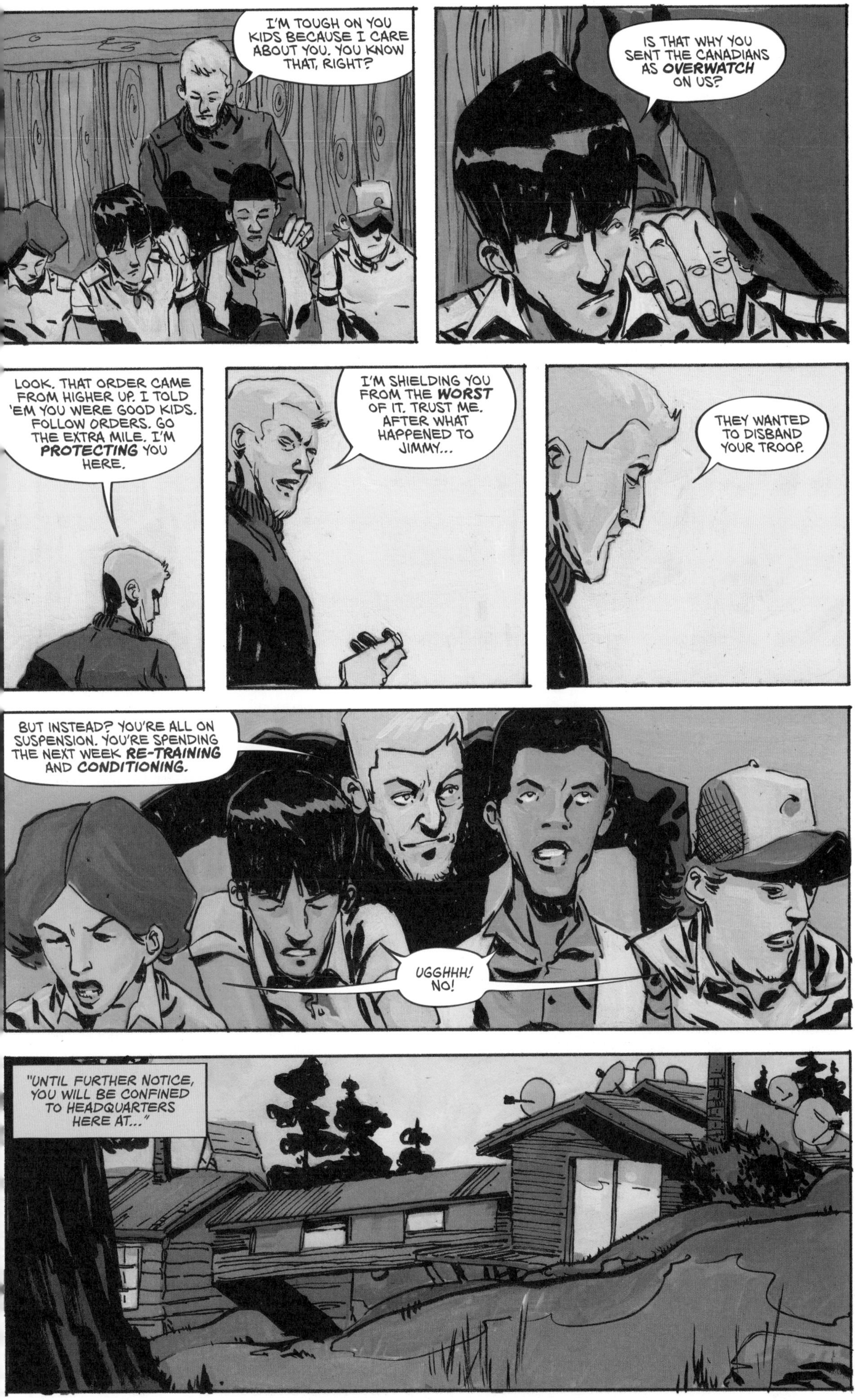
I'M TOUGH ON YOU KIDS BECAUSE I CARE ABOUT YOU. YOU KNOW THAT, RIGHT?
IS THAT WHY YOU SENT THE CANADIANS AS **OVERWATCH** ON US?
LOOK. THAT ORDER CAME FROM HIGHER UP. I TOLD 'EM YOU WERE GOOD KIDS. FOLLOW ORDERS. GO THE EXTRA MILE. I'M **PROTECTING** YOU HERE.
I'M SHIELDING YOU FROM THE **WORST** OF IT. TRUST ME. AFTER WHAT HAPPENED TO JIMMY...
THEY WANTED TO DISBAND YOUR TROOP.
BUT INSTEAD? YOU'RE ALL ON SUSPENSION. YOU'RE SPENDING THE NEXT WEEK **RE-TRAINING** AND **CONDITIONING.**
UGGHHH! NO!
"UNTIL FURTHER NOTICE, YOU WILL BE CONFINED TO HEADQUARTERS HERE AT..."

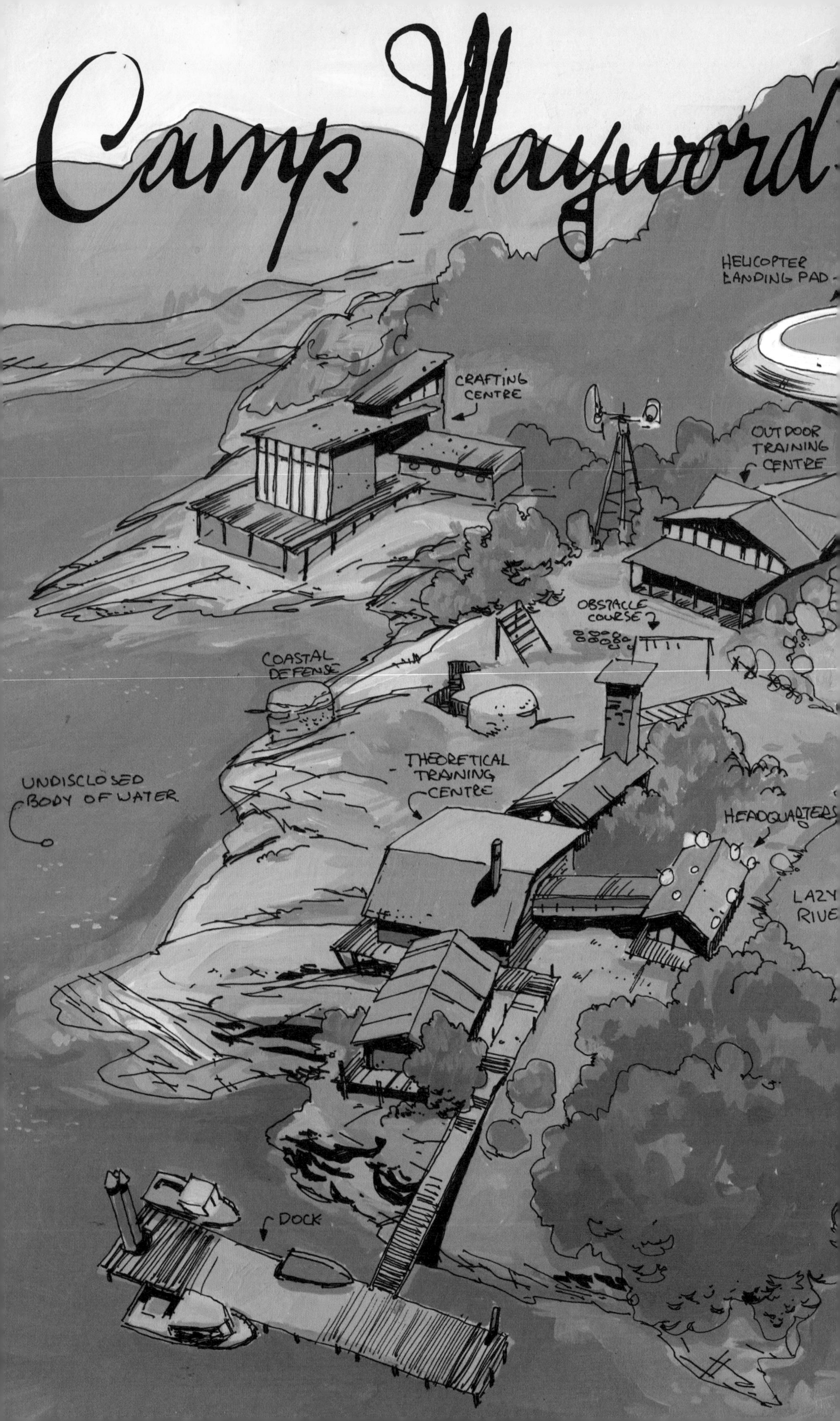
Camp Wayward
HELICOPTER LANDING PAD
CRAFTING CENTRE
OUTDOOR TRAINING CENTRE
OBSTACLE COURSE
COASTAL DEFENSE
THEORETICAL TRAINING CENTRE
UNDISCLOSED BODY OF WATER
HEADQUARTERS
LAZY RIVE
DOCK

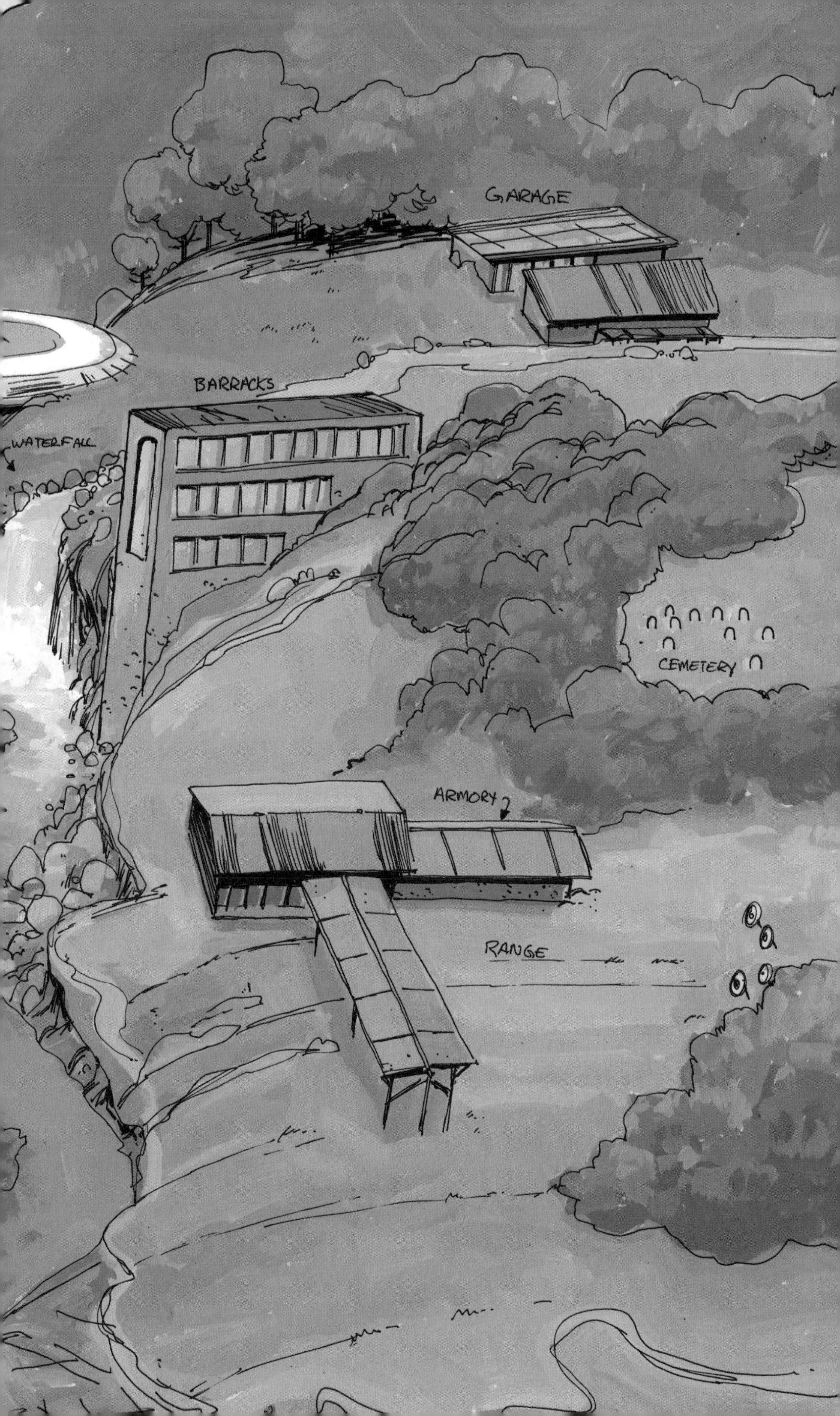
GARAGE
BARRACKS
WATERFALL
CEMETERY
ARMORY
RANGE

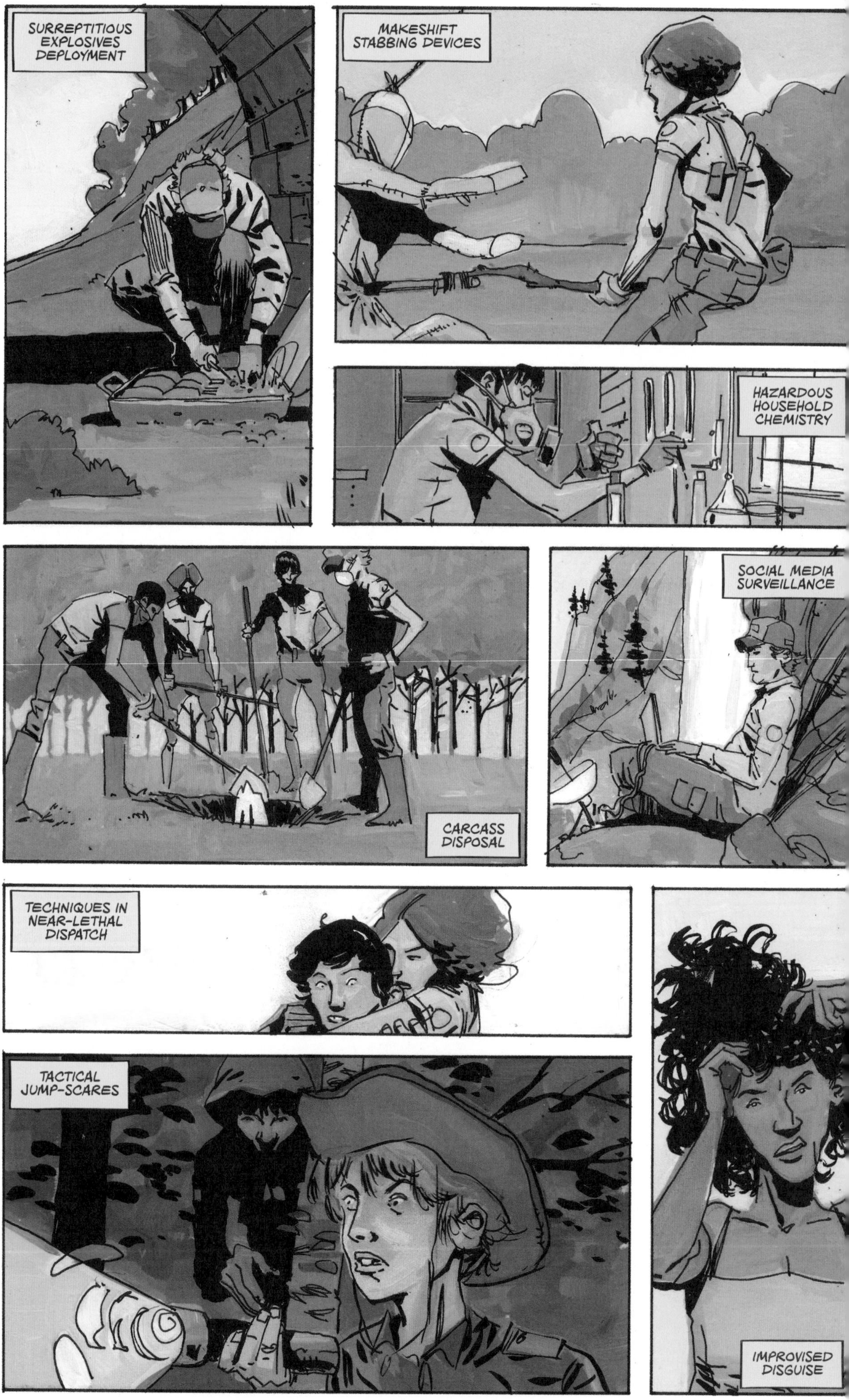
SURREPTITIOUS EXPLOSIVES DEPLOYMENT
MAKESHIFT STABBING DEVICES
HAZARDOUS HOUSEHOLD CHEMISTRY
CARCASS DISPOSAL
SOCIAL MEDIA SURVEILLANCE
TECHNIQUES IN NEAR-LETHAL DISPATCH
TACTICAL JUMP-SCARES
IMPROVISED DISGUISE

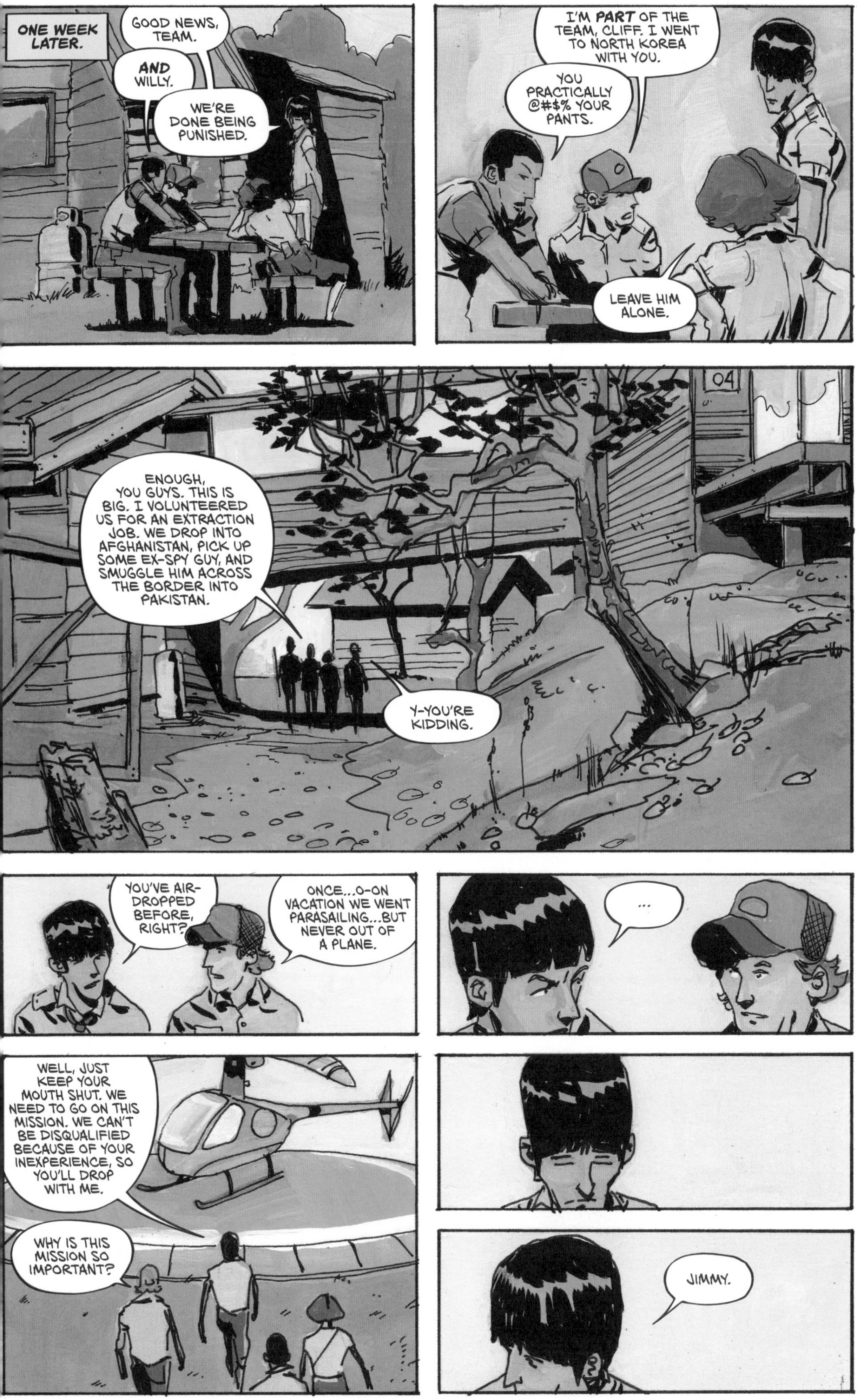
ONE WEEK LATER.
GOOD NEWS, TEAM.
AND WILLY.
WE'RE DONE BEING PUNISHED.
I'M PART OF THE TEAM, CLIFF. I WENT TO NORTH KOREA WITH YOU.
YOU PRACTICALLY @#$% YOUR PANTS.
LEAVE HIM ALONE.
ENOUGH, YOU GUYS. THIS IS BIG. I VOLUNTEERED US FOR AN EXTRACTION JOB. WE DROP INTO AFGHANISTAN, PICK UP SOME EX-SPY GUY, AND SMUGGLE HIM ACROSS THE BORDER INTO PAKISTAN.
04
Y-YOU'RE KIDDING.
YOU'VE AIR-DROPPED BEFORE, RIGHT?
ONCE...O-ON VACATION WE WENT PARASAILING...BUT NEVER OUT OF A PLANE.
...
WELL, JUST KEEP YOUR MOUTH SHUT. WE NEED TO GO ON THIS MISSION. WE CAN'T BE DISQUALIFIED BECAUSE OF YOUR INEXPERIENCE, SO YOU'LL DROP WITH ME.
WHY IS THIS MISSION SO IMPORTANT?
JIMMY.

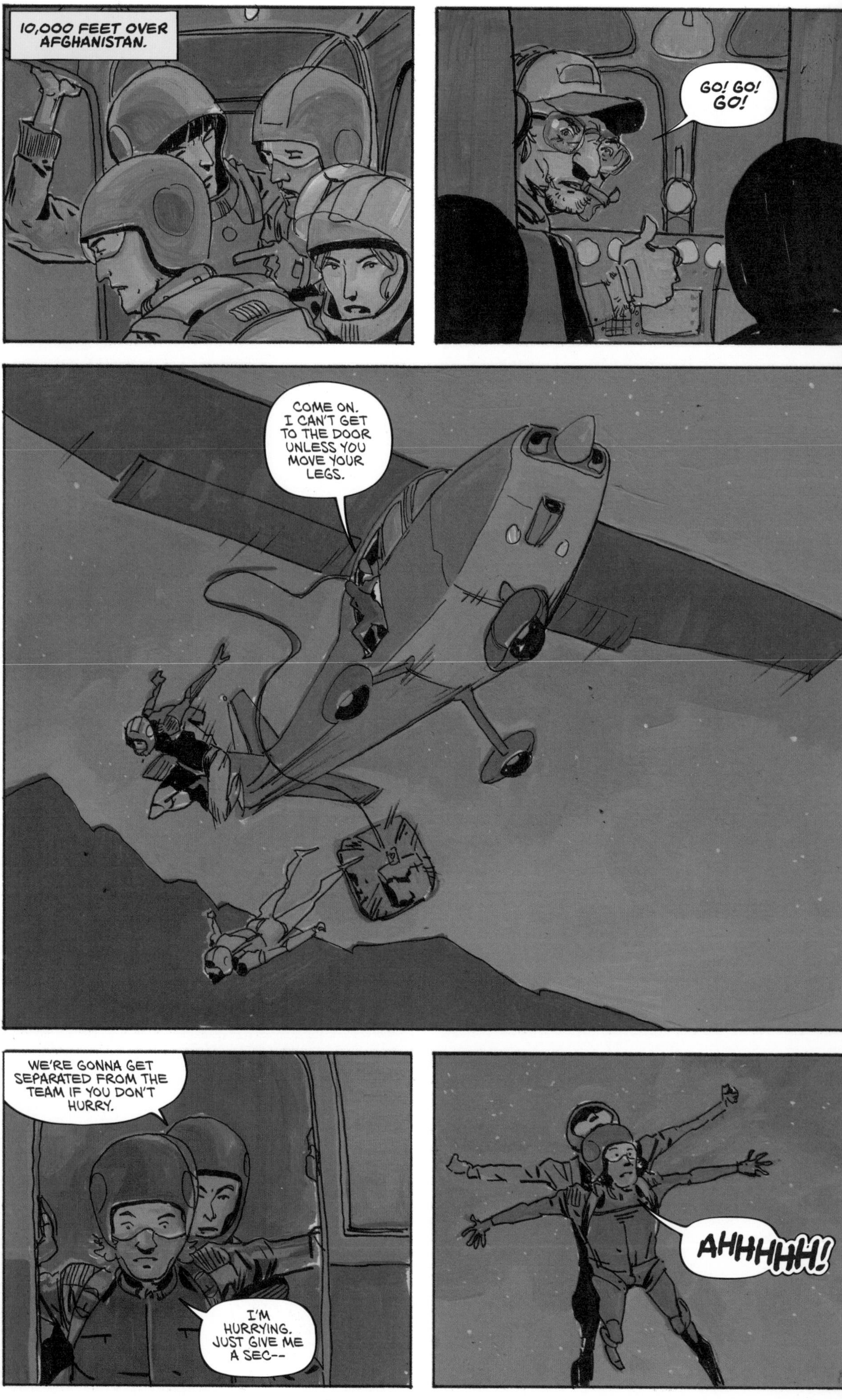
10,000 FEET OVER AFGHANISTAN.
GO! GO! GO!
COME ON. I CAN'T GET TO THE DOOR UNLESS YOU MOVE YOUR LEGS.
WE'RE GONNA GET SEPARATED FROM THE TEAM IF YOU DON'T HURRY.
I'M HURRYING. JUST GIVE ME A SEC--
AHHHHH!

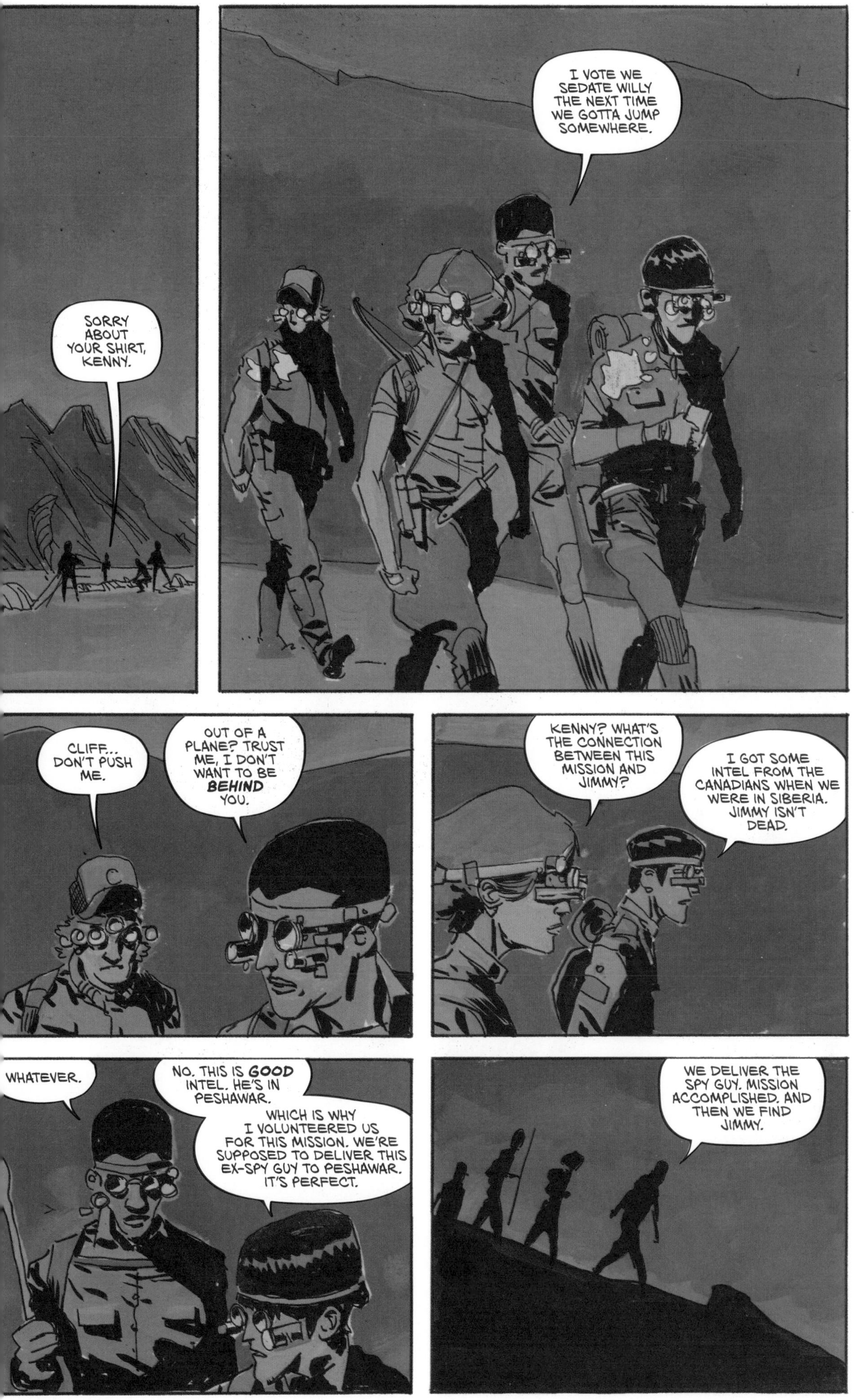
SORRY ABOUT YOUR SHIRT, KENNY.
I VOTE WE SEDATE WILLY THE NEXT TIME WE GOTTA JUMP SOMEWHERE.
CLIFF... DON'T PUSH ME.
OUT OF A PLANE? TRUST ME, I DON'T WANT TO BE **BEHIND** YOU.
KENNY? WHAT'S THE CONNECTION BETWEEN THIS MISSION AND JIMMY?
I GOT SOME INTEL FROM THE CANADIANS WHEN WE WERE IN SIBERIA. JIMMY ISN'T DEAD.
WHATEVER.
NO. THIS IS **GOOD** INTEL. HE'S IN PESHAWAR.
WHICH IS WHY I VOLUNTEERED US FOR THIS MISSION. WE'RE SUPPOSED TO DELIVER THIS EX-SPY GUY TO PESHAWAR. IT'S PERFECT.
WE DELIVER THE SPY GUY. MISSION ACCOMPLISHED. AND THEN WE FIND JIMMY.

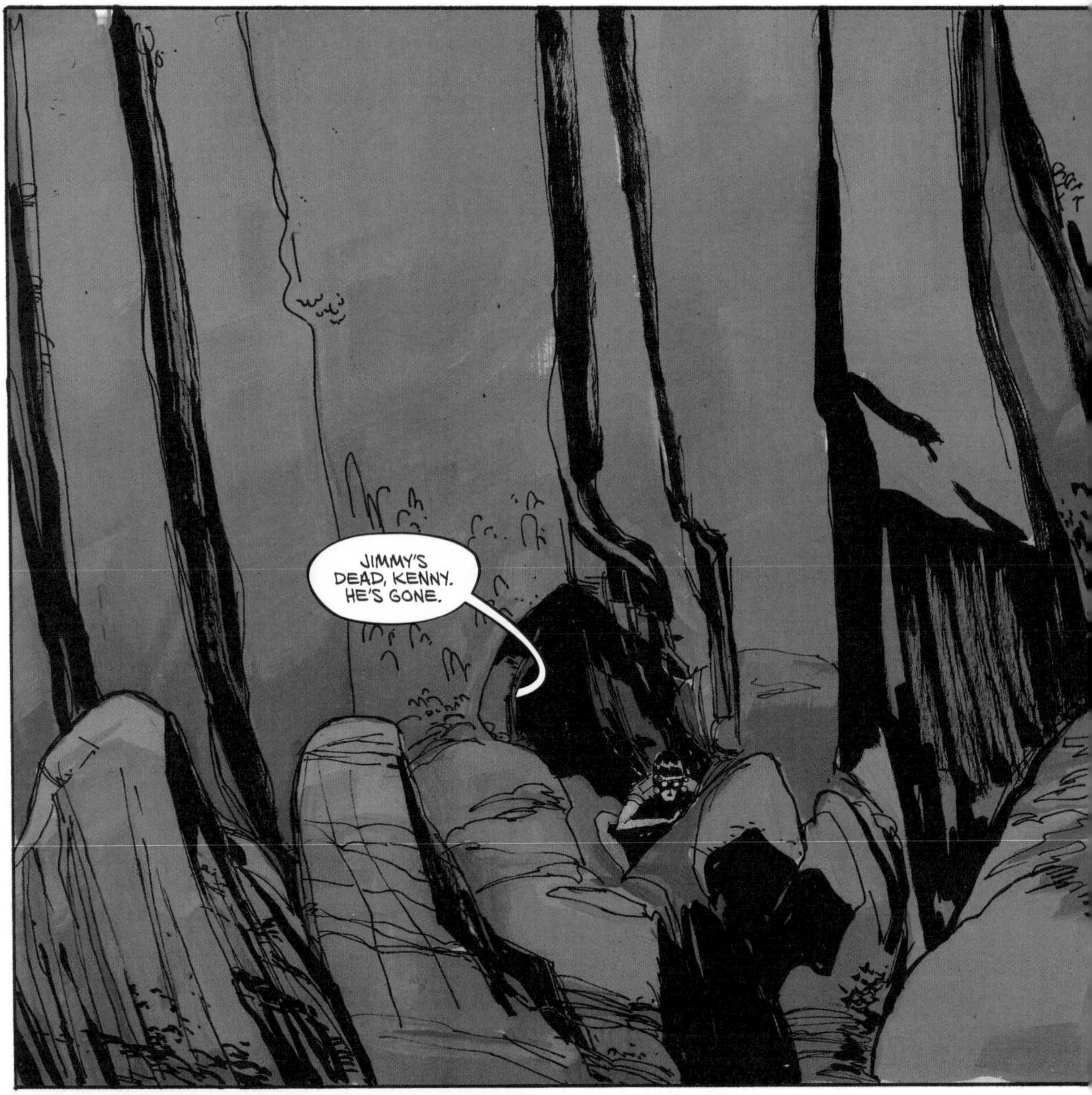
JIMMY'S DEAD, KENNY. HE'S GONE.

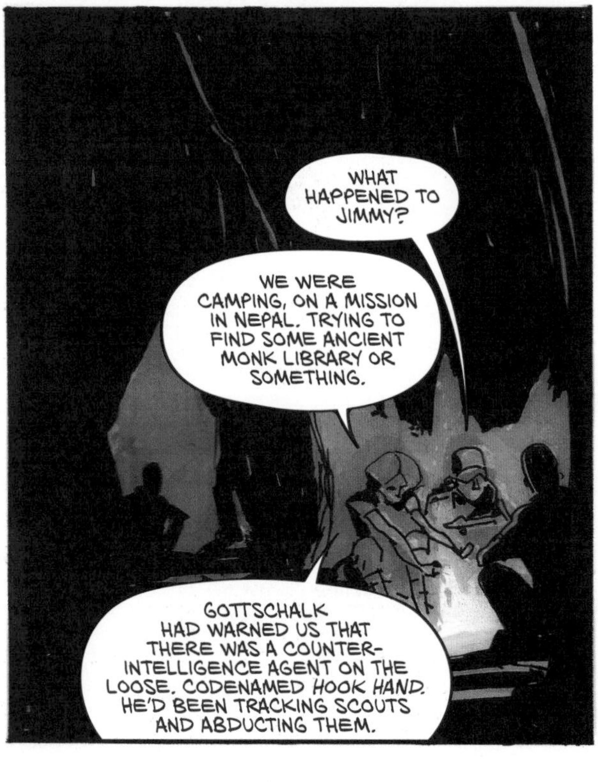
WHAT HAPPENED TO JIMMY?
WE WERE CAMPING, ON A MISSION IN NEPAL. TRYING TO FIND SOME ANCIENT MONK LIBRARY OR SOMETHING.
GOTTSCHALK HAD WARNED US THAT THERE WAS A COUNTER-INTELLIGENCE AGENT ON THE LOOSE. CODENAMED *HOOK HAND*. HE'D BEEN TRACKING SCOUTS AND ABDUCTING THEM.

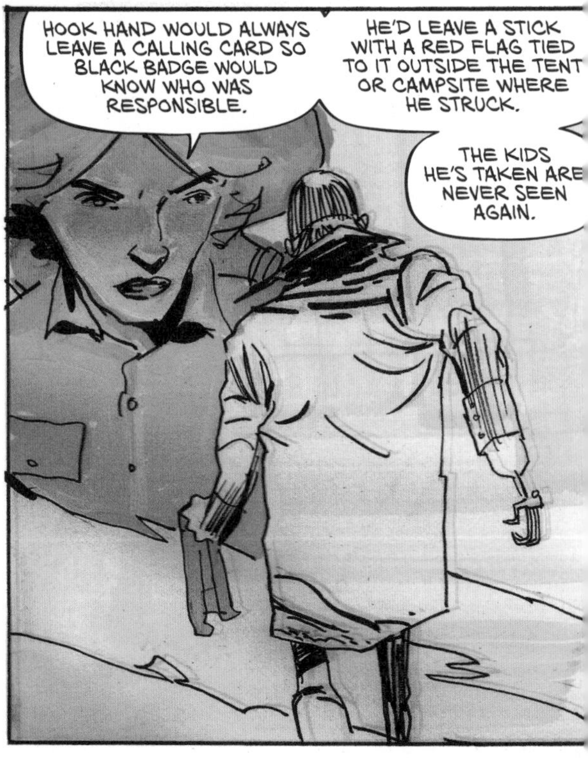
HOOK HAND WOULD ALWAYS LEAVE A CALLING CARD SO BLACK BADGE WOULD KNOW WHO WAS RESPONSIBLE.
HE'D LEAVE A STICK WITH A RED FLAG TIED TO IT OUTSIDE THE TENT OR CAMPSITE WHERE HE STRUCK.
THE KIDS HE'S TAKEN ARE NEVER SEEN AGAIN.

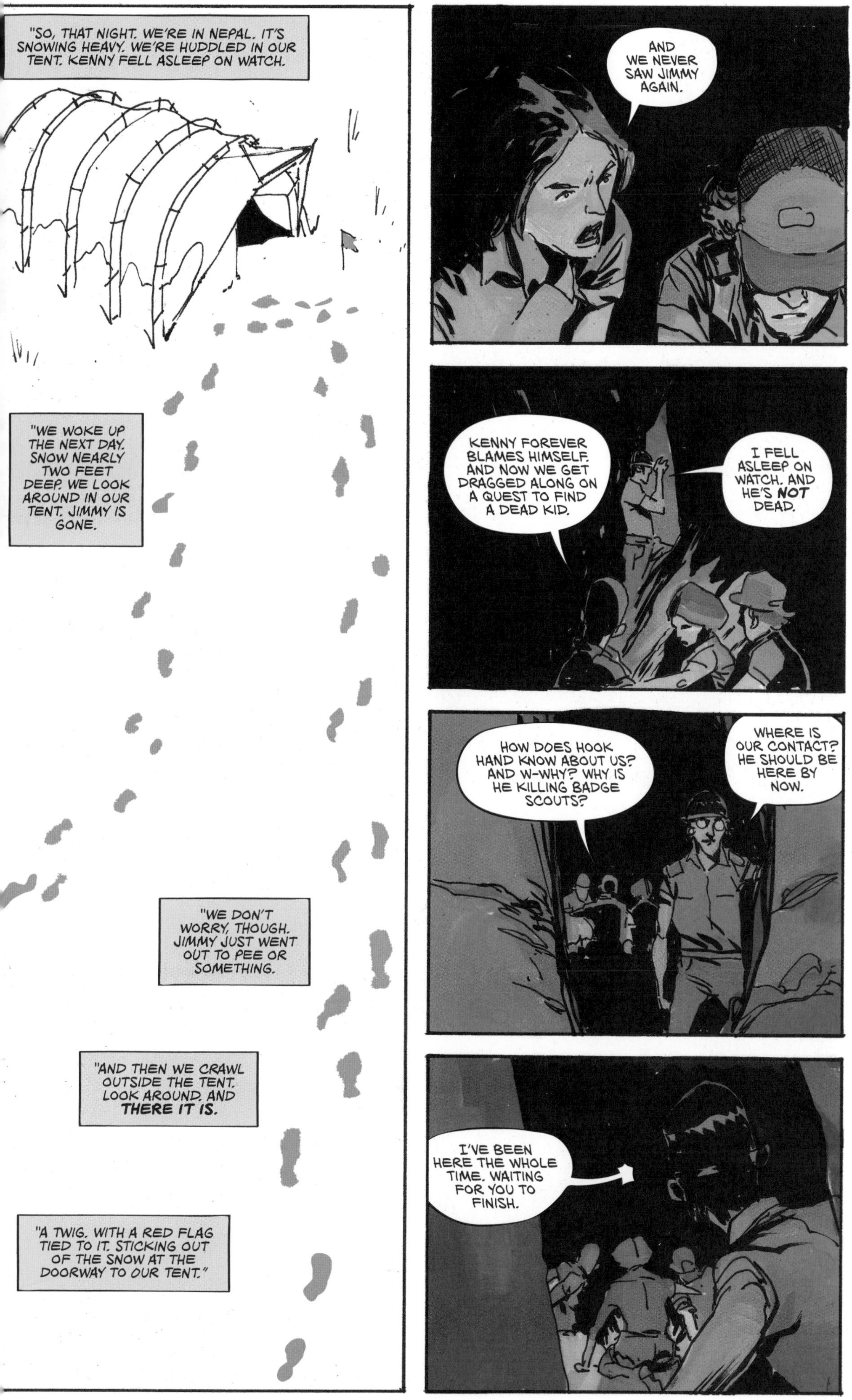
"SO, THAT NIGHT. WE'RE IN NEPAL. IT'S SNOWING HEAVY. WE'RE HUDDLED IN OUR TENT. KENNY FELL ASLEEP ON WATCH.
"WE WOKE UP THE NEXT DAY. SNOW NEARLY TWO FEET DEEP. WE LOOK AROUND IN OUR TENT. JIMMY IS GONE.
"WE DON'T WORRY, THOUGH. JIMMY JUST WENT OUT TO PEE OR SOMETHING.
"AND THEN WE CRAWL OUTSIDE THE TENT. LOOK AROUND. AND **THERE IT IS.**
"A TWIG. WITH A RED FLAG TIED TO IT. STICKING OUT OF THE SNOW AT THE DOORWAY TO OUR TENT."
AND WE NEVER SAW JIMMY AGAIN.
KENNY FOREVER BLAMES HIMSELF. AND NOW WE GET DRAGGED ALONG ON A QUEST TO FIND A DEAD KID.
I FELL ASLEEP ON WATCH. AND HE'S **NOT** DEAD.
HOW DOES HOOK HAND KNOW ABOUT US? AND W-WHY? WHY IS HE KILLING BADGE SCOUTS?
WHERE IS OUR CONTACT? HE SHOULD BE HERE BY NOW.
I'VE BEEN HERE THE WHOLE TIME. WAITING FOR YOU TO FINISH.

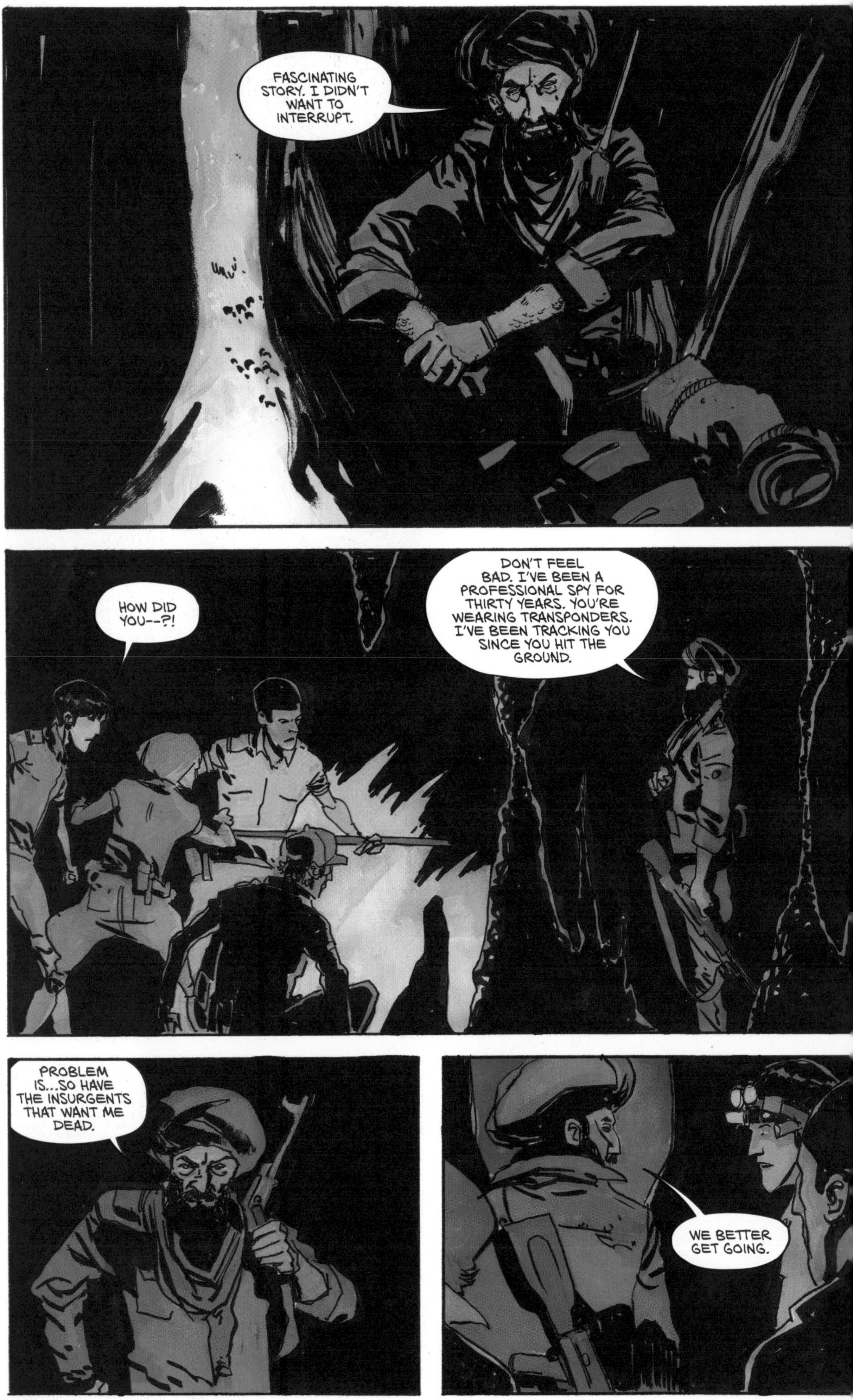
FASCINATING STORY. I DIDN'T WANT TO INTERRUPT.
HOW DID YOU--?!
DON'T FEEL BAD. I'VE BEEN A PROFESSIONAL SPY FOR THIRTY YEARS. YOU'RE WEARING TRANSPONDERS. I'VE BEEN TRACKING YOU SINCE YOU HIT THE GROUND.
PROBLEM IS...SO HAVE THE INSURGENTS THAT WANT ME DEAD.
WE BETTER GET GOING.

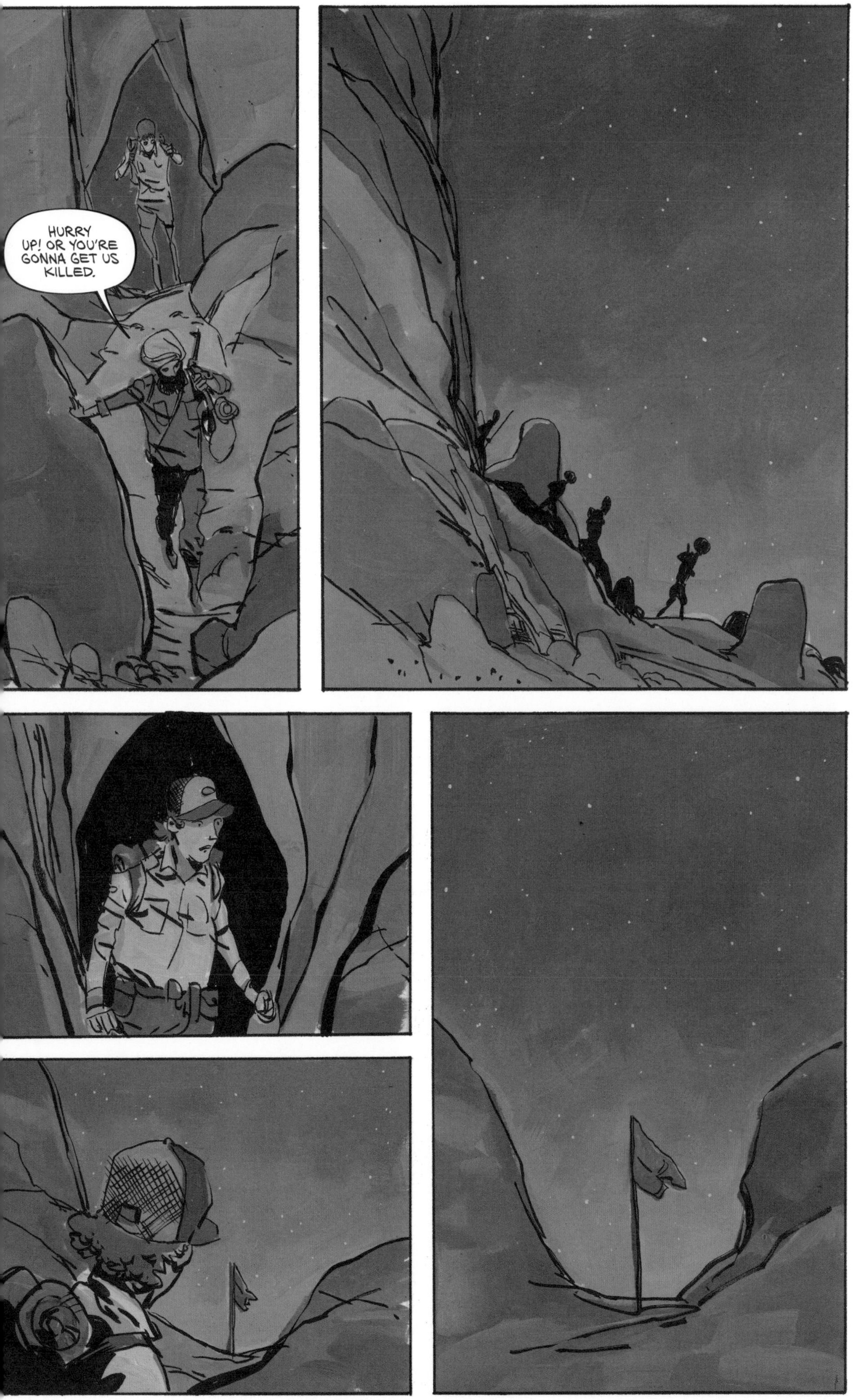
HURRY UP! OR YOU'RE GONNA GET US KILLED.

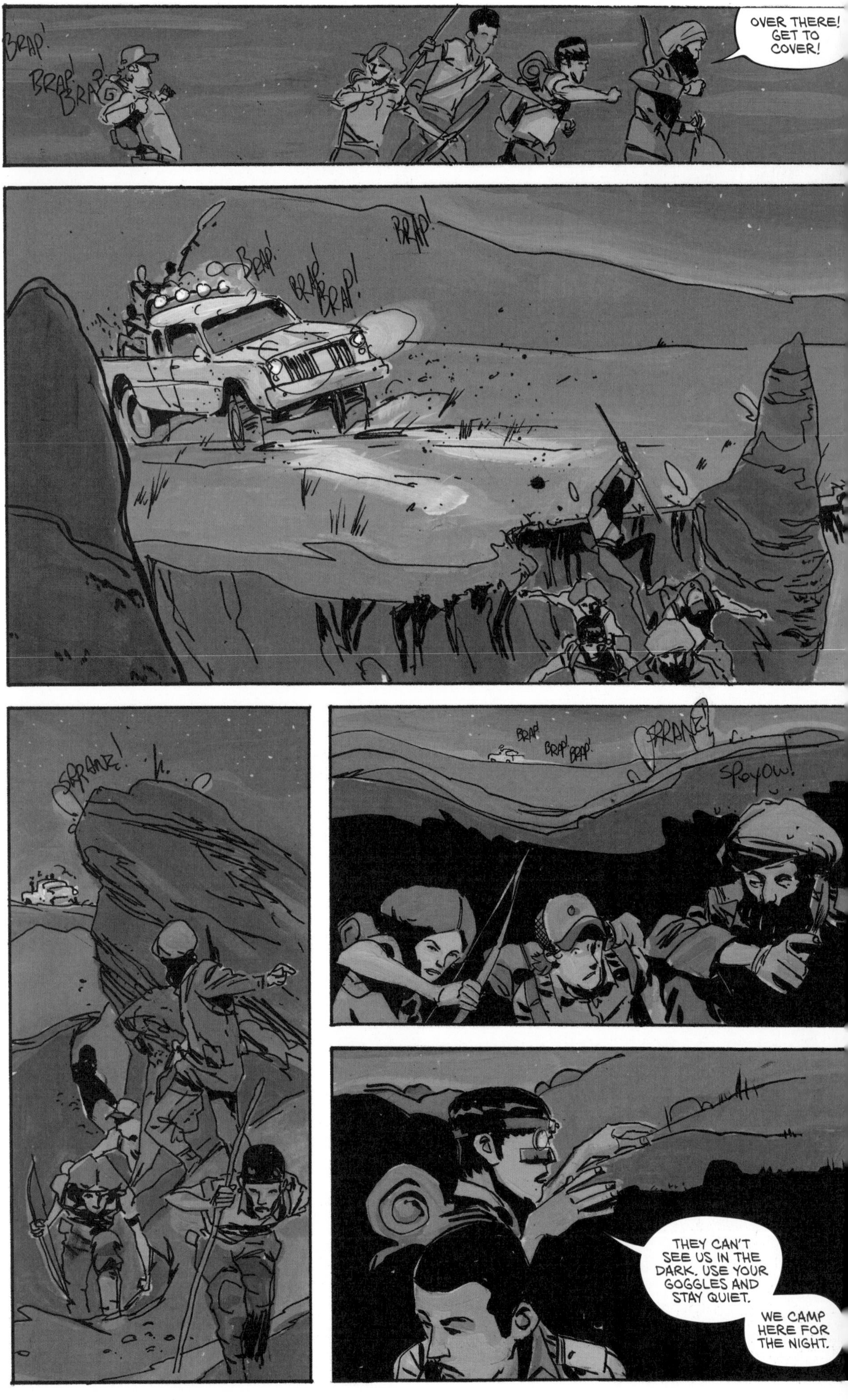
BRAP!
BRAP! BRAP!
OVER THERE! GET TO COVER!
BRAP!
BRAP!
BRAP! BRAP!
SRRANZ!
BRAP!
BRAP! BRAP!
SRRANZ!
SPOYOW!
THEY CAN'T SEE US IN THE DARK. USE YOUR GOGGLES AND STAY QUIET.
WE CAMP HERE FOR THE NIGHT.

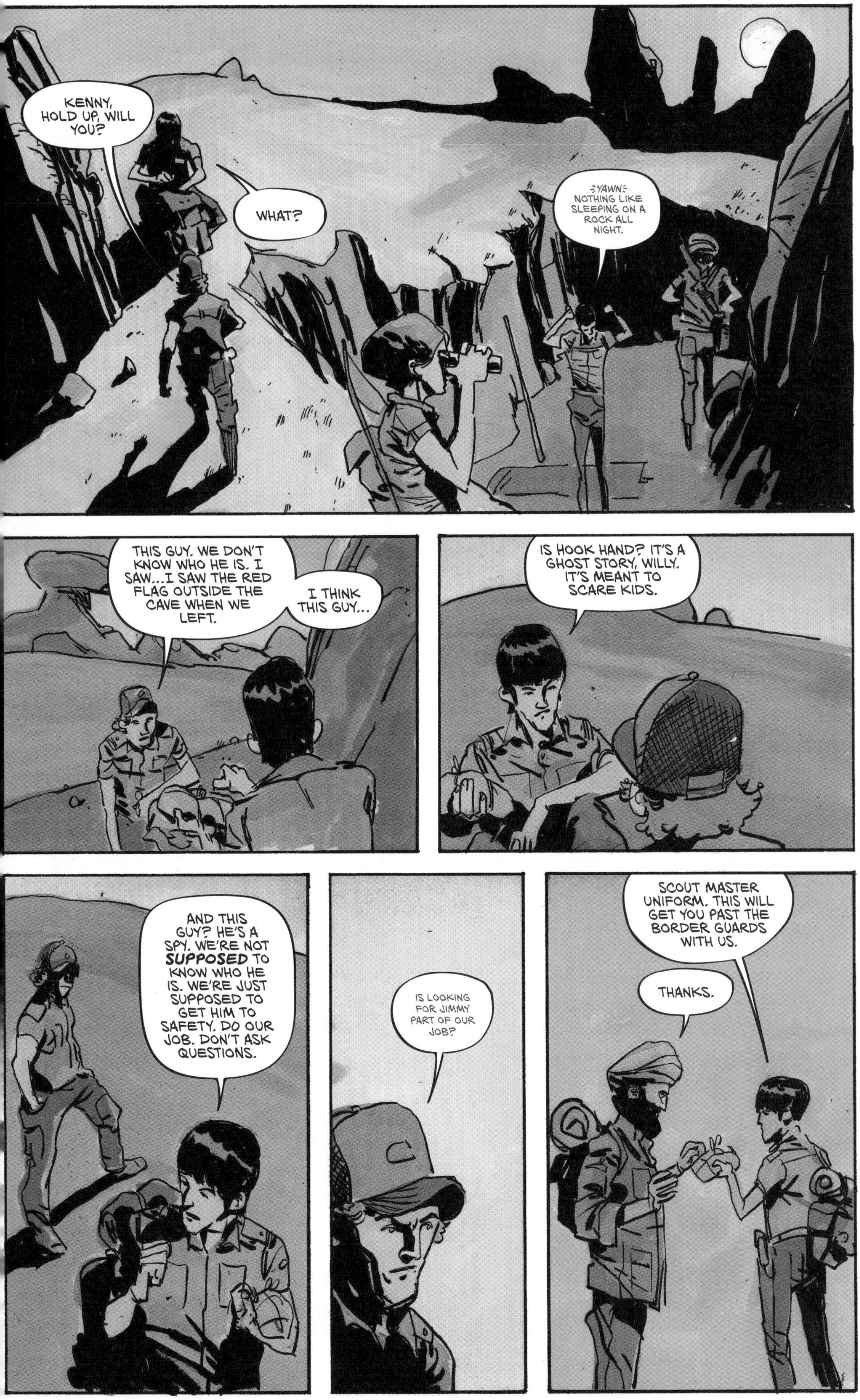
KENNY, HOLD UP, WILL YOU?
WHAT?
-YAWN- NOTHING LIKE SLEEPING ON A ROCK ALL NIGHT.
THIS GUY. WE DON'T KNOW WHO HE IS. I SAW...I SAW THE RED FLAG OUTSIDE THE CAVE WHEN WE LEFT.
I THINK THIS GUY...
IS HOOK HAND? IT'S A GHOST STORY, WILLY. IT'S MEANT TO SCARE KIDS.
AND THIS GUY? HE'S A SPY. WE'RE NOT **SUPPOSED** TO KNOW WHO HE IS. WE'RE JUST SUPPOSED TO GET HIM TO SAFETY. DO OUR JOB. DON'T ASK QUESTIONS.
IS LOOKING FOR JIMMY PART OF OUR JOB?
SCOUT MASTER UNIFORM. THIS WILL GET YOU PAST THE BORDER GUARDS WITH US.
THANKS.

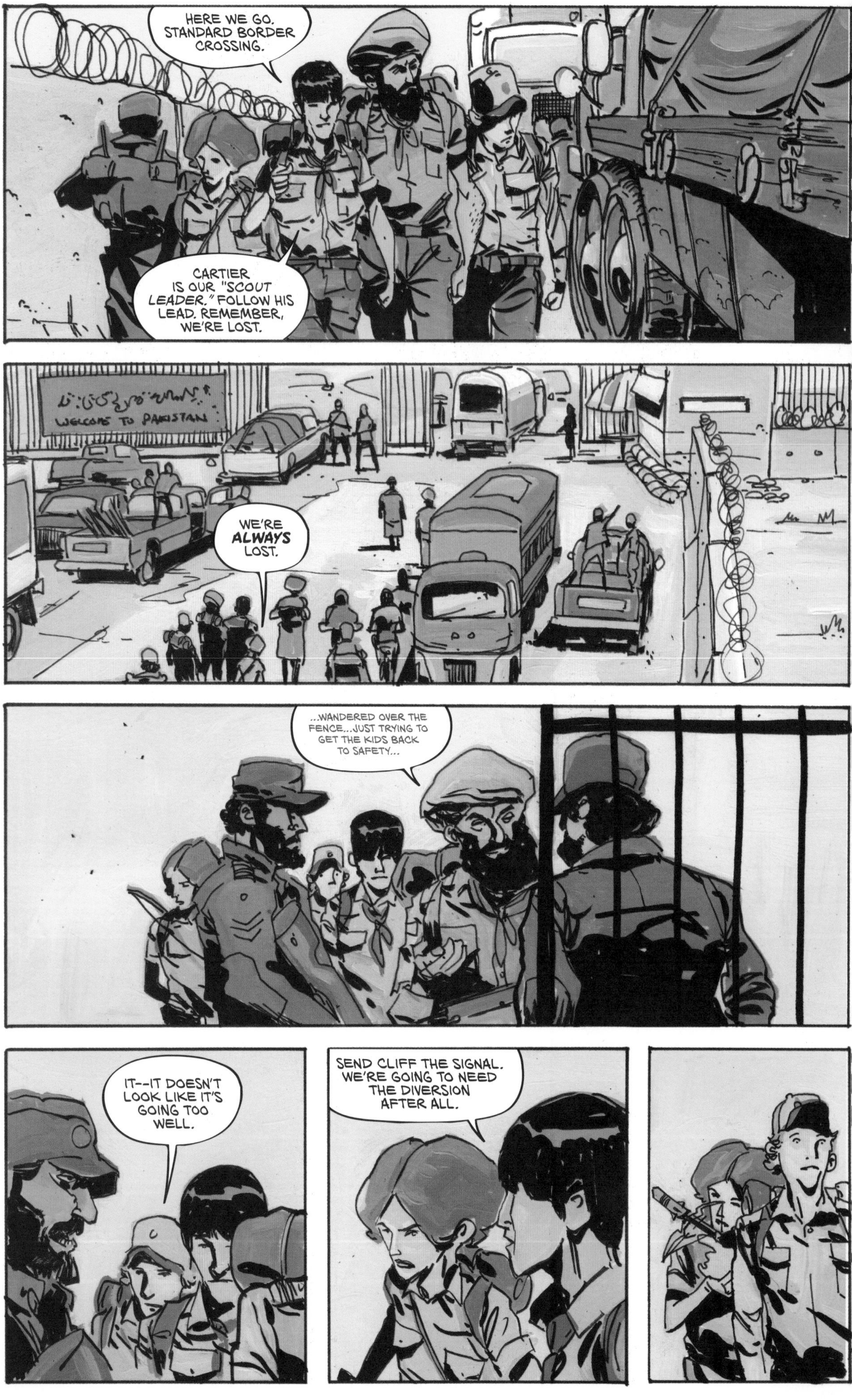
HERE WE GO. STANDARD BORDER CROSSING.
CARTIER IS OUR "SCOUT LEADER." FOLLOW HIS LEAD. REMEMBER, WE'RE LOST.
WELCOME TO PAKISTAN
WE'RE **ALWAYS** LOST.
...WANDERED OVER THE FENCE...JUST TRYING TO GET THE KIDS BACK TO SAFETY...
IT--IT DOESN'T LOOK LIKE IT'S GOING TOO WELL.
SEND CLIFF THE SIGNAL. WE'RE GOING TO NEED THE DIVERSION AFTER ALL.

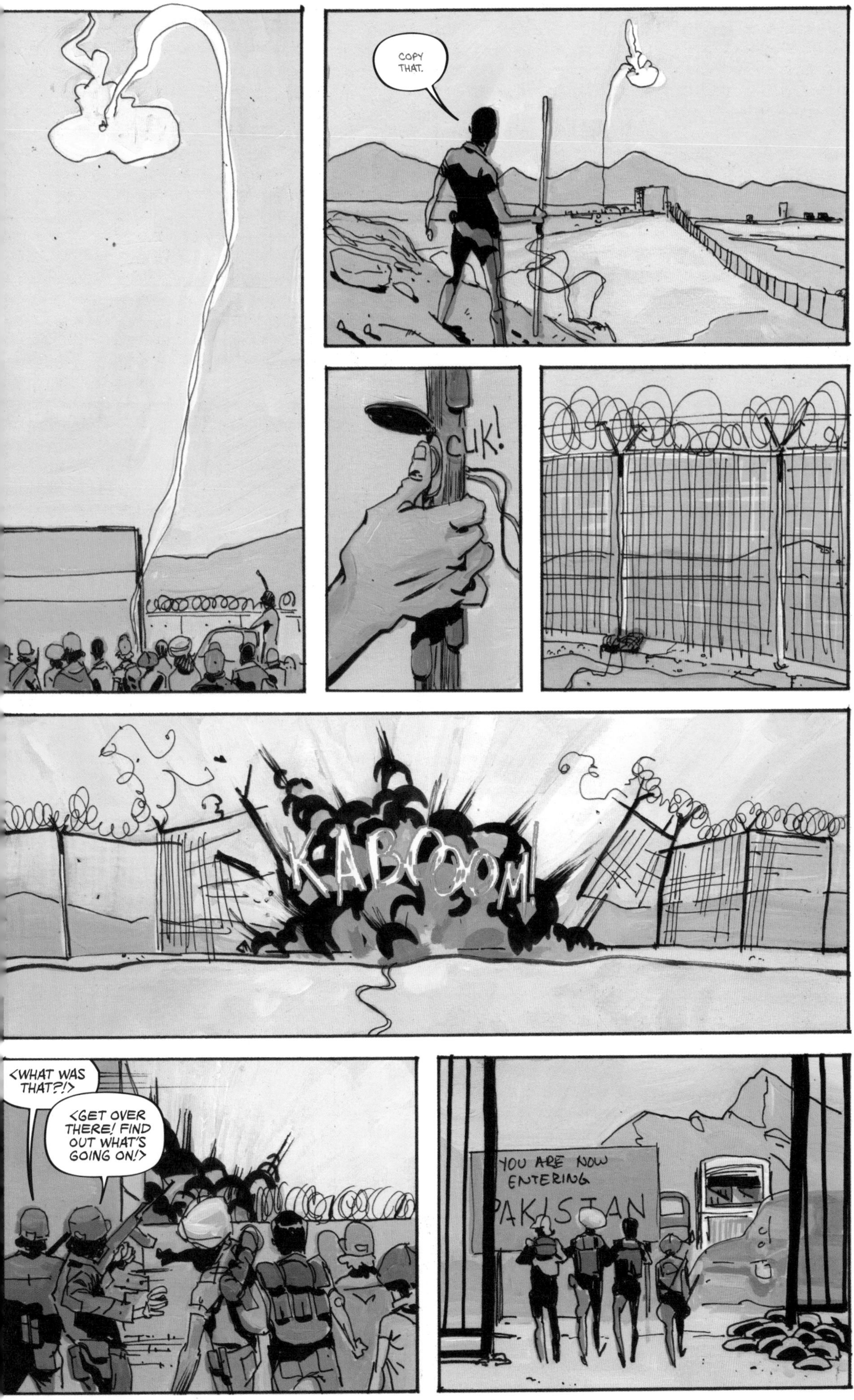
COPY THAT.
CLIK!
KABOOOM!
<WHAT WAS THAT?!>
<GET OVER THERE! FIND OUT WHAT'S GOING ON!>
YOU ARE NOW ENTERING PAKISTAN

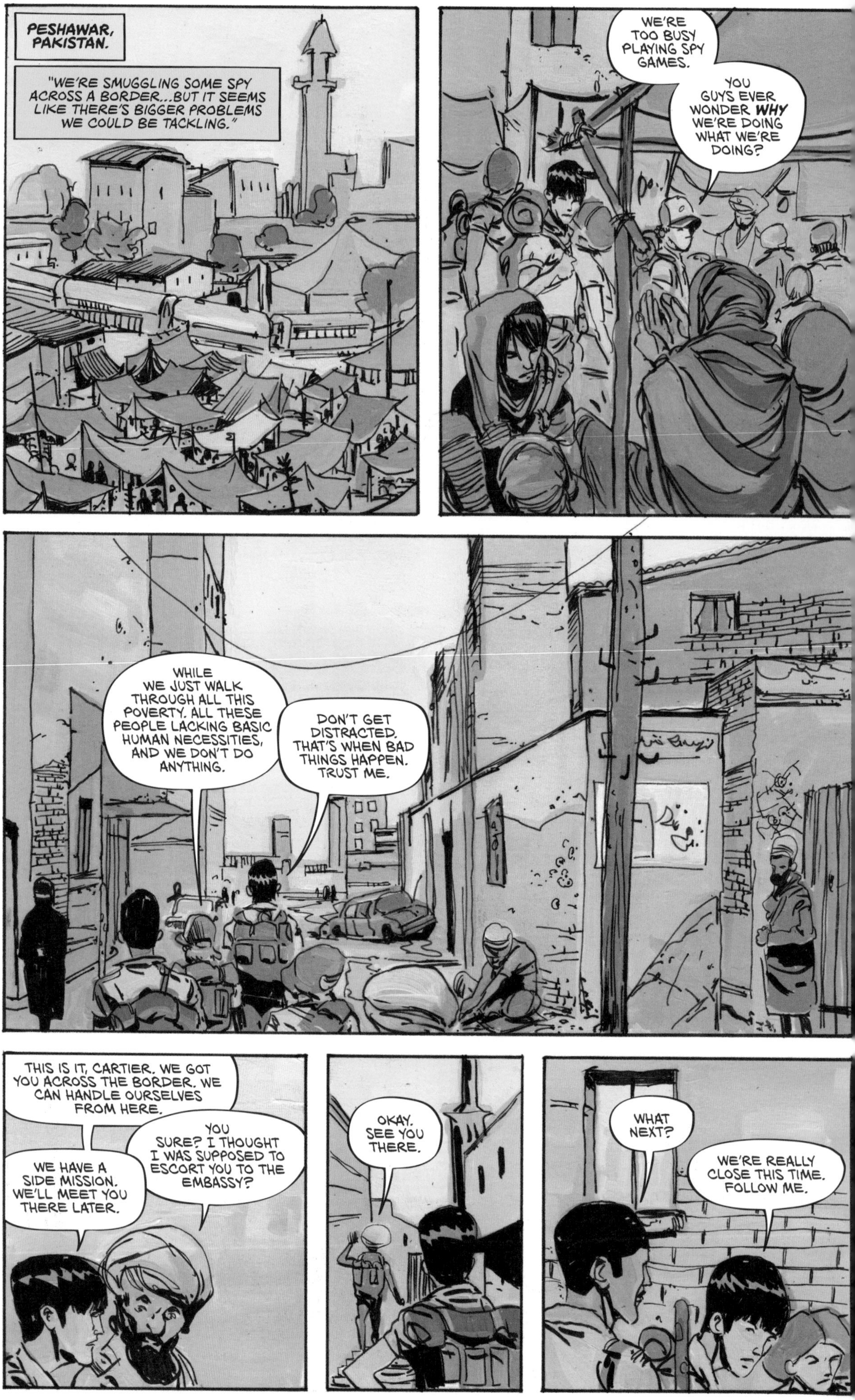
PESHAWAR, PAKISTAN.
"WE'RE SMUGGLING SOME SPY ACROSS A BORDER...BUT IT SEEMS LIKE THERE'S BIGGER PROBLEMS WE COULD BE TACKLING."
WE'RE TOO BUSY PLAYING SPY GAMES.
YOU GUYS EVER WONDER **WHY** WE'RE DOING WHAT WE'RE DOING?
WHILE WE JUST WALK THROUGH ALL THIS POVERTY. ALL THESE PEOPLE LACKING BASIC HUMAN NECESSITIES, AND WE DON'T DO ANYTHING.
DON'T GET DISTRACTED. THAT'S WHEN BAD THINGS HAPPEN. TRUST ME.
THIS IS IT, CARTIER. WE GOT YOU ACROSS THE BORDER. WE CAN HANDLE OURSELVES FROM HERE.
YOU SURE? I THOUGHT I WAS SUPPOSED TO ESCORT YOU TO THE EMBASSY?
WE HAVE A SIDE MISSION. WE'LL MEET YOU THERE LATER.
OKAY. SEE YOU THERE.
WHAT NEXT?
WE'RE REALLY CLOSE THIS TIME. FOLLOW ME.

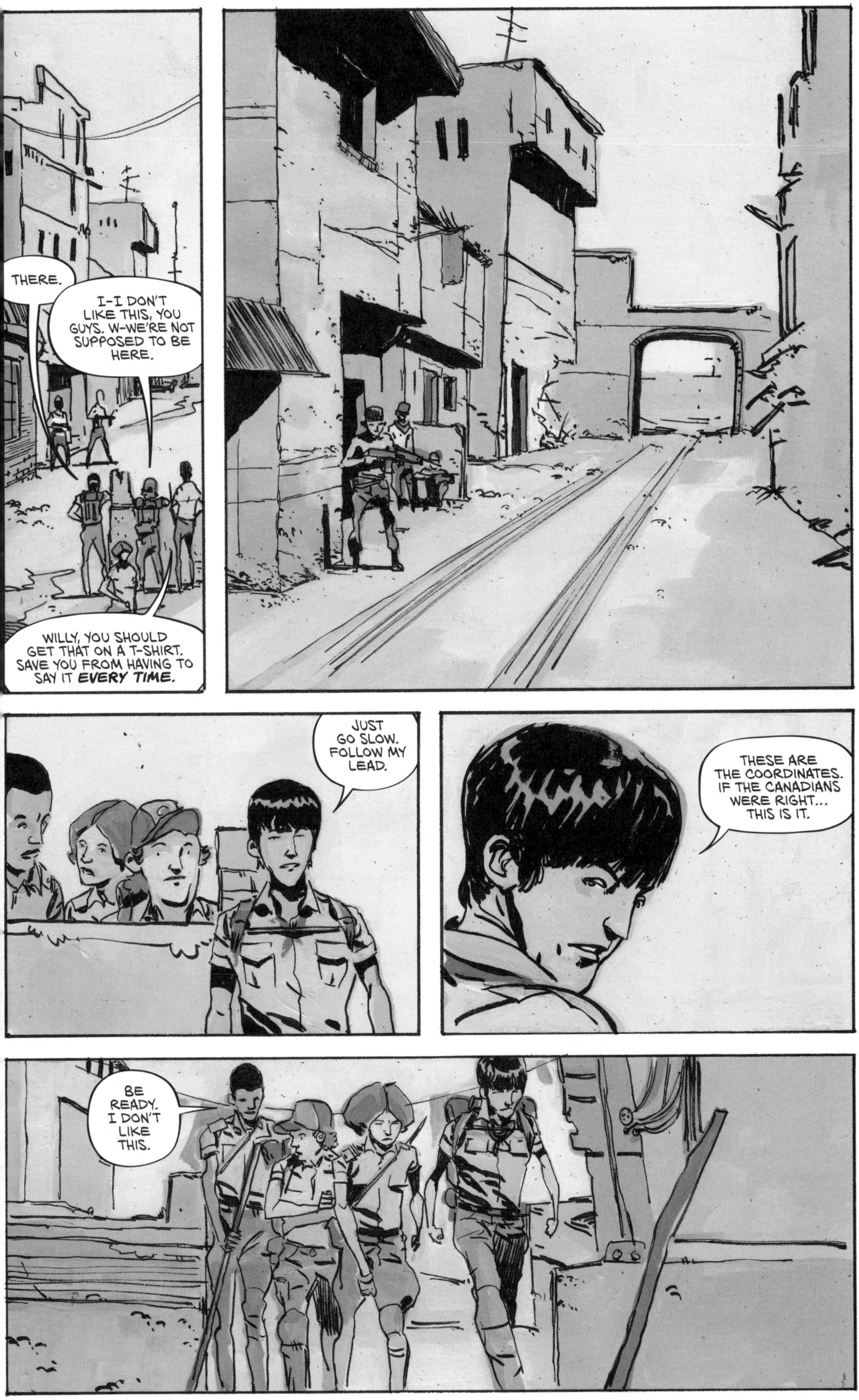
THERE.
I-I DON'T LIKE THIS, YOU GUYS. W-WE'RE NOT SUPPOSED TO BE HERE.
WILLY, YOU SHOULD GET THAT ON A T-SHIRT. SAVE YOU FROM HAVING TO SAY IT EVERY TIME.
JUST GO SLOW. FOLLOW MY LEAD.
THESE ARE THE COORDINATES. IF THE CANADIANS WERE RIGHT... THIS IS IT.
BE READY. I DON'T LIKE THIS.

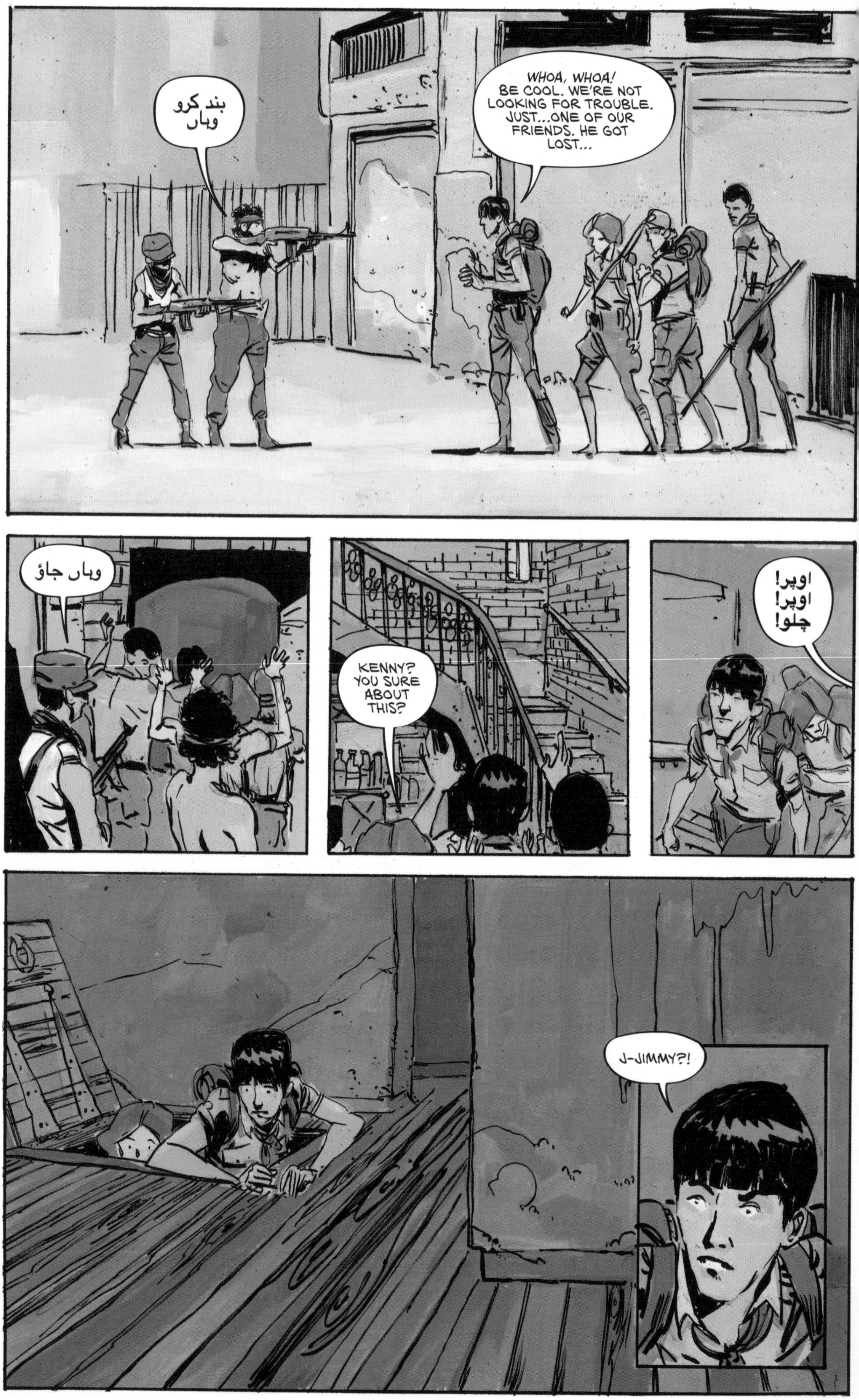
بند کرو
وہاں
WHOA, WHOA! BE COOL. WE'RE NOT LOOKING FOR TROUBLE. JUST...ONE OF OUR FRIENDS. HE GOT LOST...
وہاں جاؤ
KENNY? YOU SURE ABOUT THIS?
اوپر!
اوپر!
چلو!
J-JIMMY?!

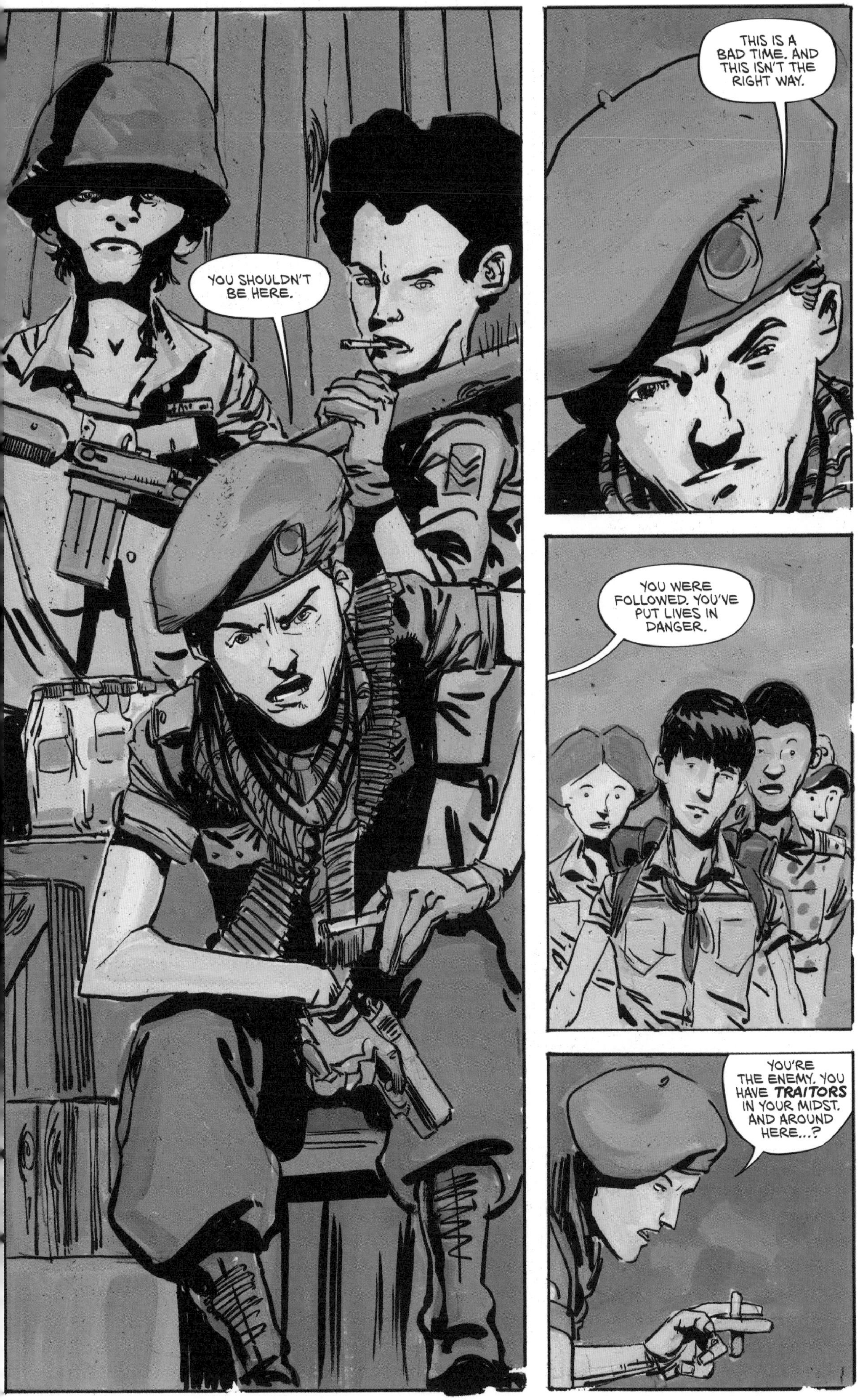
YOU SHOULDN'T BE HERE.
THIS IS A BAD TIME. AND THIS ISN'T THE RIGHT WAY.
YOU WERE FOLLOWED. YOU'VE PUT LIVES IN DANGER.
YOU'RE THE ENEMY. YOU HAVE **TRAITORS** IN YOUR MIDST. AND AROUND HERE...?

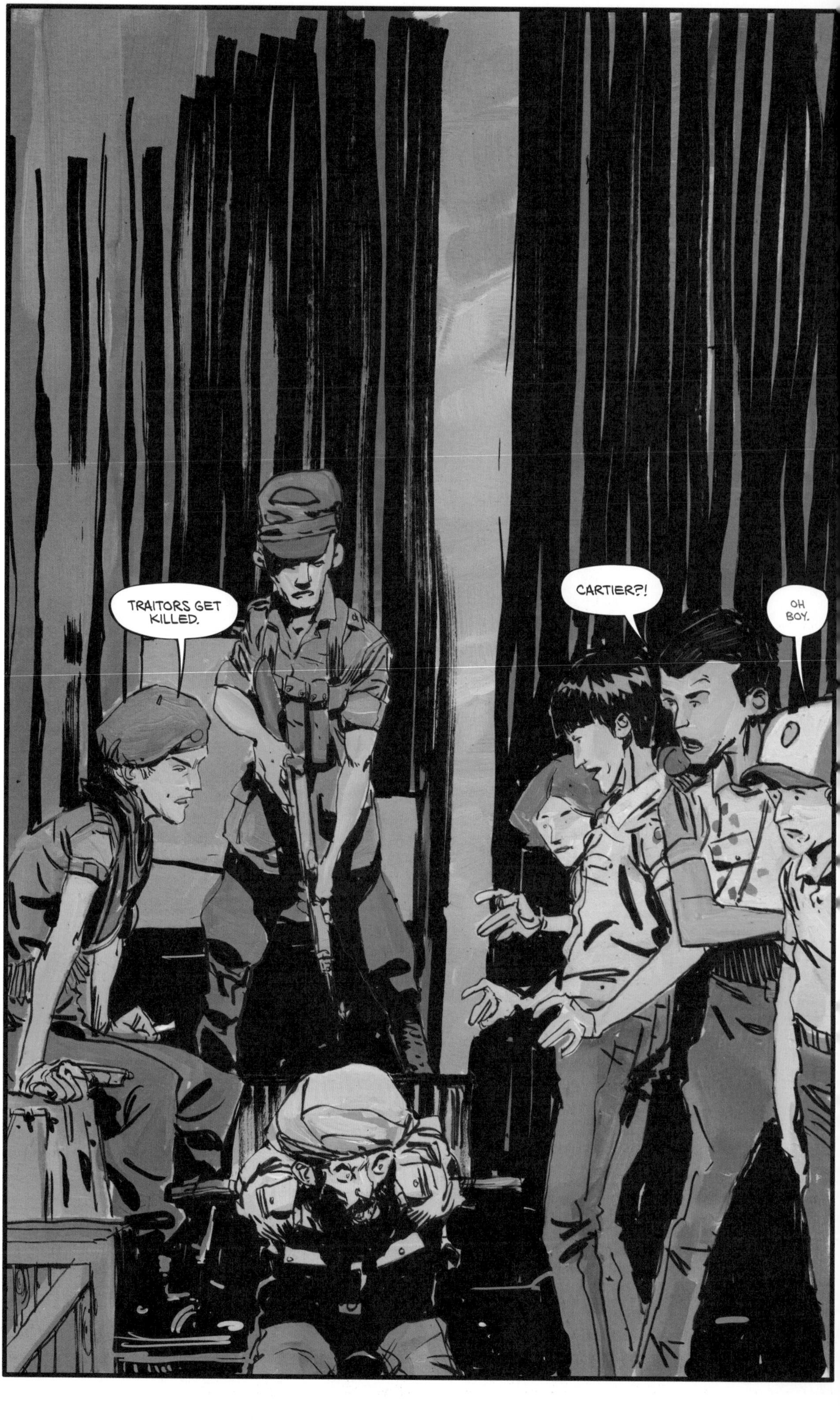
TRAITORS GET KILLED.
CARTIER?!
OH BOY.

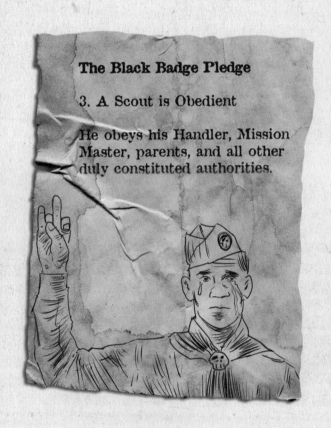

The Black Badge Pledge

3. A Scout is Obedient

He obeys his Handler, Mission Master, parents, and all other duly constituted authorities.

Black Badge was founded in 1910 by William Randolph He
sub-branch of the American Boy Scouts. After the Boy Sc
America sued Hearst for use of the name, the ABS was di
but Black Badge remained* - becoming active during bot
Wars and as a sort of elite scouting club in present d

Chapter Four

[redacted] Peshawar, Pakistan [redacted] second. [redacted] cyanide capsule [redacted] S.W.O.B. [redacted] makeshift comms [redacted] "the Grass Kingdom" [redacted] strategic bullying [redacted]

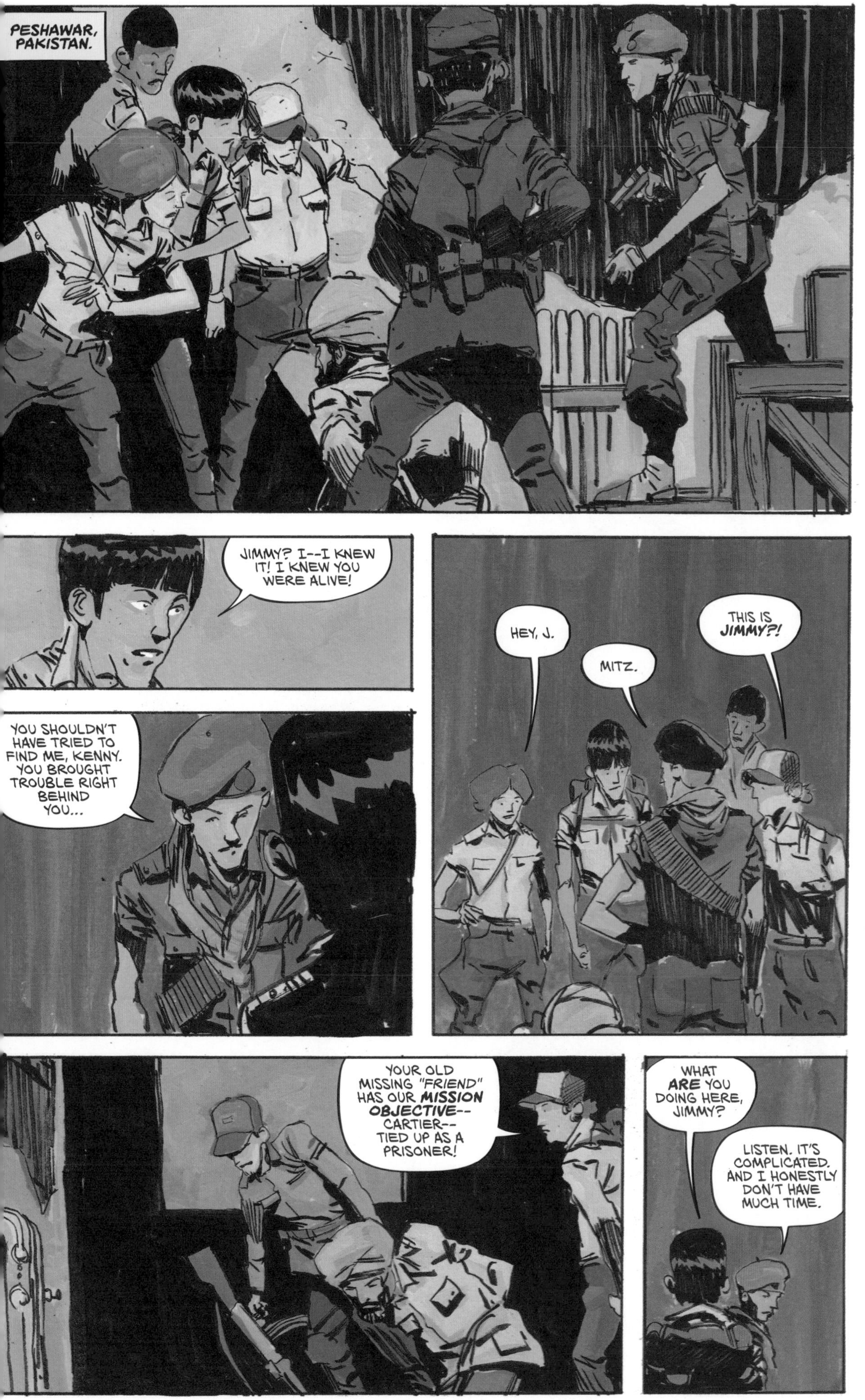
PESHAWAR, PAKISTAN.
JIMMY? I--I KNEW IT! I KNEW YOU WERE ALIVE!
YOU SHOULDN'T HAVE TRIED TO FIND ME, KENNY. YOU BROUGHT TROUBLE RIGHT BEHIND YOU...
HEY, J.
MITZ.
THIS IS JIMMY?!
YOUR OLD MISSING "FRIEND" HAS OUR MISSION OBJECTIVE-- CARTIER-- TIED UP AS A PRISONER!
WHAT ARE YOU DOING HERE, JIMMY?
LISTEN. IT'S COMPLICATED. AND I HONESTLY DON'T HAVE MUCH TIME.

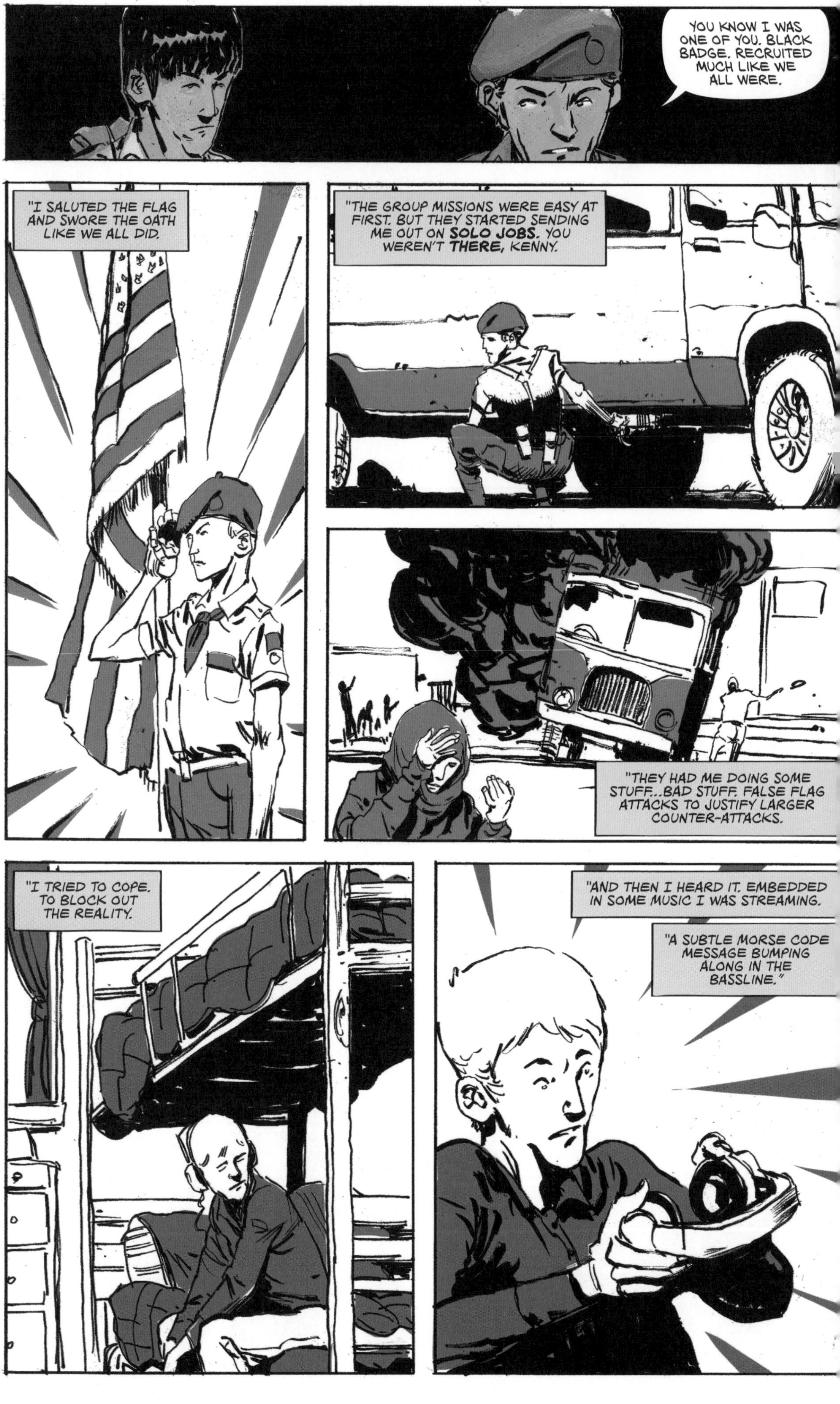
YOU KNOW I WAS ONE OF YOU. BLACK BADGE. RECRUITED MUCH LIKE WE ALL WERE.
"I SALUTED THE FLAG AND SWORE THE OATH LIKE WE ALL DID.
"THE GROUP MISSIONS WERE EASY AT FIRST. BUT THEY STARTED SENDING ME OUT ON SOLO JOBS. YOU WEREN'T THERE, KENNY.
"THEY HAD ME DOING SOME STUFF...BAD STUFF. FALSE FLAG ATTACKS TO JUSTIFY LARGER COUNTER-ATTACKS.
"I TRIED TO COPE. TO BLOCK OUT THE REALITY.
"AND THEN I HEARD IT. EMBEDDED IN SOME MUSIC I WAS STREAMING.
"A SUBTLE MORSE CODE MESSAGE BUMPING ALONG IN THE BASSLINE."

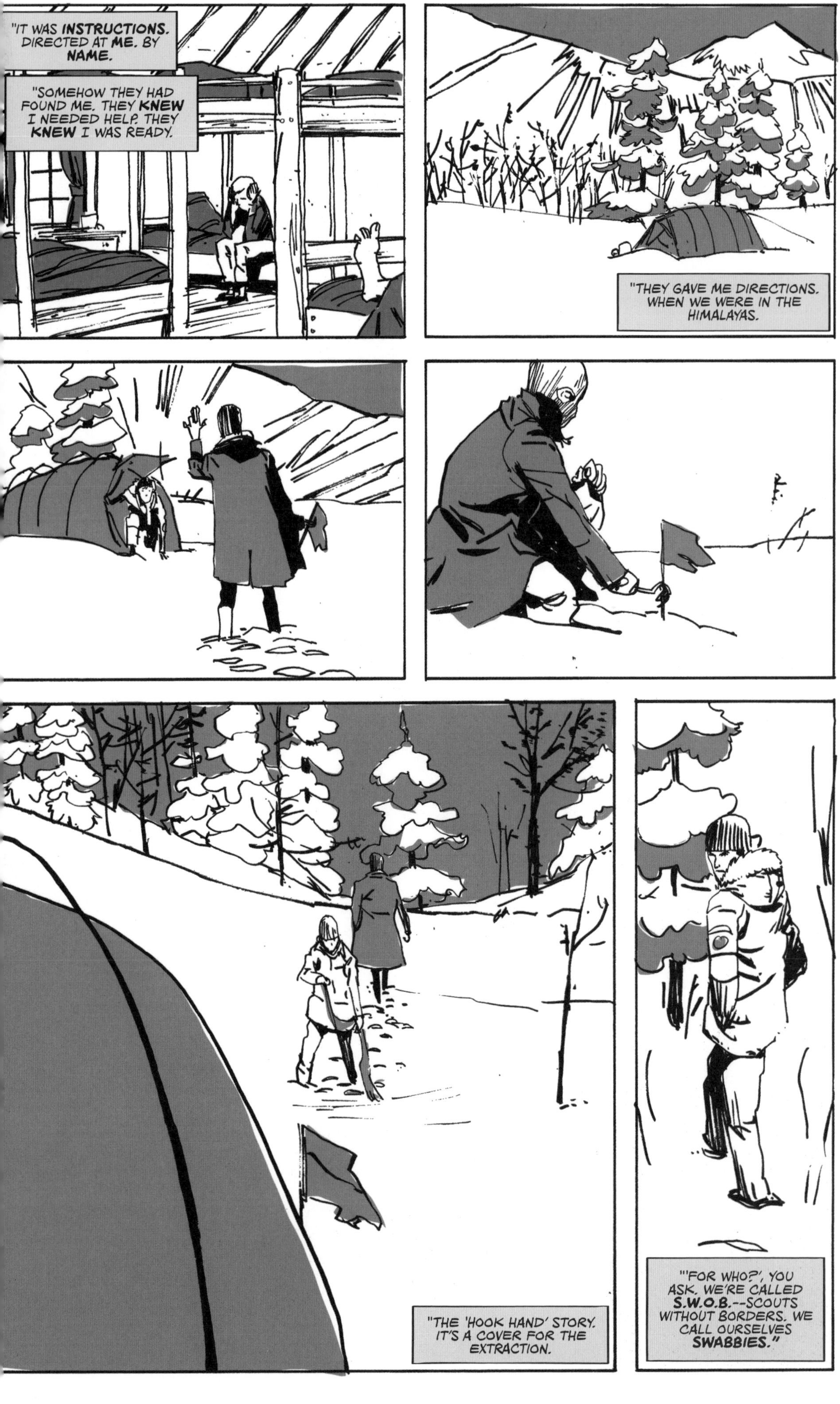
"IT WAS **INSTRUCTIONS.** DIRECTED AT **ME.** BY **NAME.**
"SOMEHOW THEY HAD FOUND ME. THEY **KNEW** I NEEDED HELP. THEY **KNEW** I WAS READY.
"THEY GAVE ME DIRECTIONS. WHEN WE WERE IN THE HIMALAYAS.
"THE 'HOOK HAND' STORY. IT'S A COVER FOR THE EXTRACTION.
"'FOR WHO?', YOU ASK. WE'RE CALLED **S.W.O.B.**--SCOUTS WITHOUT BORDERS. WE CALL OURSELVES **SWABBIES.**"

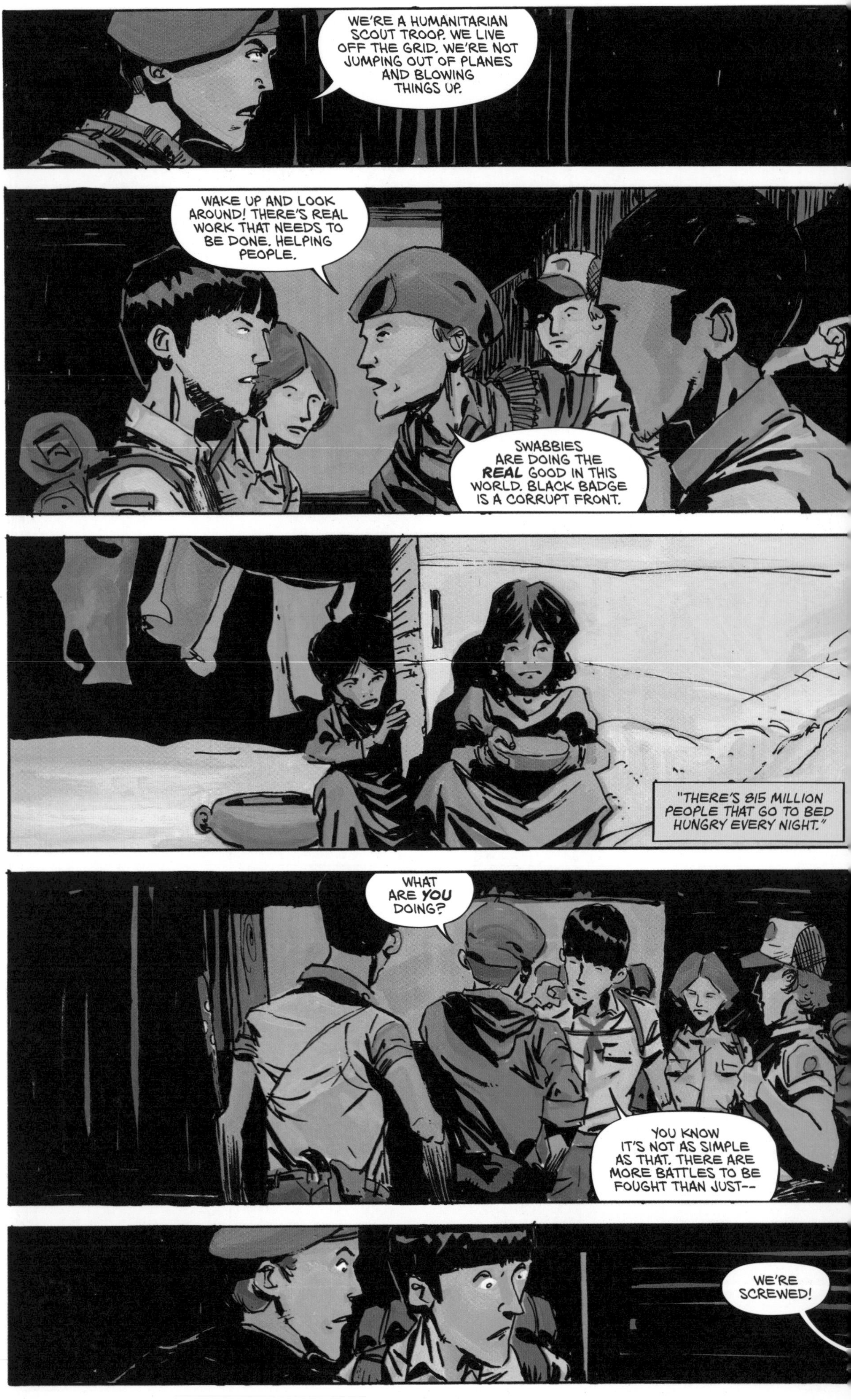
WE'RE A HUMANITARIAN SCOUT TROOP. WE LIVE OFF THE GRID. WE'RE NOT JUMPING OUT OF PLANES AND BLOWING THINGS UP.
WAKE UP AND LOOK AROUND! THERE'S REAL WORK THAT NEEDS TO BE DONE. HELPING PEOPLE.
SWABBIES ARE DOING THE **REAL** GOOD IN THIS WORLD. BLACK BADGE IS A CORRUPT FRONT.
"THERE'S 815 MILLION PEOPLE THAT GO TO BED HUNGRY EVERY NIGHT."
WHAT ARE ***YOU*** DOING?
YOU KNOW IT'S NOT AS SIMPLE AS THAT. THERE ARE MORE BATTLES TO BE FOUGHT THAN JUST--
WE'RE SCREWED!

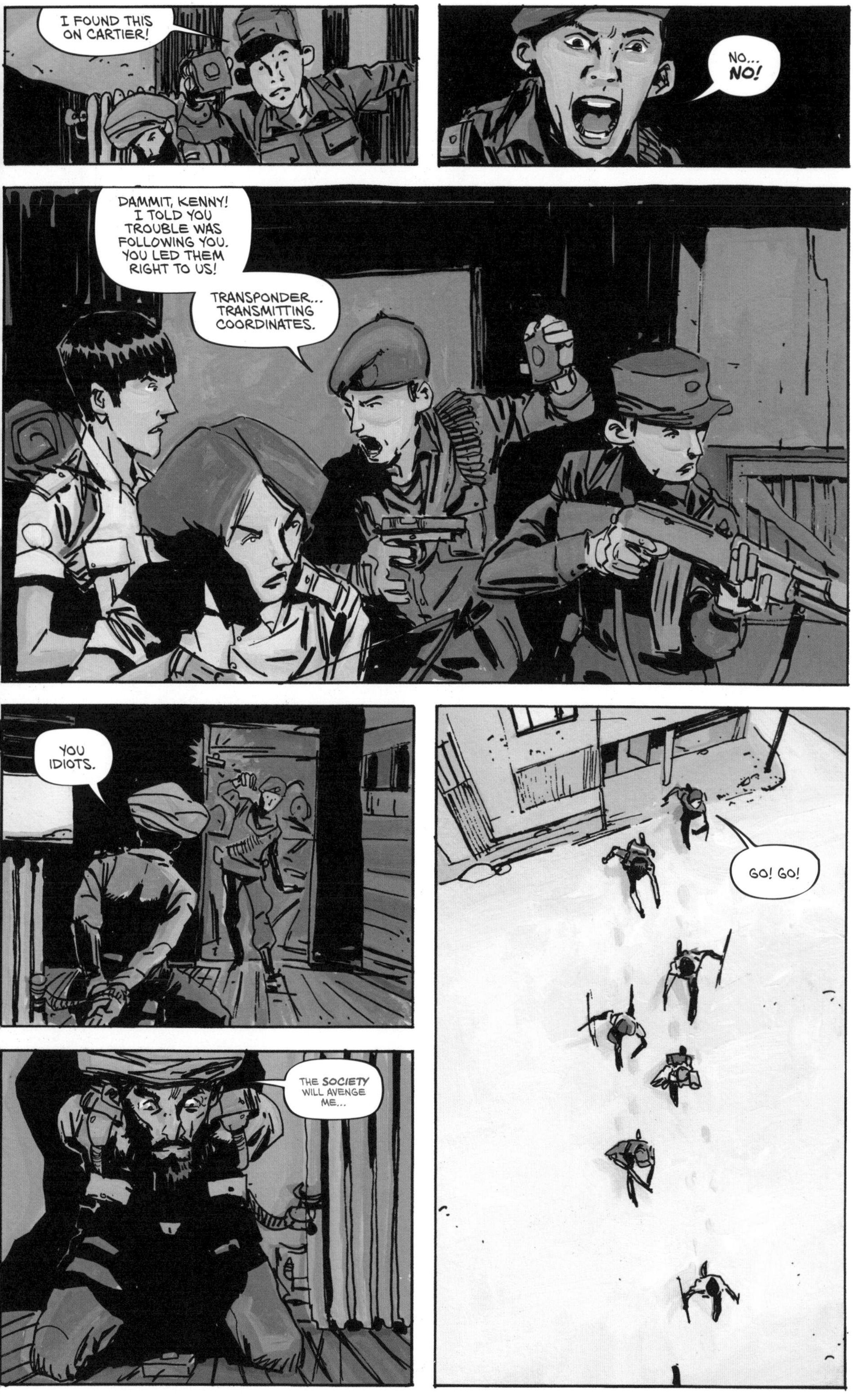
I FOUND THIS ON CARTIER!
NO... NO!
DAMMIT, KENNY! I TOLD YOU TROUBLE WAS FOLLOWING YOU. YOU LED THEM RIGHT TO US!
TRANSPONDER... TRANSMITTING COORDINATES.
YOU IDIOTS.
THE SOCIETY WILL AVENGE ME...
GO! GO!

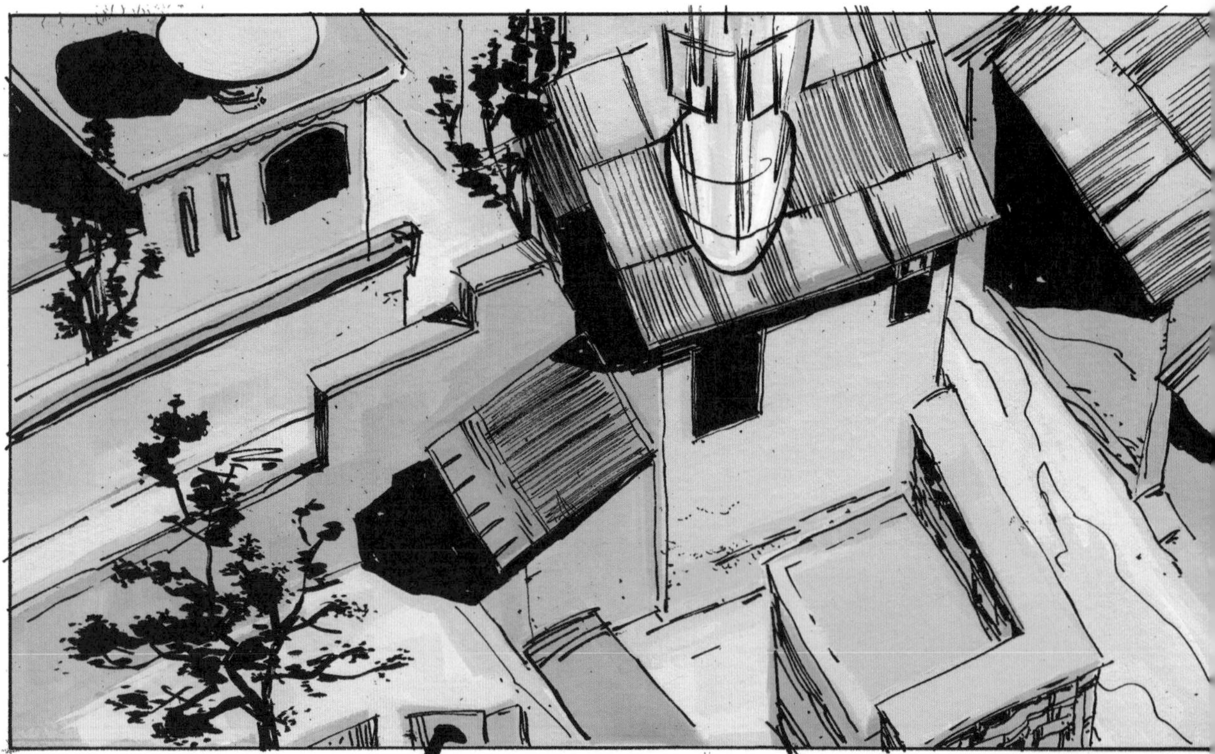

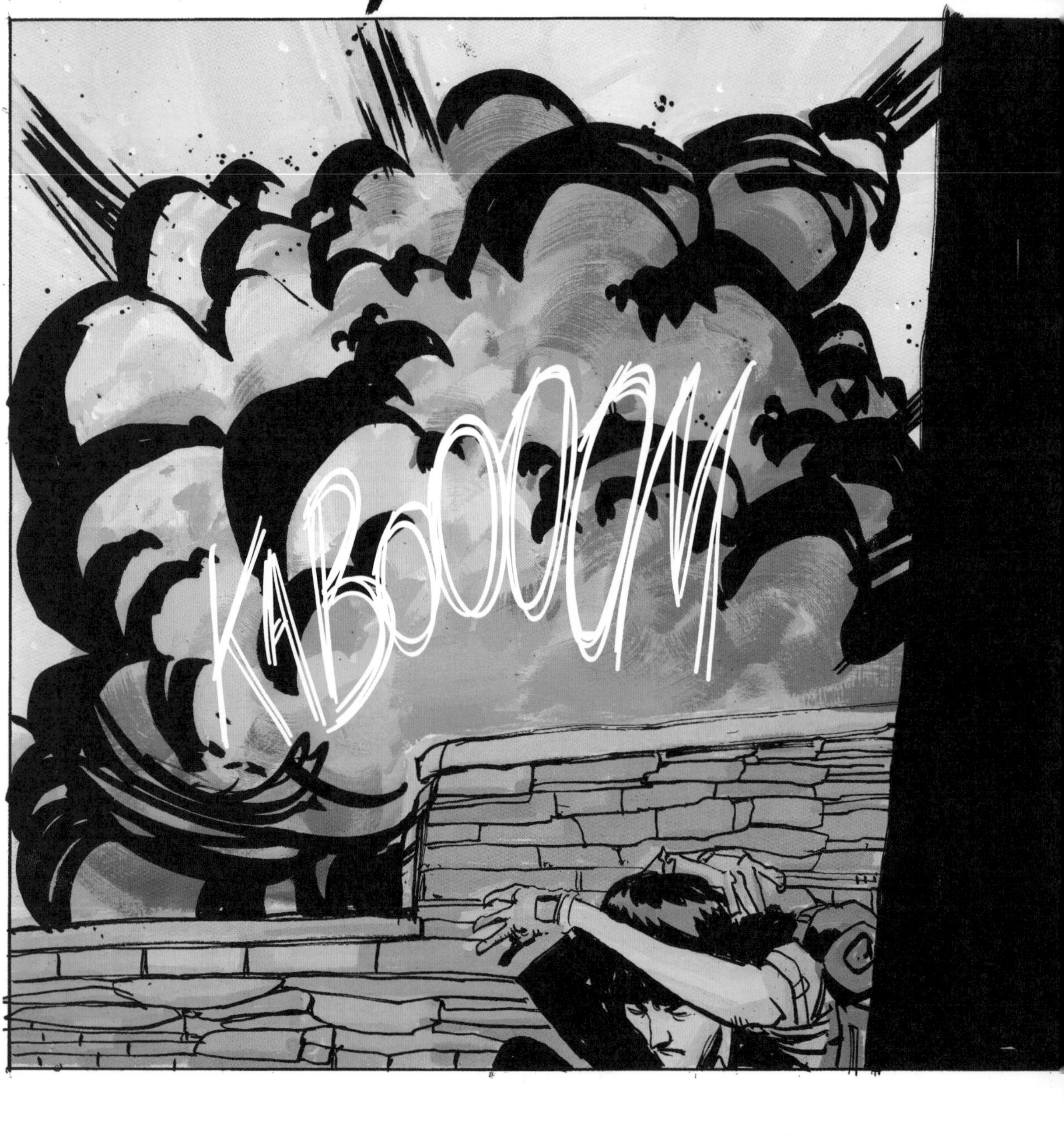
KABOOOOM

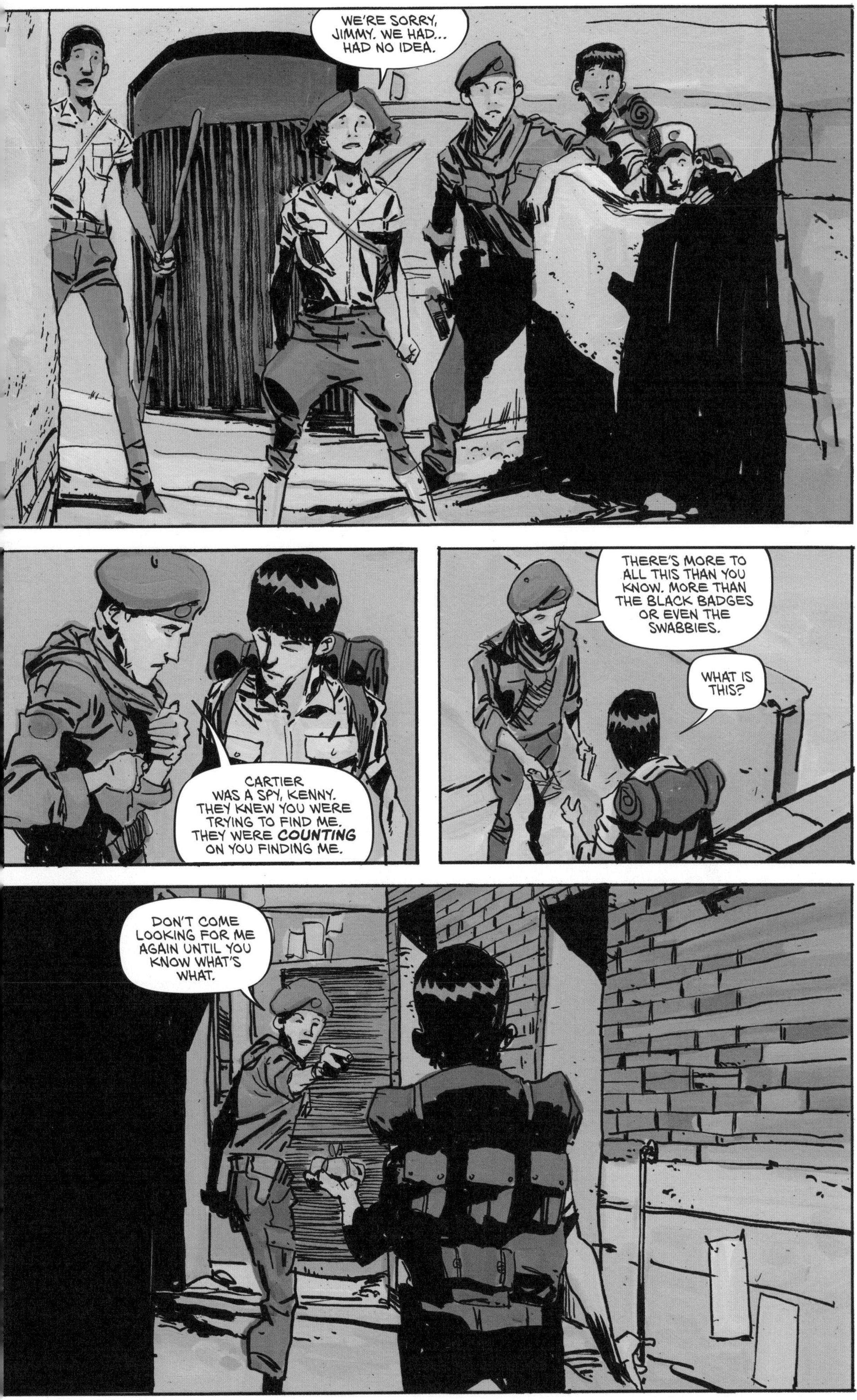
WE'RE SORRY, JIMMY. WE HAD... HAD NO IDEA.
CARTIER WAS A SPY, KENNY. THEY KNEW YOU WERE TRYING TO FIND ME. THEY WERE **COUNTING** ON YOU FINDING ME.
THERE'S MORE TO ALL THIS THAN YOU KNOW. MORE THAN THE BLACK BADGES OR EVEN THE SWABBIES.
WHAT IS THIS?
DON'T COME LOOKING FOR ME AGAIN UNTIL YOU KNOW WHAT'S WHAT.

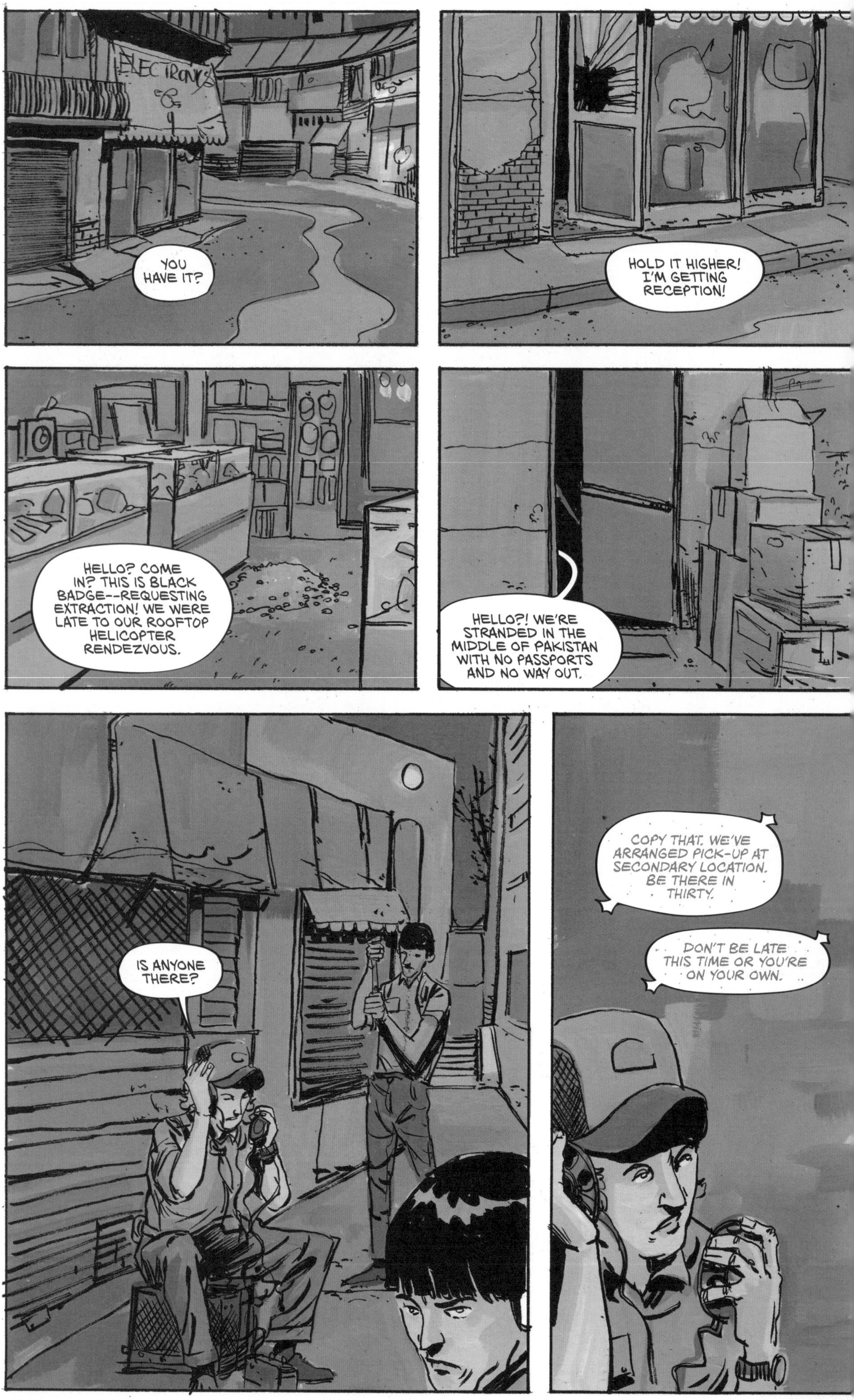
ELECTRONICS
YOU HAVE IT?
HOLD IT HIGHER! I'M GETTING RECEPTION!
HELLO? COME IN? THIS IS BLACK BADGE--REQUESTING EXTRACTION! WE WERE LATE TO OUR ROOFTOP HELICOPTER RENDEZVOUS.
HELLO?! WE'RE STRANDED IN THE MIDDLE OF PAKISTAN WITH NO PASSPORTS AND NO WAY OUT.
IS ANYONE THERE?
COPY THAT. WE'VE ARRANGED PICK-UP AT SECONDARY LOCATION. BE THERE IN THIRTY.
DON'T BE LATE THIS TIME OR YOU'RE ON YOUR OWN.

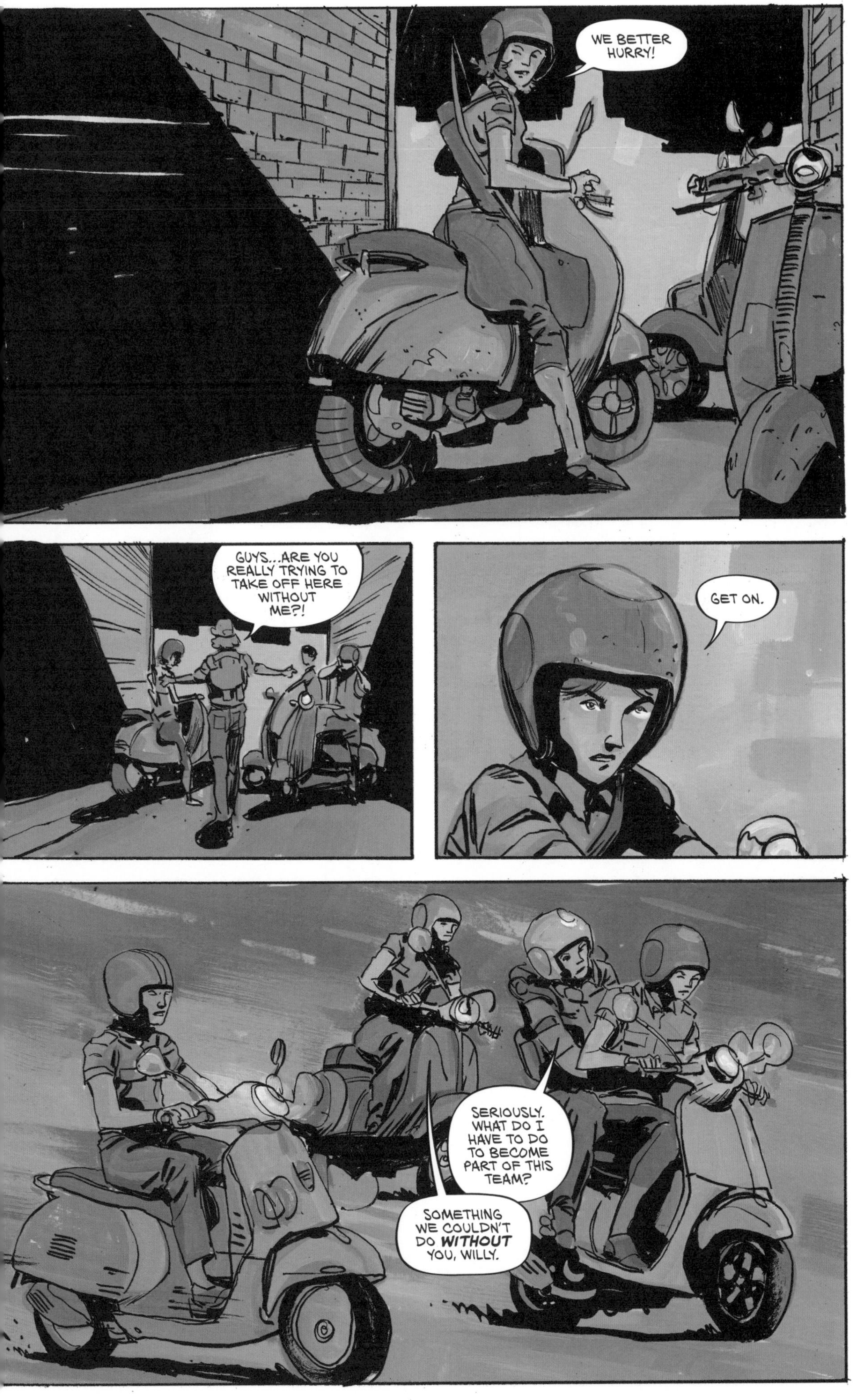
WE BETTER HURRY!
GUYS...ARE YOU REALLY TRYING TO TAKE OFF HERE WITHOUT ME?!
GET ON.
SERIOUSLY. WHAT DO I HAVE TO DO TO BECOME PART OF THIS TEAM?
SOMETHING WE COULDN'T DO **WITHOUT** YOU, WILLY.

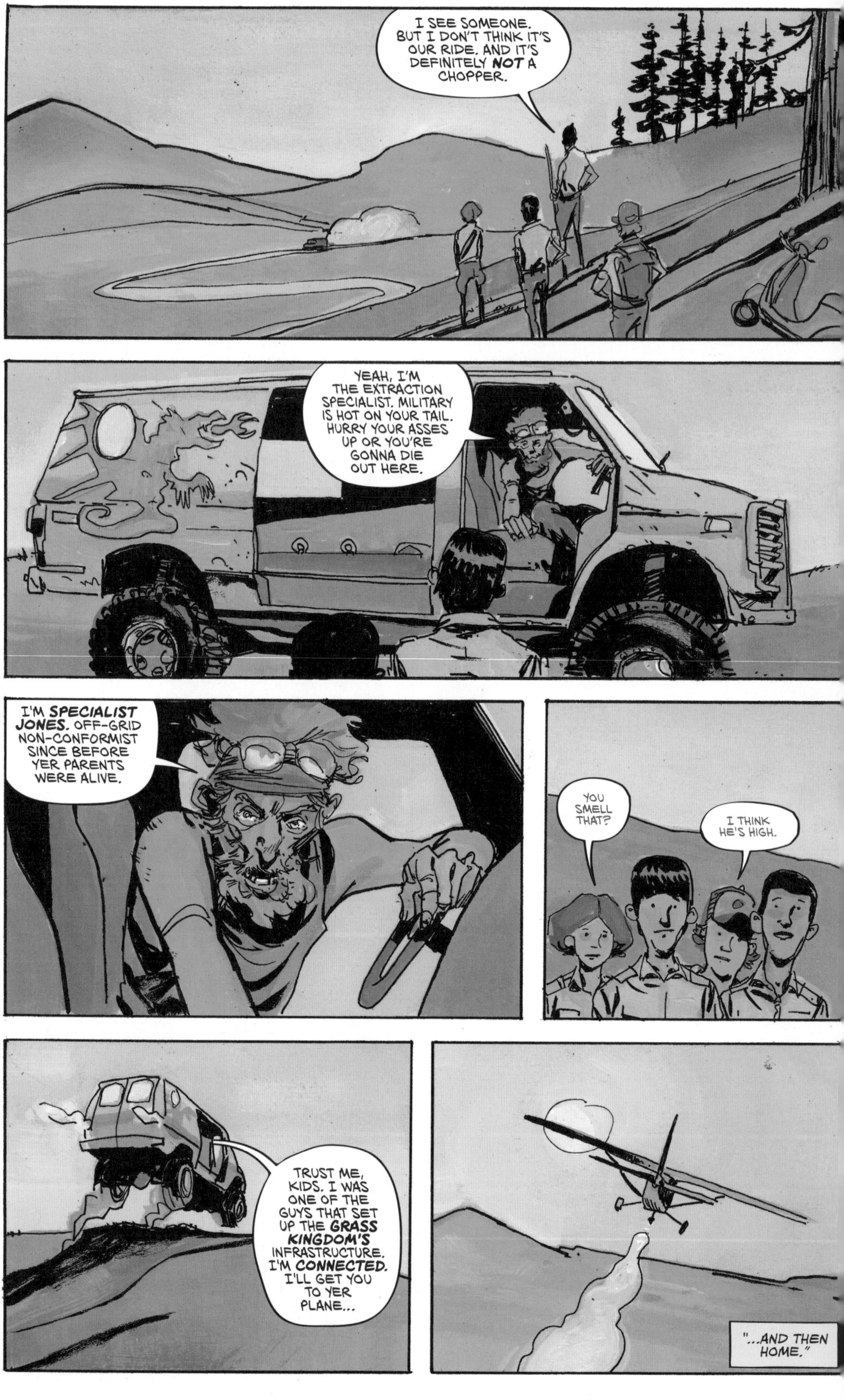
I SEE SOMEONE. BUT I DON'T THINK IT'S OUR RIDE. AND IT'S DEFINITELY **NOT** A CHOPPER.
YEAH, I'M THE EXTRACTION SPECIALIST. MILITARY IS HOT ON YOUR TAIL. HURRY YOUR ASSES UP OR YOU'RE GONNA DIE OUT HERE.
I'M **SPECIALIST JONES.** OFF-GRID NON-CONFORMIST SINCE BEFORE YER PARENTS WERE ALIVE.
YOU SMELL THAT?
I THINK HE'S HIGH.
TRUST ME, KIDS. I WAS ONE OF THE GUYS THAT SET UP THE **GRASS KINGDOM'S** INFRASTRUCTURE. I'M **CONNECTED.** I'LL GET YOU TO YER PLANE...
"...AND THEN HOME."

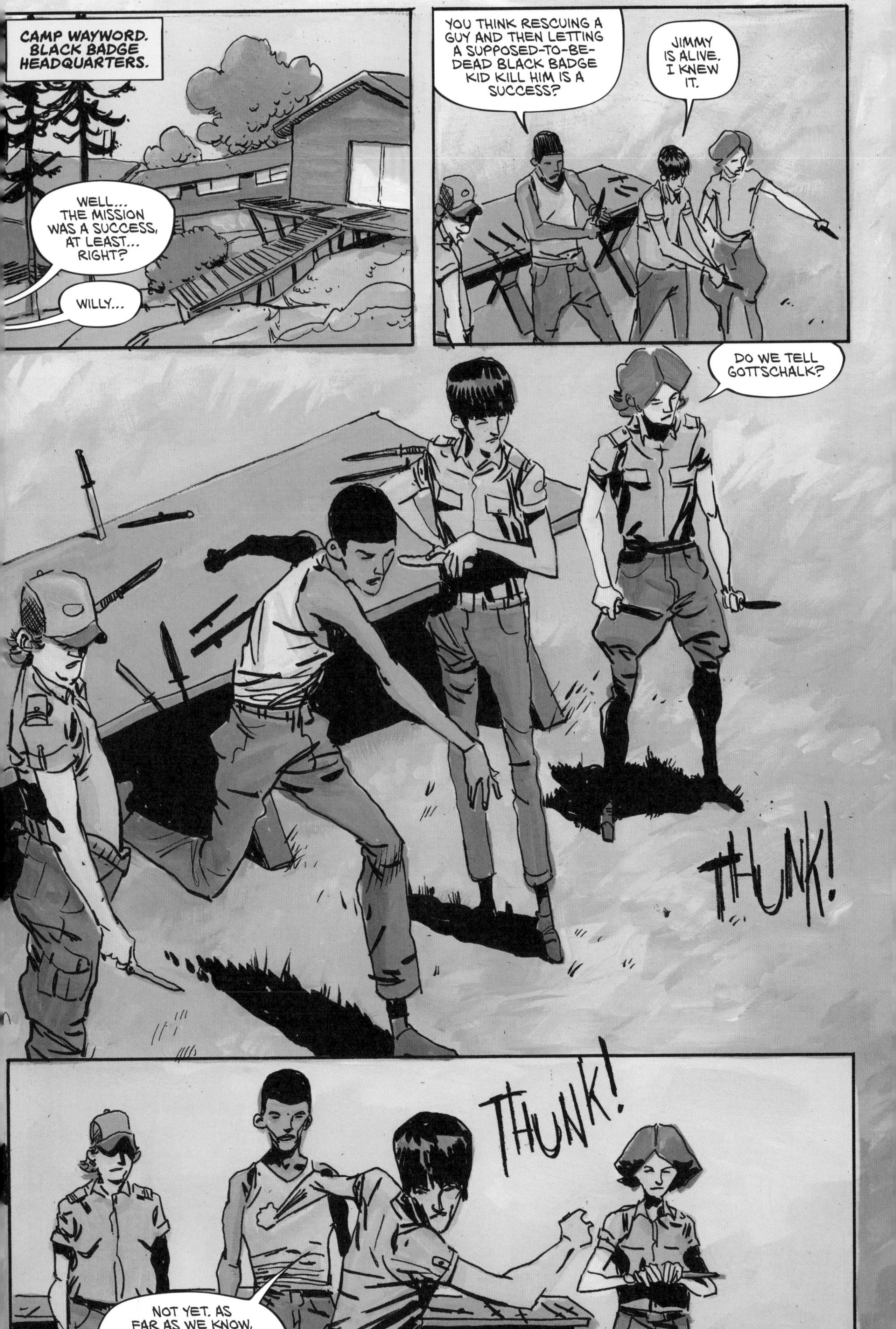
CAMP WAYWORD. BLACK BADGE HEADQUARTERS.
WELL... THE MISSION WAS A SUCCESS, AT LEAST... RIGHT?
WILLY...
YOU THINK RESCUING A GUY AND THEN LETTING A SUPPOSED-TO-BE-DEAD BLACK BADGE KID KILL HIM IS A SUCCESS?
JIMMY IS ALIVE. I KNEW IT.
DO WE TELL GOTTSCHALK?
THUNK!
THUNK!
NOT YET. AS FAR AS WE KNOW, JIMMY IS TELLING THE TRUTH. SO WE CAN'T TRUST ANYBODY UNTIL WE'RE SURE.

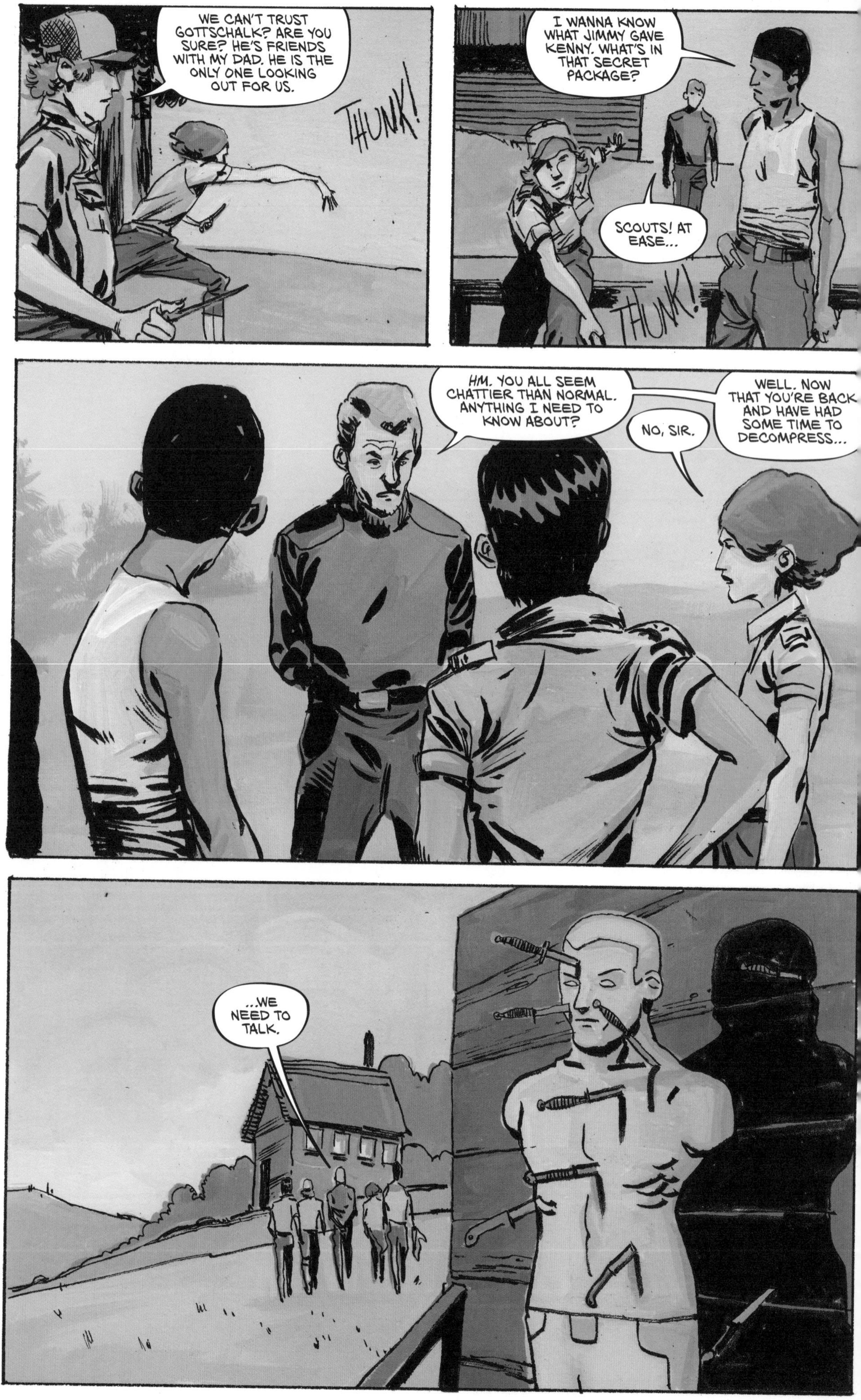
WE CAN'T TRUST GOTTSCHALK? ARE YOU SURE? HE'S FRIENDS WITH MY DAD. HE IS THE ONLY ONE LOOKING OUT FOR US.
THUNK!
I WANNA KNOW WHAT JIMMY GAVE KENNY. WHAT'S IN THAT SECRET PACKAGE?
SCOUTS! AT EASE...
THUNK!
HM. YOU ALL SEEM CHATTIER THAN NORMAL. ANYTHING I NEED TO KNOW ABOUT?
NO, SIR.
WELL. NOW THAT YOU'RE BACK AND HAVE HAD SOME TIME TO DECOMPRESS...
...WE NEED TO TALK.

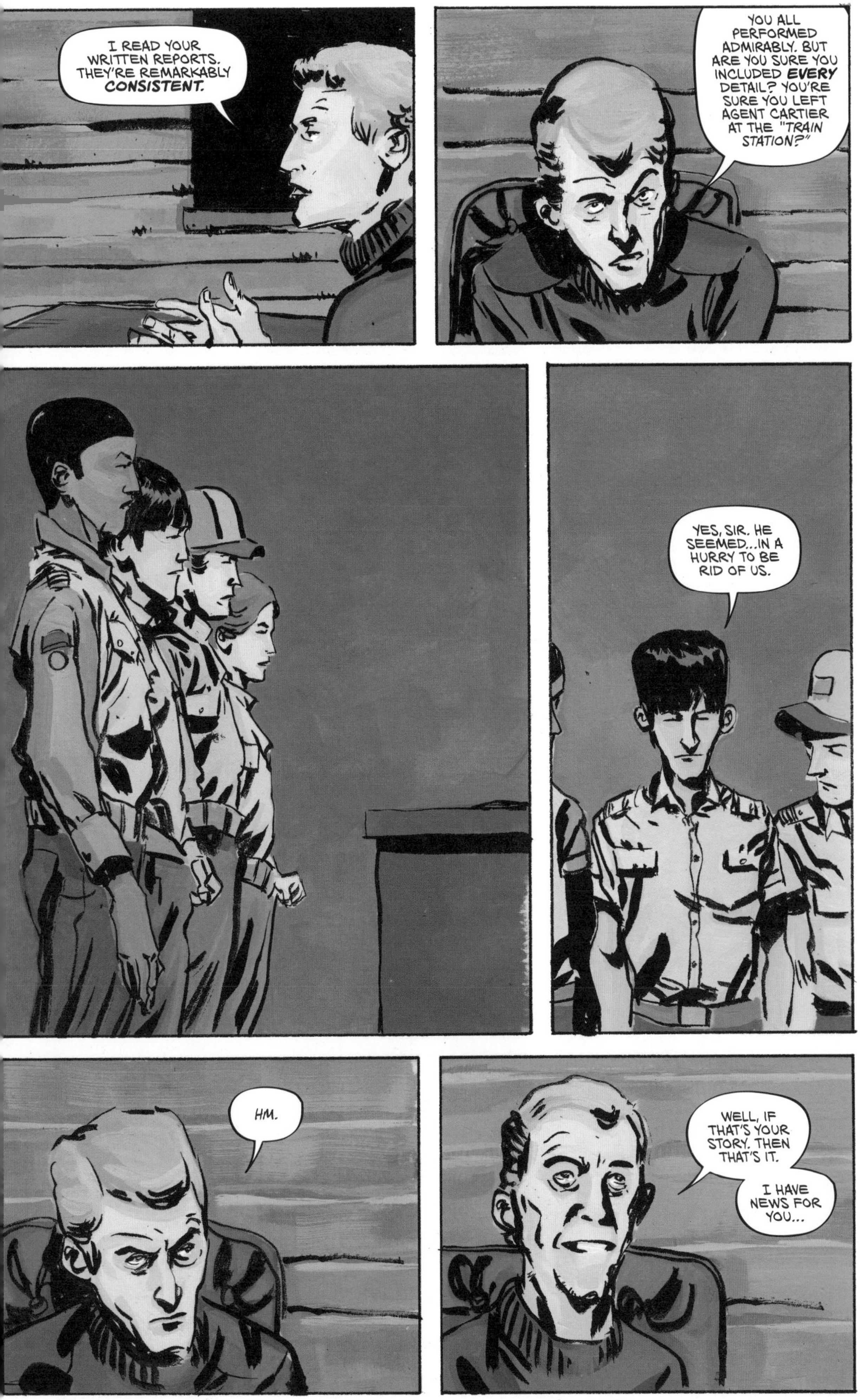
I READ YOUR WRITTEN REPORTS. THEY'RE REMARKABLY **CONSISTENT.**
YOU ALL PERFORMED ADMIRABLY. BUT ARE YOU SURE YOU INCLUDED **EVERY** DETAIL? YOU'RE SURE YOU LEFT AGENT CARTIER AT THE *"TRAIN STATION?"*
YES, SIR. HE SEEMED...IN A HURRY TO BE RID OF US.
HM.
WELL, IF THAT'S YOUR STORY. THEN THAT'S IT.
I HAVE NEWS FOR YOU...

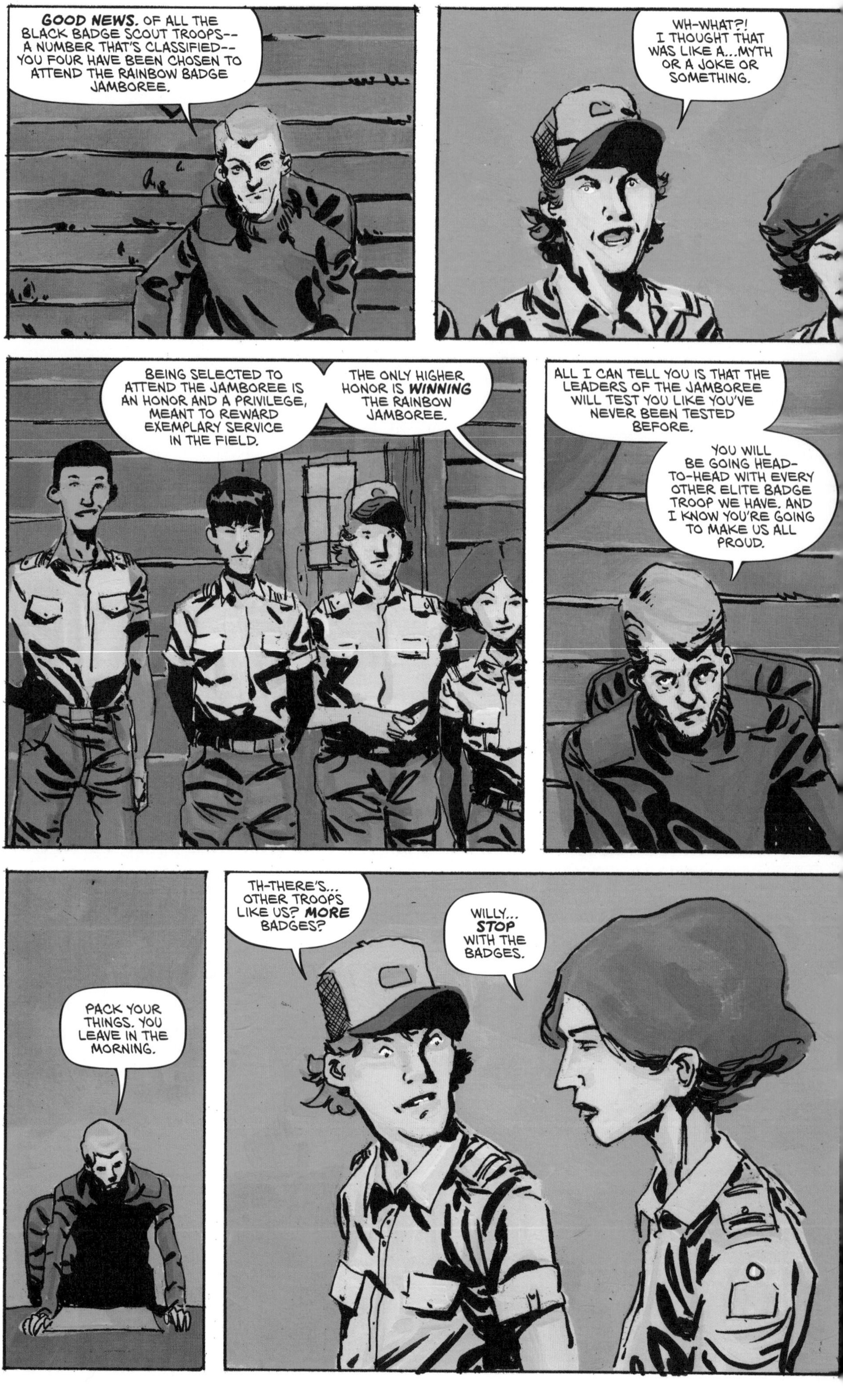

GOOD NEWS. OF ALL THE BLACK BADGE SCOUT TROOPS-- A NUMBER THAT'S CLASSIFIED-- YOU FOUR HAVE BEEN CHOSEN TO ATTEND THE RAINBOW BADGE JAMBOREE.
WH-WHAT?! I THOUGHT THAT WAS LIKE A...MYTH OR A JOKE OR SOMETHING.
BEING SELECTED TO ATTEND THE JAMBOREE IS AN HONOR AND A PRIVILEGE, MEANT TO REWARD EXEMPLARY SERVICE IN THE FIELD.
THE ONLY HIGHER HONOR IS WINNING THE RAINBOW JAMBOREE.
ALL I CAN TELL YOU IS THAT THE LEADERS OF THE JAMBOREE WILL TEST YOU LIKE YOU'VE NEVER BEEN TESTED BEFORE.
YOU WILL BE GOING HEAD-TO-HEAD WITH EVERY OTHER ELITE BADGE TROOP WE HAVE. AND I KNOW YOU'RE GOING TO MAKE US ALL PROUD.
PACK YOUR THINGS. YOU LEAVE IN THE MORNING.
TH-THERE'S... OTHER TROOPS LIKE US? MORE BADGES?
WILLY... STOP WITH THE BADGES.

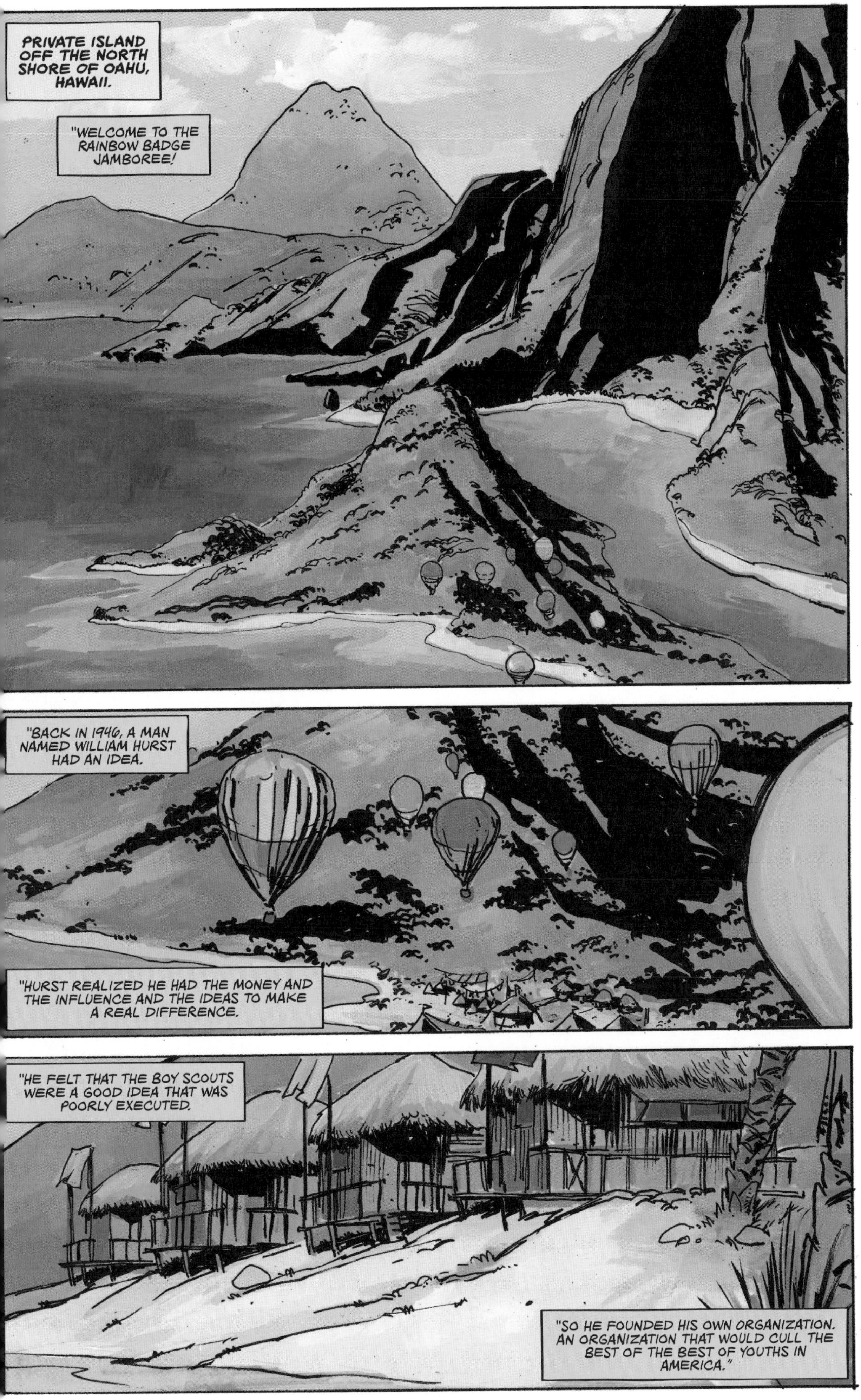
PRIVATE ISLAND OFF THE NORTH SHORE OF OAHU, HAWAII.
"WELCOME TO THE RAINBOW BADGE JAMBOREE!
"BACK IN 1946, A MAN NAMED WILLIAM HURST HAD AN IDEA.
"HURST REALIZED HE HAD THE MONEY AND THE INFLUENCE AND THE IDEAS TO MAKE A REAL DIFFERENCE.
"HE FELT THAT THE BOY SCOUTS WERE A GOOD IDEA THAT WAS POORLY EXECUTED.
"SO HE FOUNDED HIS OWN ORGANIZATION. AN ORGANIZATION THAT WOULD CULL THE BEST OF THE BEST OF YOUTHS IN AMERICA."

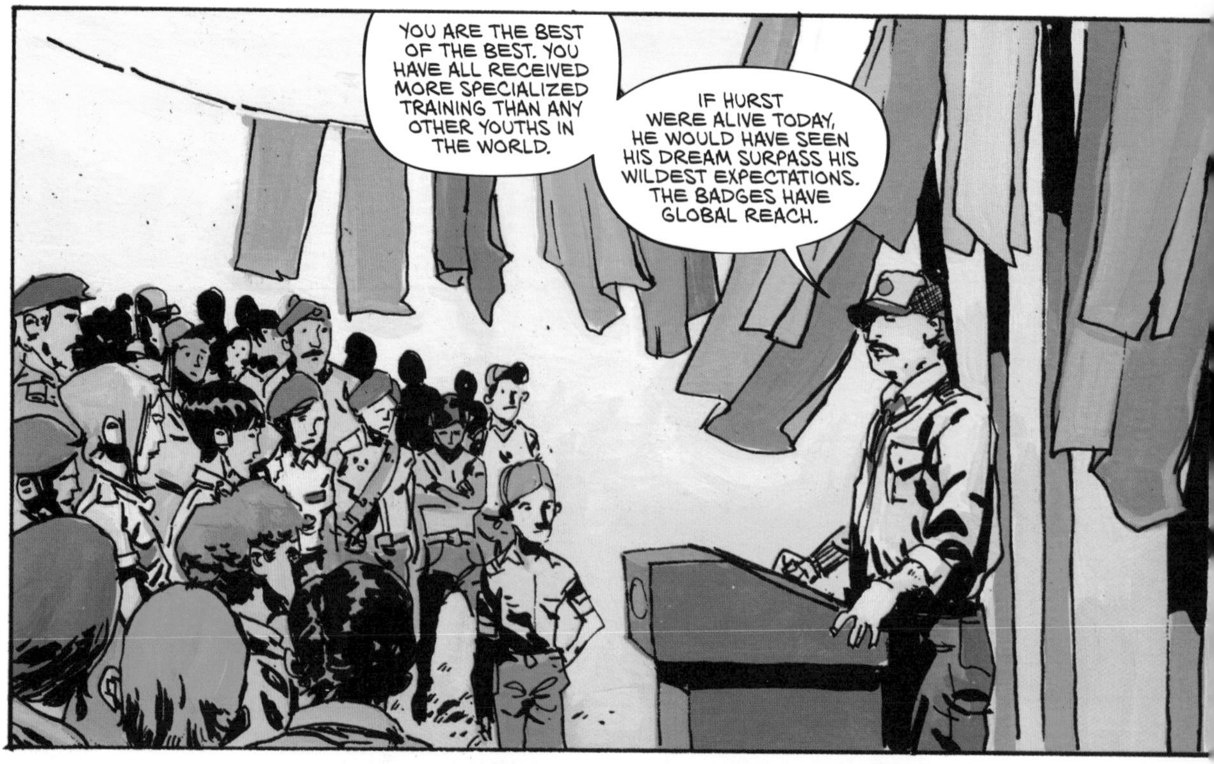
YOU ARE THE BEST OF THE BEST. YOU HAVE ALL RECEIVED MORE SPECIALIZED TRAINING THAN ANY OTHER YOUTHS IN THE WORLD.
IF HURST WERE ALIVE TODAY, HE WOULD HAVE SEEN HIS DREAM SURPASS HIS WILDEST EXPECTATIONS. THE BADGES HAVE GLOBAL REACH.

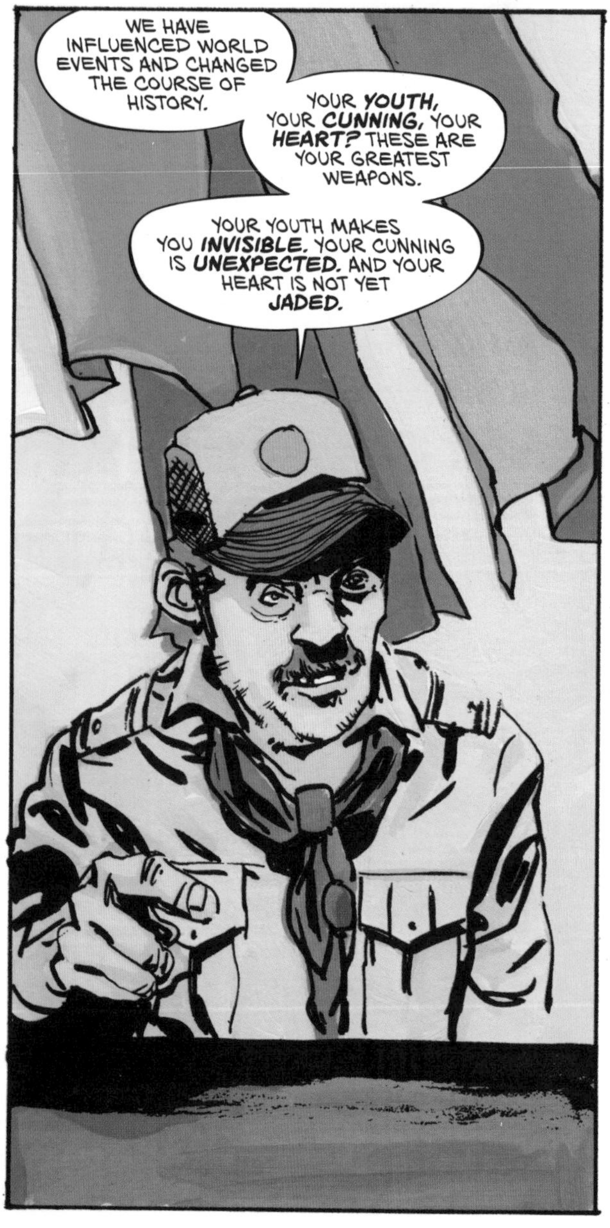
WE HAVE INFLUENCED WORLD EVENTS AND CHANGED THE COURSE OF HISTORY.
YOUR **YOUTH,** YOUR **CUNNING,** YOUR **HEART?** THESE ARE YOUR GREATEST WEAPONS.
YOUR YOUTH MAKES YOU **INVISIBLE.** YOUR CUNNING IS **UNEXPECTED.** AND YOUR HEART IS NOT YET **JADED.**

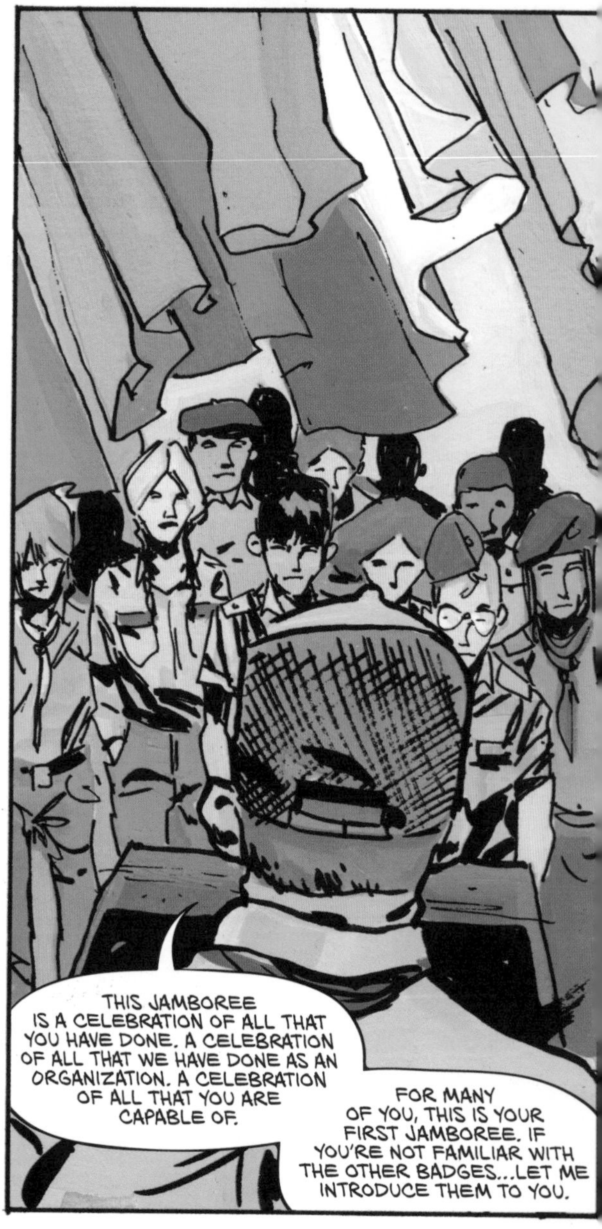
THIS JAMBOREE IS A CELEBRATION OF ALL THAT YOU HAVE DONE. A CELEBRATION OF ALL THAT WE HAVE DONE AS AN ORGANIZATION. A CELEBRATION OF ALL THAT YOU ARE CAPABLE OF.
FOR MANY OF YOU, THIS IS YOUR FIRST JAMBOREE. IF YOU'RE NOT FAMILIAR WITH THE OTHER BADGES...LET ME INTRODUCE THEM TO YOU.

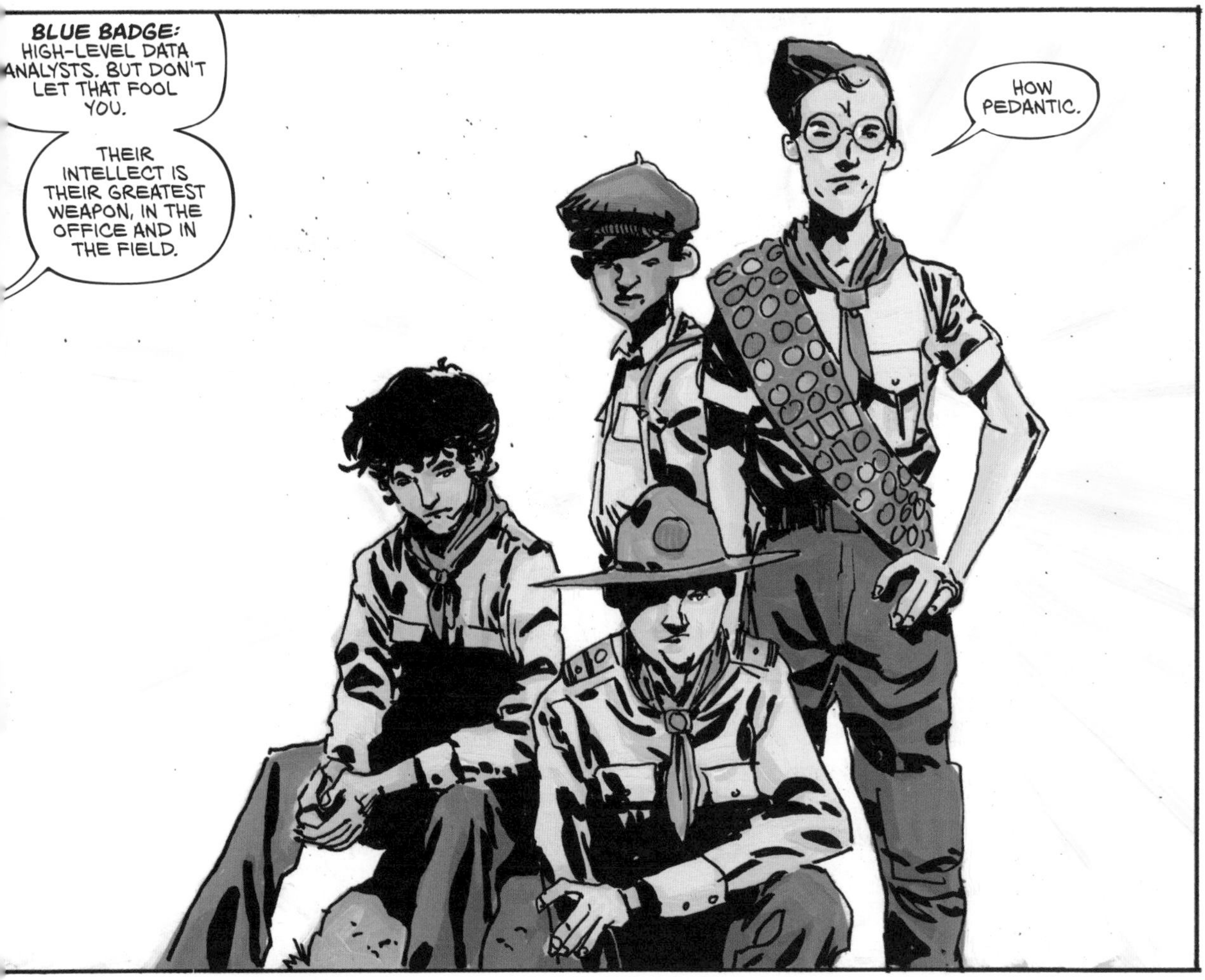
BLUE BADGE: HIGH-LEVEL DATA ANALYSTS. BUT DON'T LET THAT FOOL YOU.
THEIR INTELLECT IS THEIR GREATEST WEAPON, IN THE OFFICE AND IN THE FIELD.
HOW PEDANTIC.

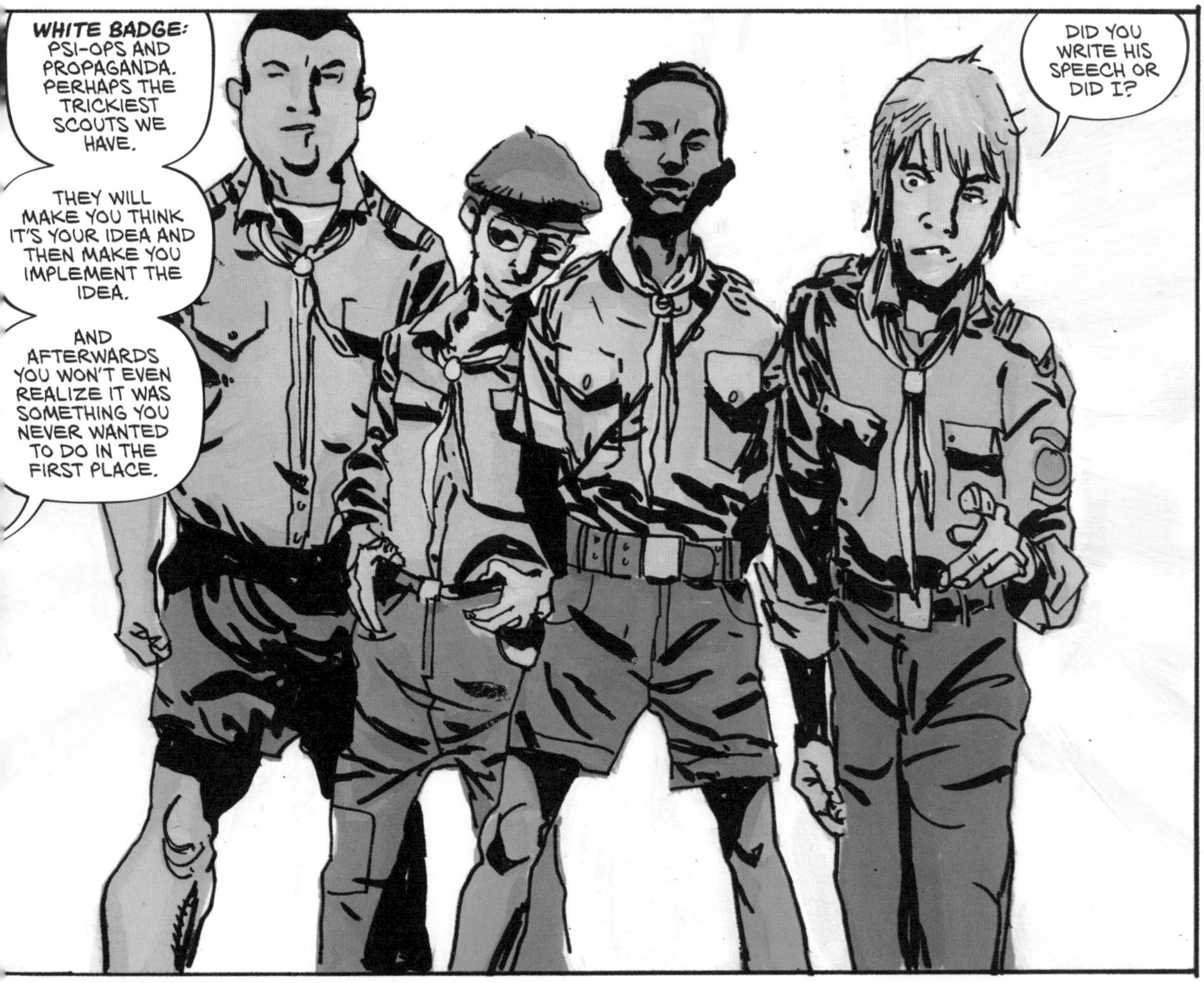
WHITE BADGE: PSI-OPS AND PROPAGANDA. PERHAPS THE TRICKIEST SCOUTS WE HAVE.
THEY WILL MAKE YOU THINK IT'S YOUR IDEA AND THEN MAKE YOU IMPLEMENT THE IDEA.
AND AFTERWARDS YOU WON'T EVEN REALIZE IT WAS SOMETHING YOU NEVER WANTED TO DO IN THE FIRST PLACE.
DID YOU WRITE HIS SPEECH OR DID I?

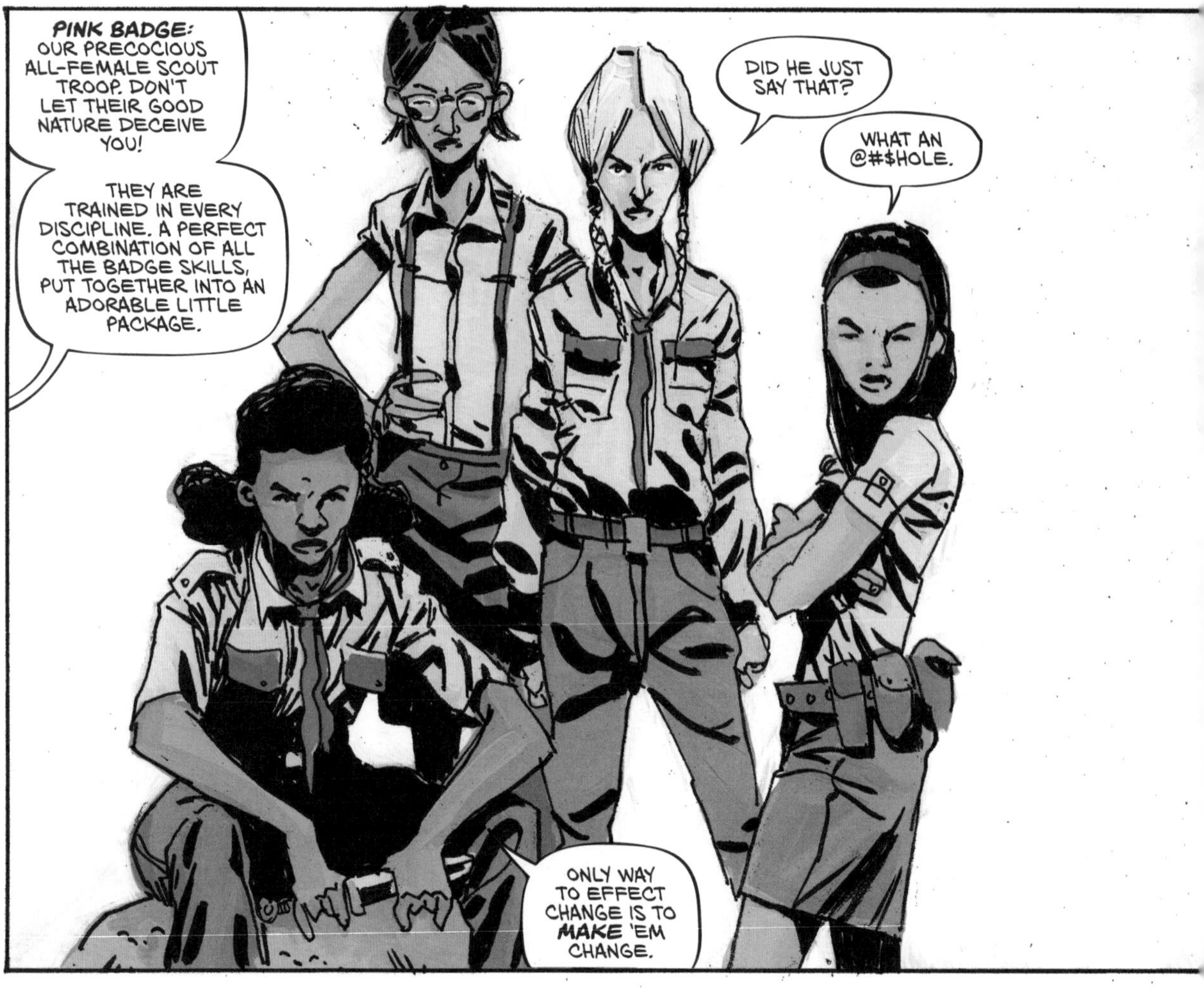
PINK BADGE: OUR PRECOCIOUS ALL-FEMALE SCOUT TROOP. DON'T LET THEIR GOOD NATURE DECEIVE YOU!
THEY ARE TRAINED IN EVERY DISCIPLINE. A PERFECT COMBINATION OF ALL THE BADGE SKILLS, PUT TOGETHER INTO AN ADORABLE LITTLE PACKAGE.
DID HE JUST SAY THAT?
WHAT AN @#$HOLE.
ONLY WAY TO EFFECT CHANGE IS TO **MAKE** 'EM CHANGE.

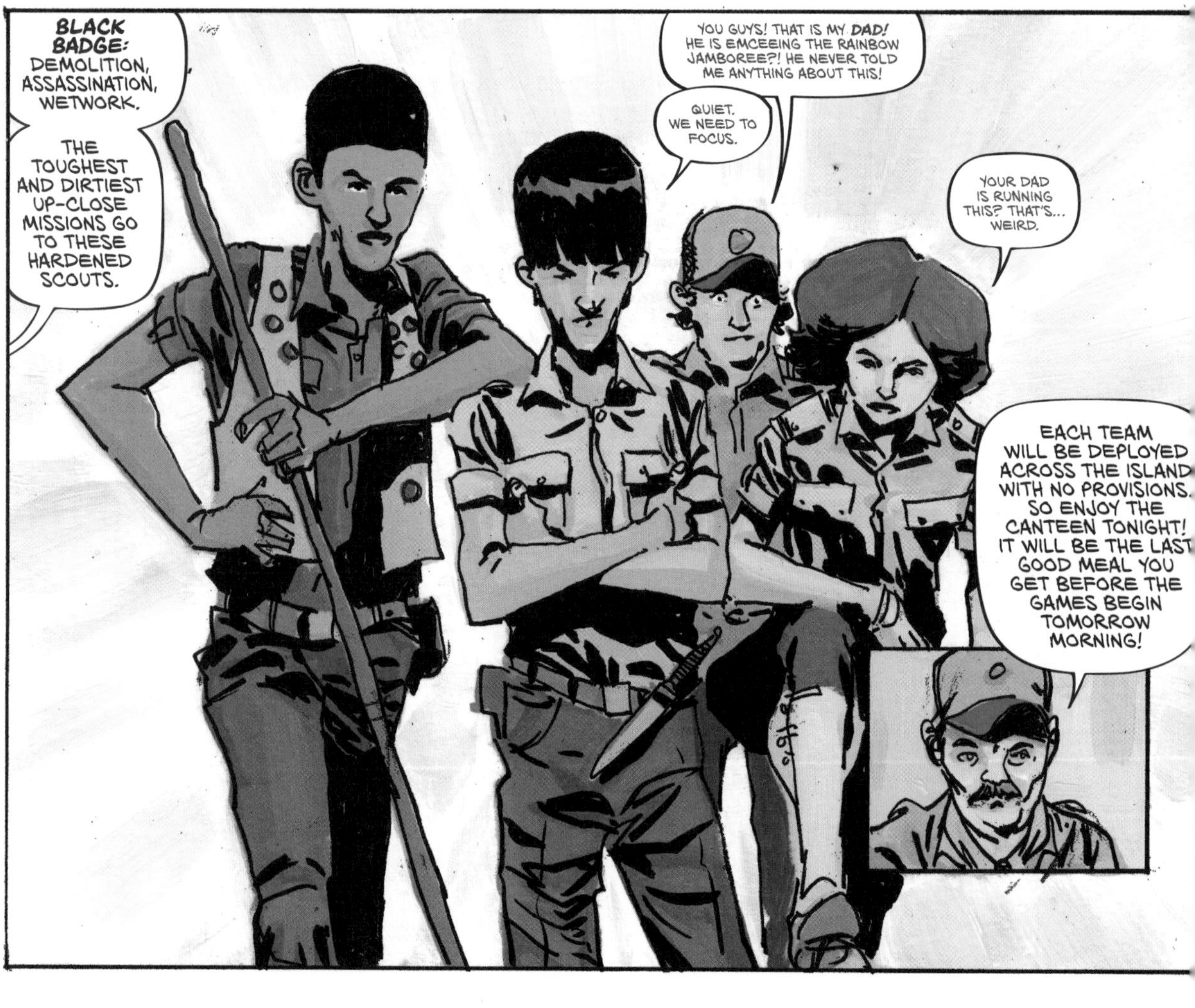
BLACK BADGE: DEMOLITION, ASSASSINATION, WETWORK.
THE TOUGHEST AND DIRTIEST UP-CLOSE MISSIONS GO TO THESE HARDENED SCOUTS.
YOU GUYS! THAT IS MY ***DAD!*** HE IS EMCEEING THE RAINBOW JAMBOREE?! HE NEVER TOLD ME ANYTHING ABOUT THIS!
QUIET. WE NEED TO FOCUS.
YOUR DAD IS RUNNING THIS? THAT'S... WEIRD.
EACH TEAM WILL BE DEPLOYED ACROSS THE ISLAND WITH NO PROVISIONS. SO ENJOY THE CANTEEN TONIGHT! IT WILL BE THE LAST GOOD MEAL YOU GET BEFORE THE GAMES BEGIN TOMORROW MORNING!

IT'S JUST AMAZING, ISN'T IT? WE GO FROM BEING BULLIED BY SOME PUNKS IN NORTH KOREA, TO STARTING A PRISON RIOT IN SIBERIA, TO BLOWING UP A BUILDING IN PAKISTAN. HOW DID WE *GET* HERE?

ARE THEY SERIOUS WITH THIS *HUNGER GAMES/LORD OF THE FLIES* CRAP?

THEY WOULDN'T DO IT JUST FOR FUN. THIS HAS GOT TO BE A TEST.

IT'S *SICK* AND *DERIVATIVE*, IS WHAT IT IS. NOTHING WORSE THAN ADULTS PRETENDING THEY KNOW WHAT MAKES KIDS TICK.

THEY MUST BE DOING SOMETHING RIGHT. LOOK AT ALL WE'VE DONE.

WE DO WHAT WE'RE TOLD, WILLY.

AND DOING WHAT WE'RE TOLD...? IT'S STARTING TO--

HEY, LOSERS!

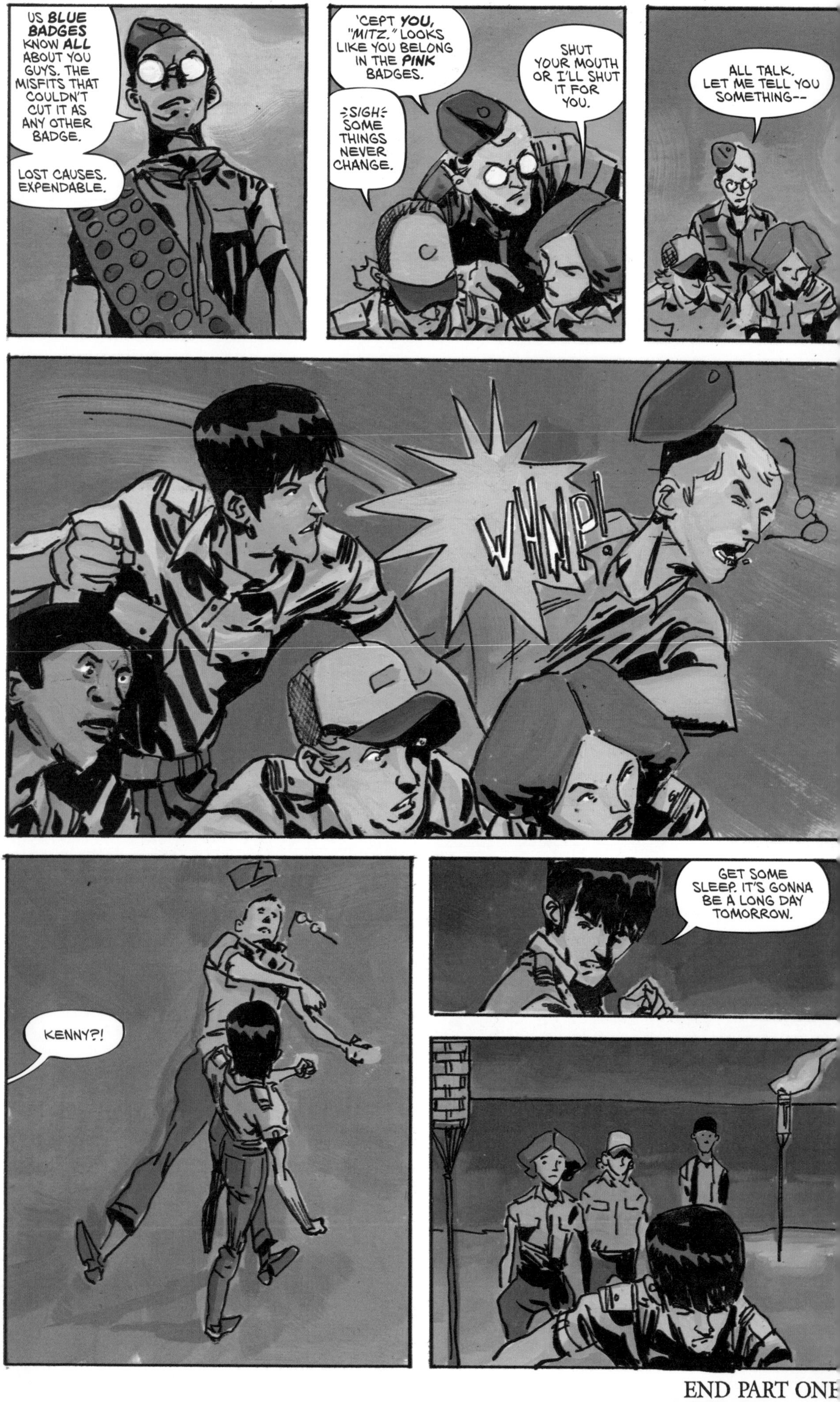
US BLUE BADGES KNOW ALL ABOUT YOU GUYS. THE MISFITS THAT COULDN'T CUT IT AS ANY OTHER BADGE.
LOST CAUSES. EXPENDABLE.
'CEPT YOU, "MITZ." LOOKS LIKE YOU BELONG IN THE PINK BADGES.
SIGH SOME THINGS NEVER CHANGE.
SHUT YOUR MOUTH OR I'LL SHUT IT FOR YOU.
ALL TALK. LET ME TELL YOU SOMETHING--
WHMP!
KENNY?!
GET SOME SLEEP. IT'S GONNA BE A LONG DAY TOMORROW.

END PART ONE

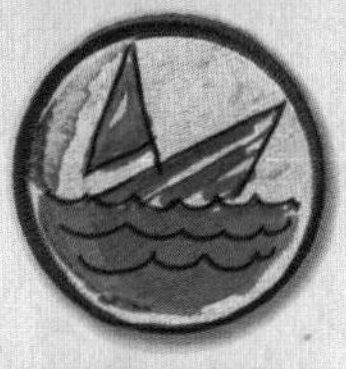

BOAT SCUTTLING

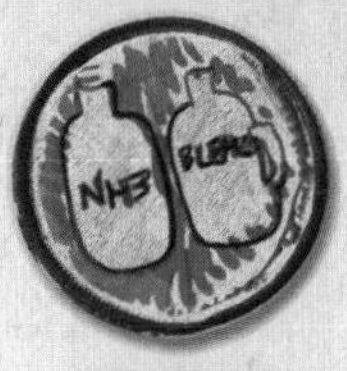

HOUSEHOLD EXPLOSIVES

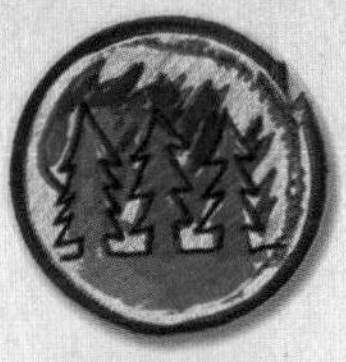

FOREST FIRES

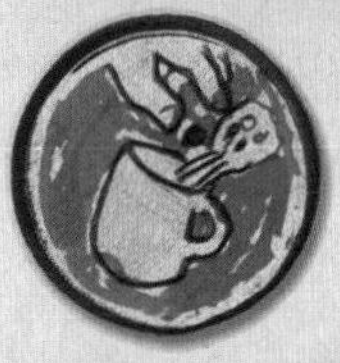

SURREPTITIOUS POISONING

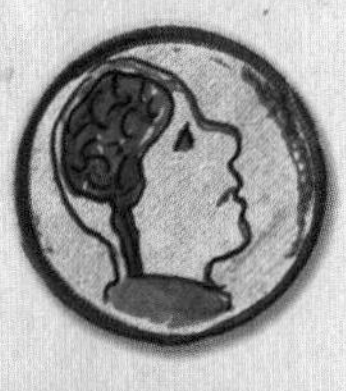

MIND MANAGEMENT

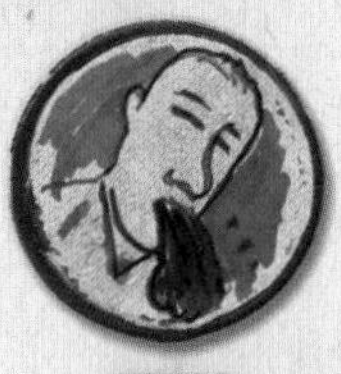

VOMIT INDUCEMENT

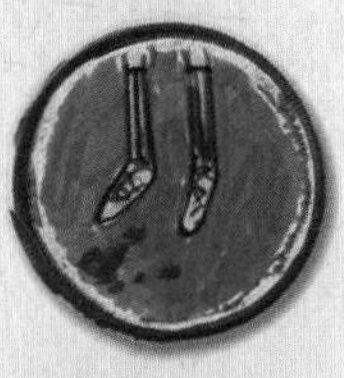

CRIME SCENE CLEANSING

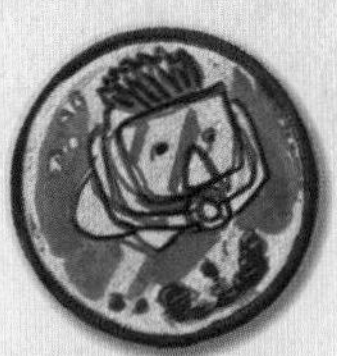

WET WORK

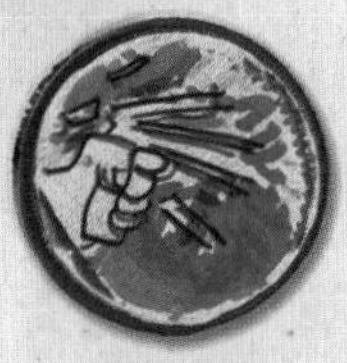

WEAPON SABOTAGE

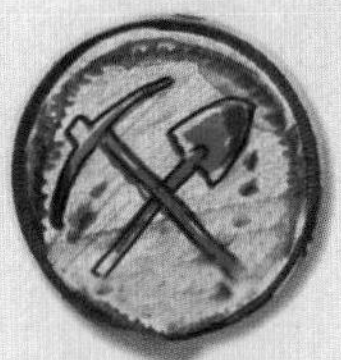

ALTERNATIVE WEAPONRY

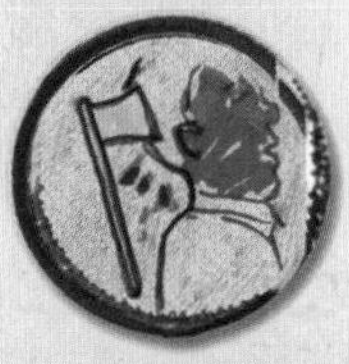

AXE THROWING

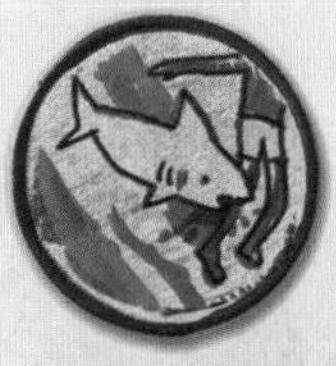

SHARK ATTACK

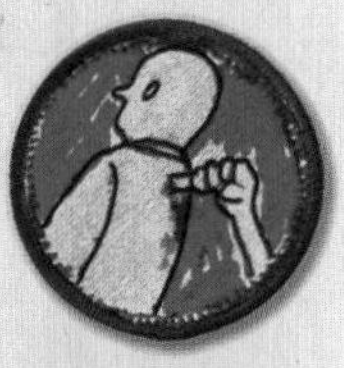

IMPROVISED WEAPONRY

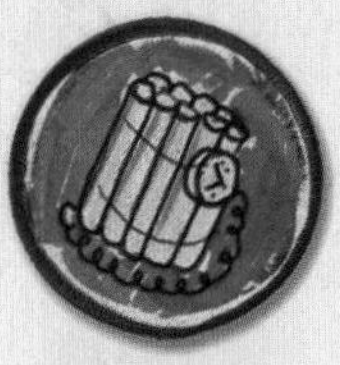

DEMOLITIONS

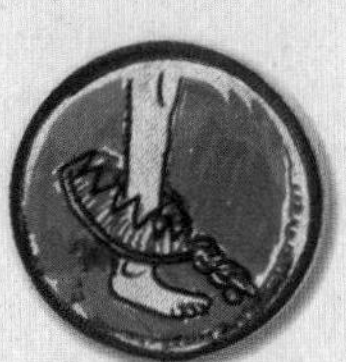

TRAPS

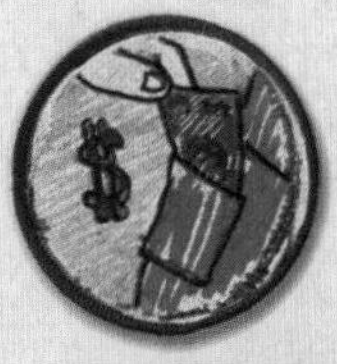

POCKET PICKING

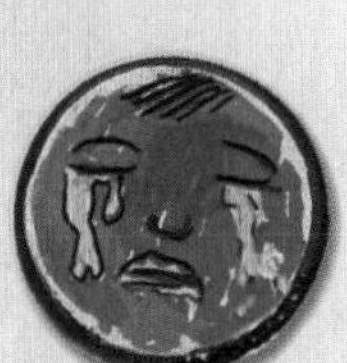

STRATEGIC BULLYING

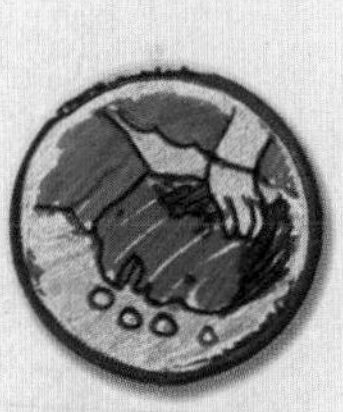

WATER TORTURE

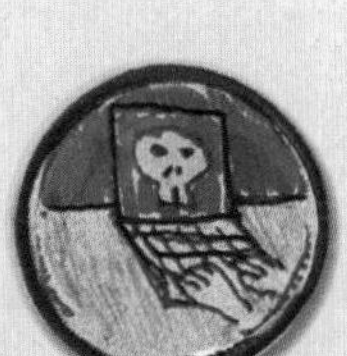

CYBER BULLYING

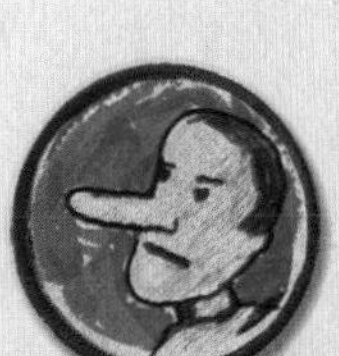

LYING

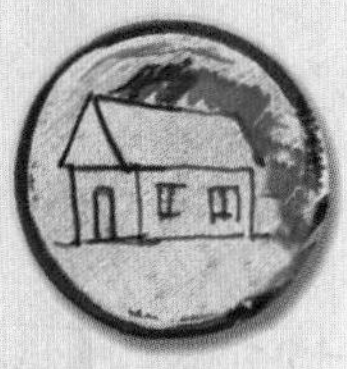

ARSON

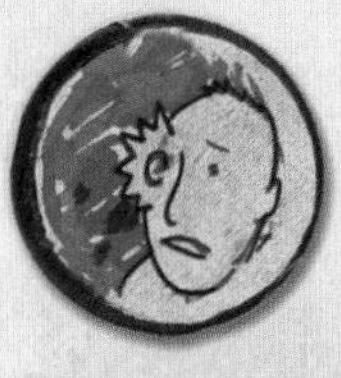

NINJA STARS

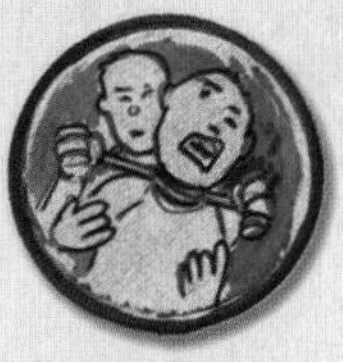

GARROTE

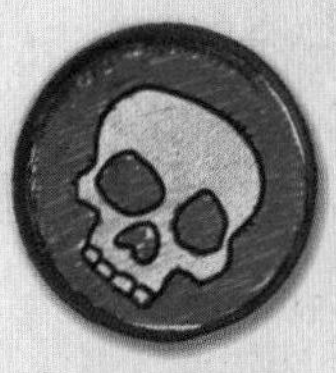

BLACK BADGE

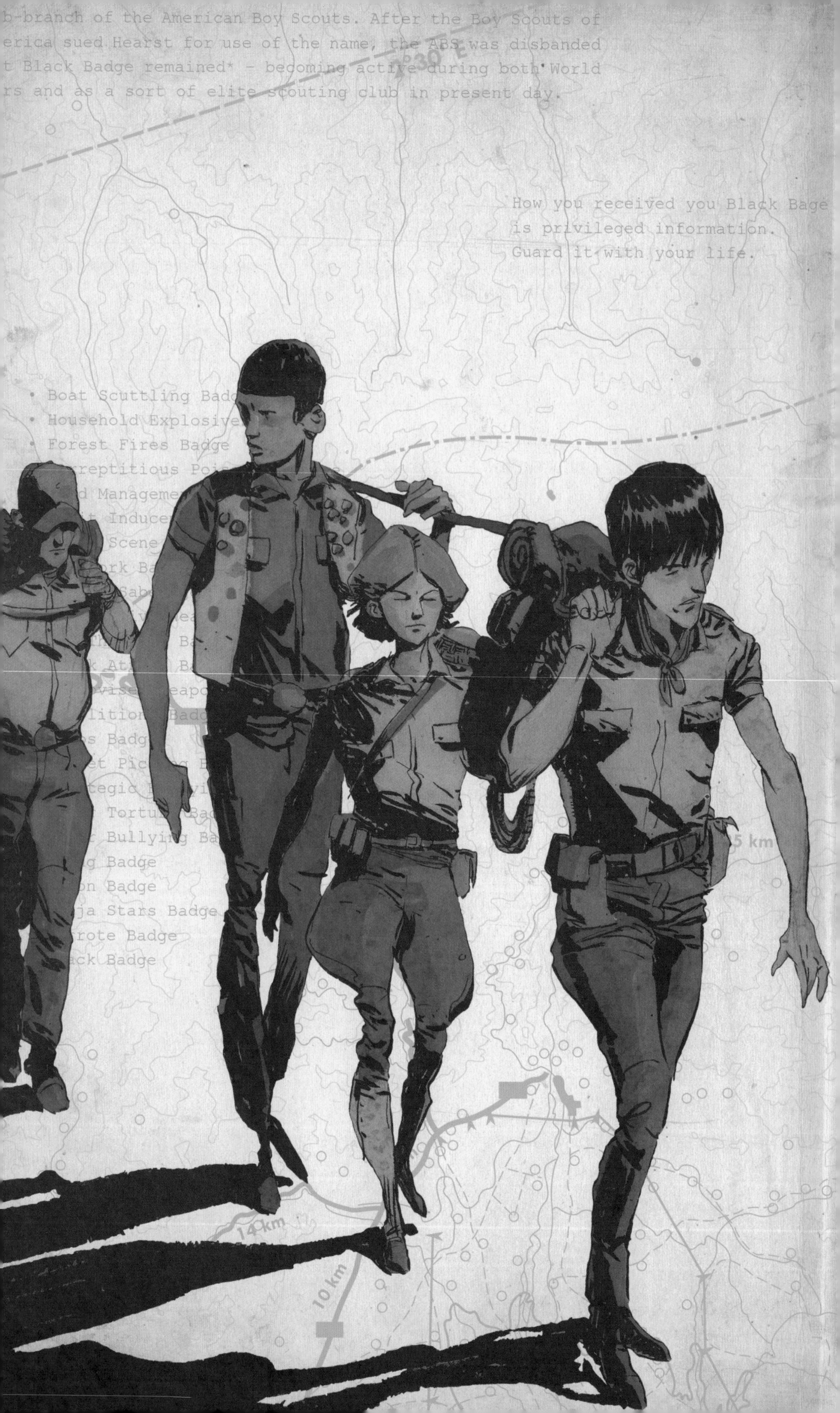
b-branch of the American Boy Scouts. After the Boy Scouts of
erica sued Hearst for use of the name, the ABS was disbanded
t Black Badge remained* - becoming active during both World
rs and as a sort of elite scouting club in present day.
How you received you Black Bage
is privileged information.
Guard it with your life.
• Boat Scuttling Badg
• Household Explosive
• Forest Fires Badge
Garrote Badge
14 km
10 km

Your Black Badge doubles as an explosive throwing star.

Behind the Badge

[redacted] Cover Gallery [redacted]

Development Artwork [redacted]

Making of the Badge [redacted]

From Script to Page [redacted]

New Recruit Questionnaire [redacted]

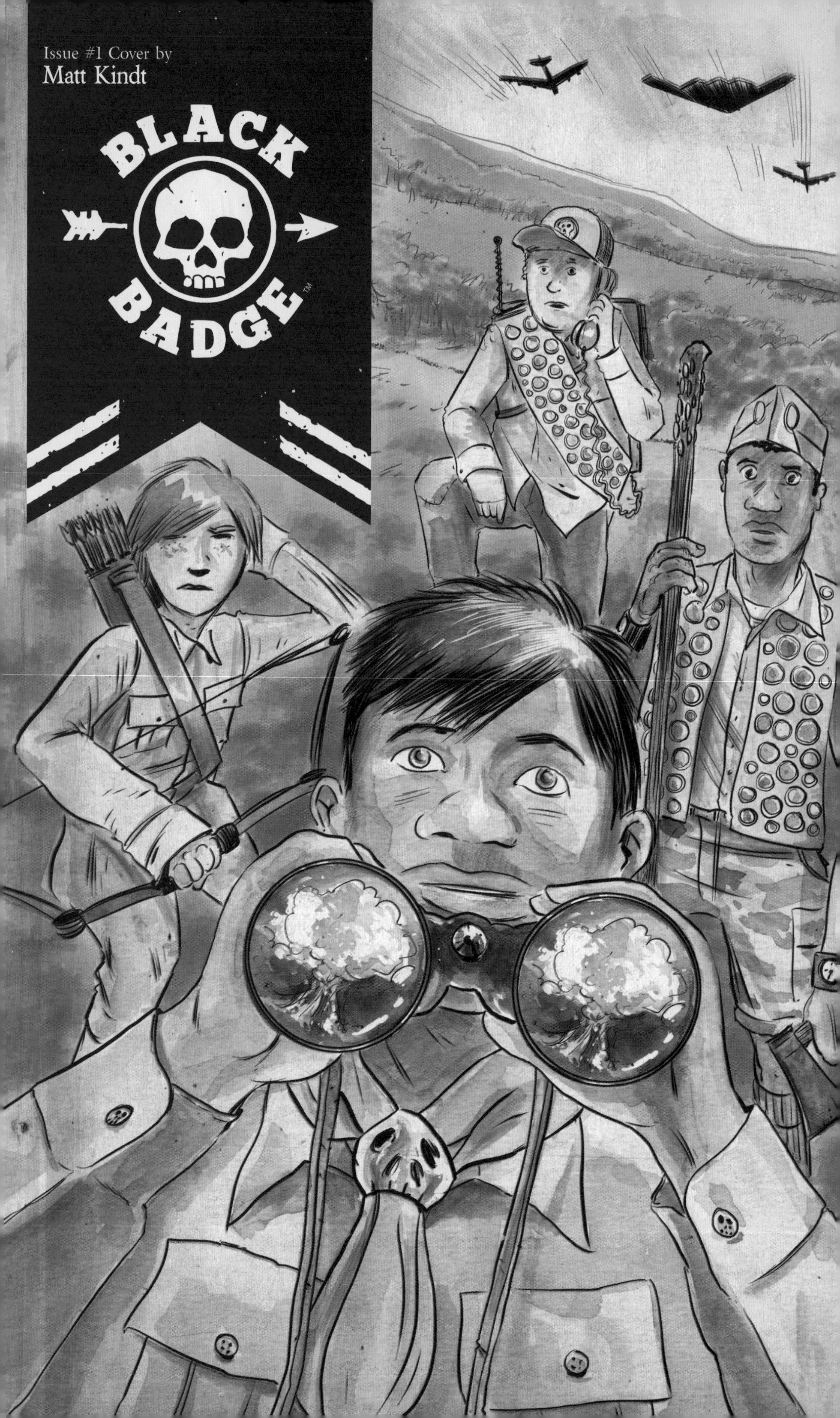
BLACK
BADGE™

Issue #1 Cover by
Matt Kindt

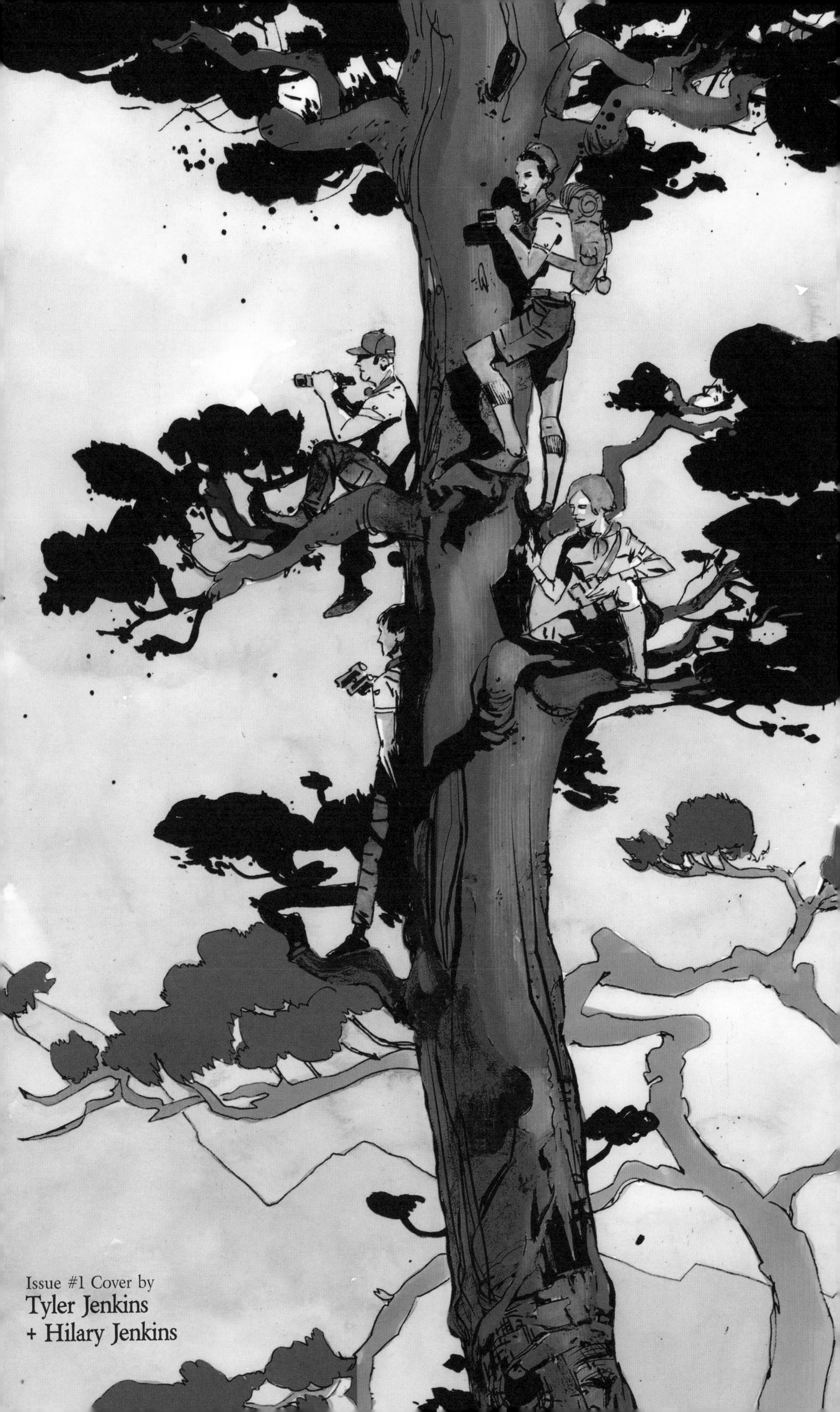

Issue #1 Cover by
Tyler Jenkins
+ Hilary Jenkins

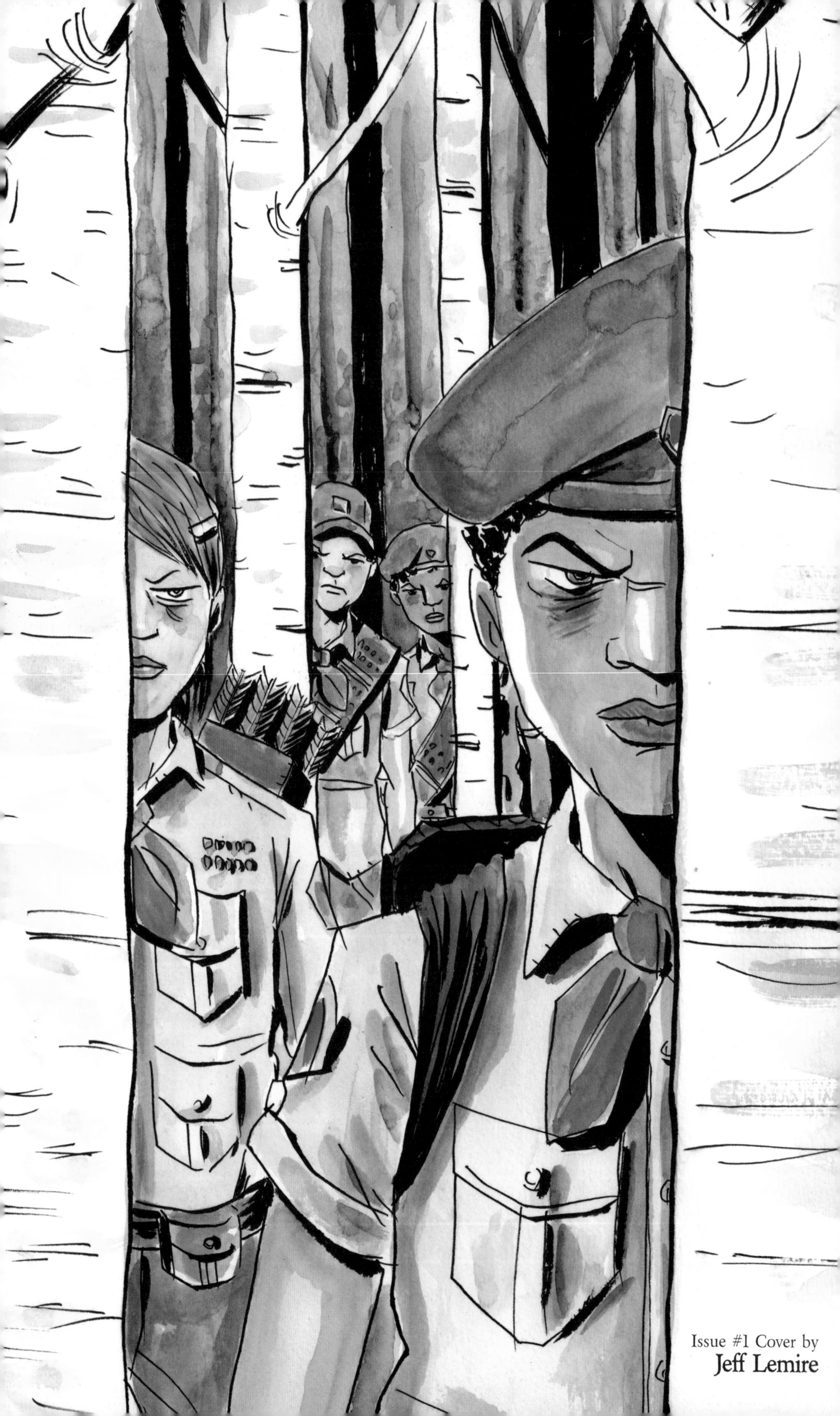

Issue #1 Cover by
Jeff Lemire

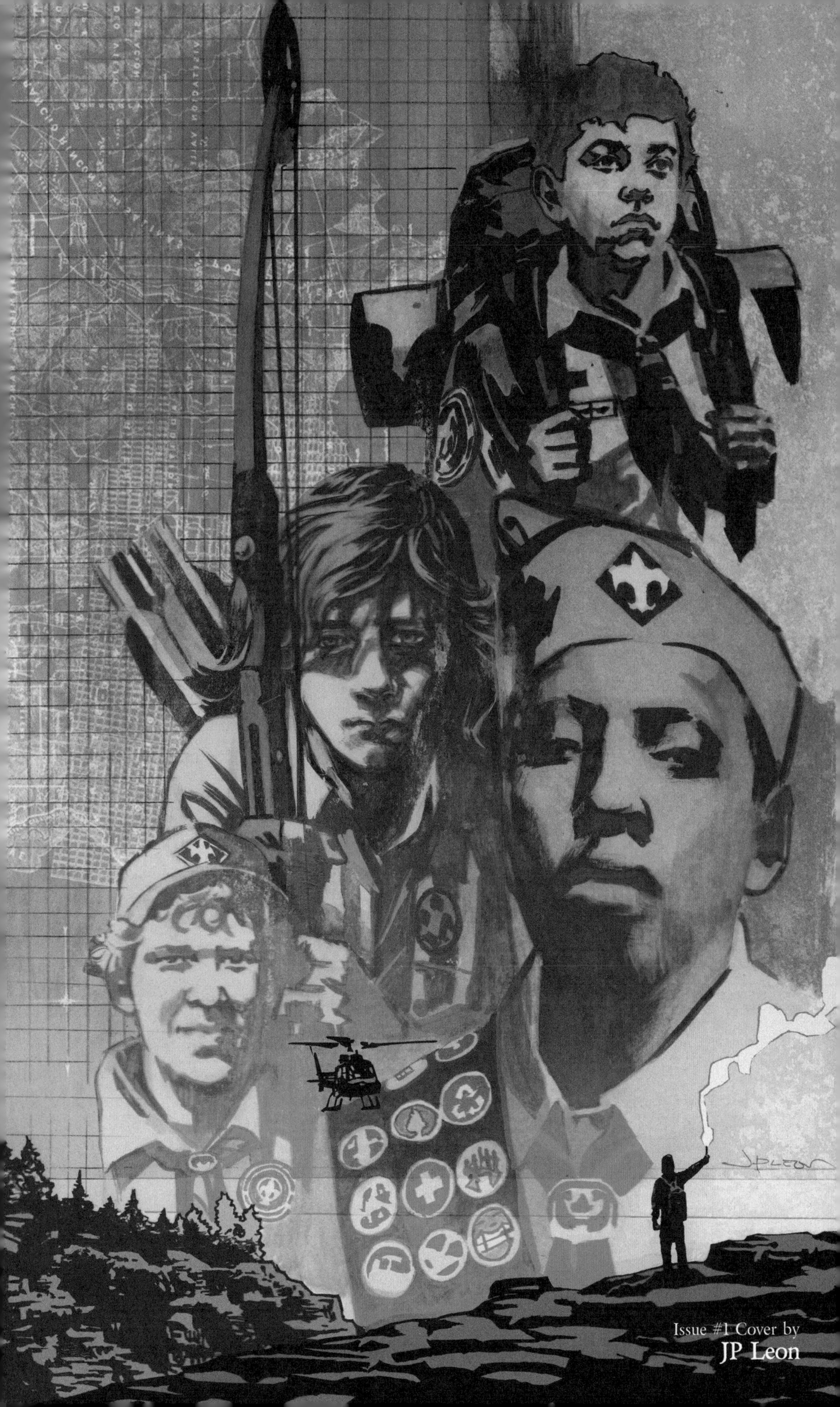

Issue #1 Cover by
JP Leon

Issue #2 Cover by
Matt Kindt

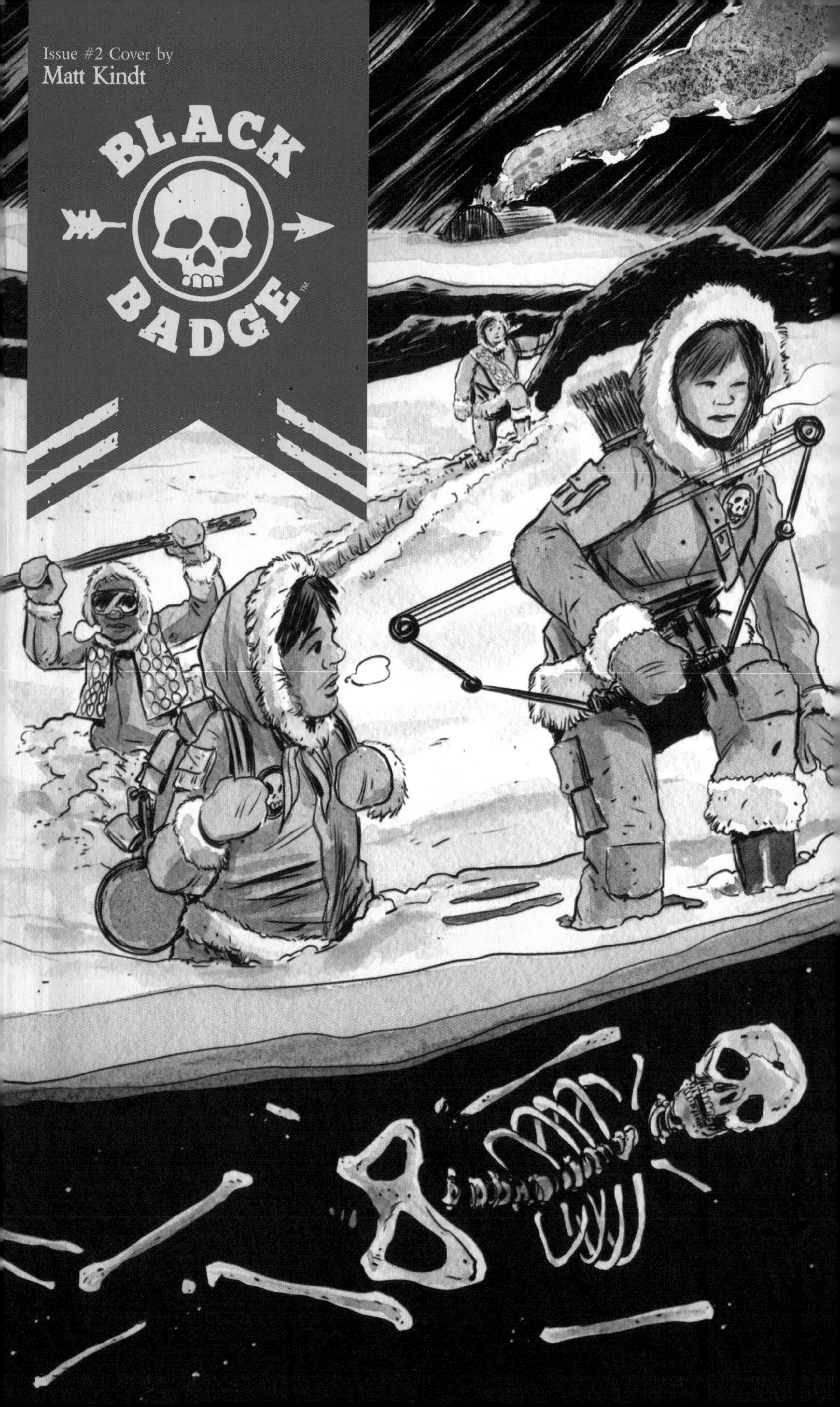
BLACK
BADGE™

Issue #2 Cover by
Tyler Jenkins
+ Hilary Jenkins

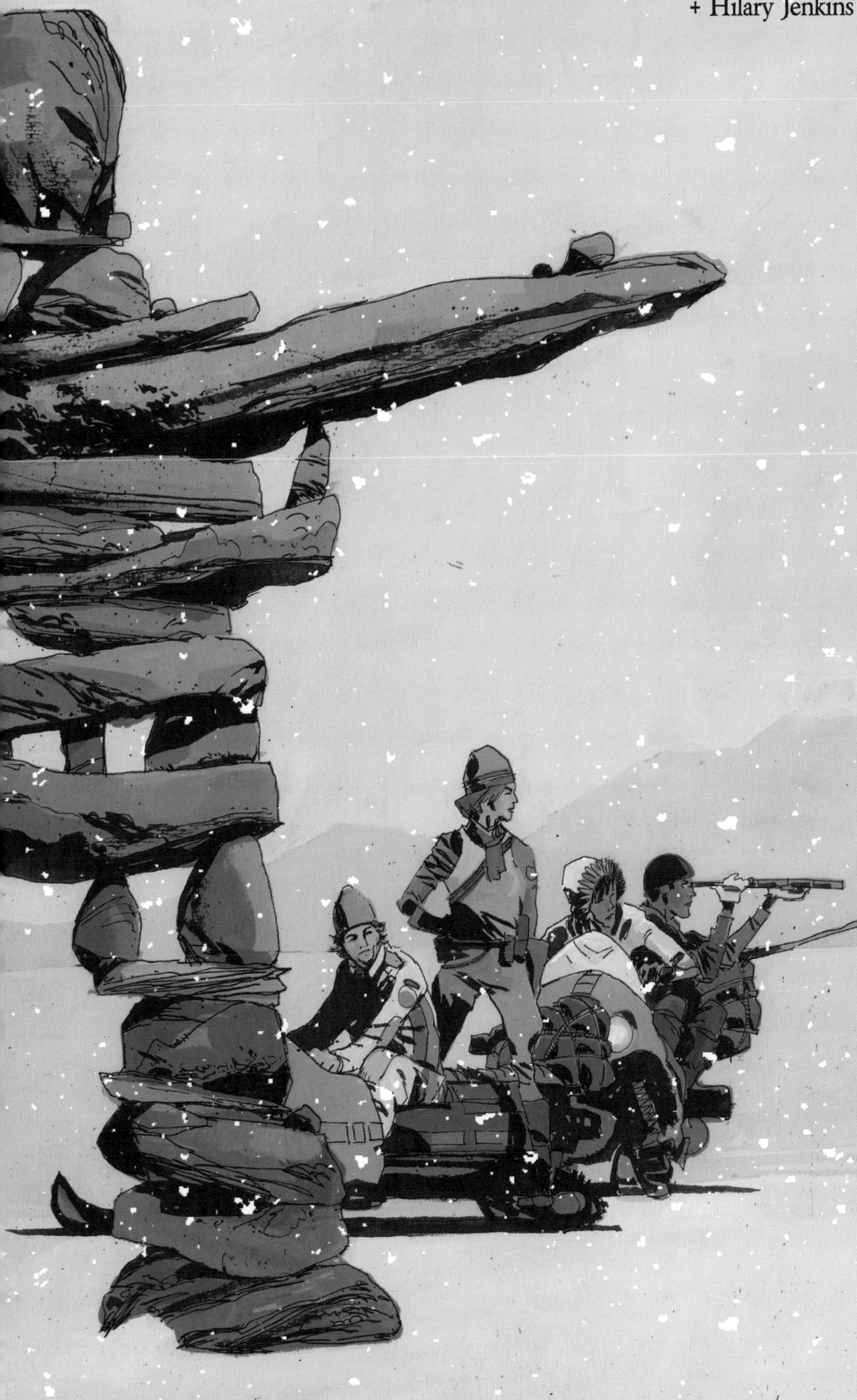

Issue #2 Cover by
Greg Smallwood

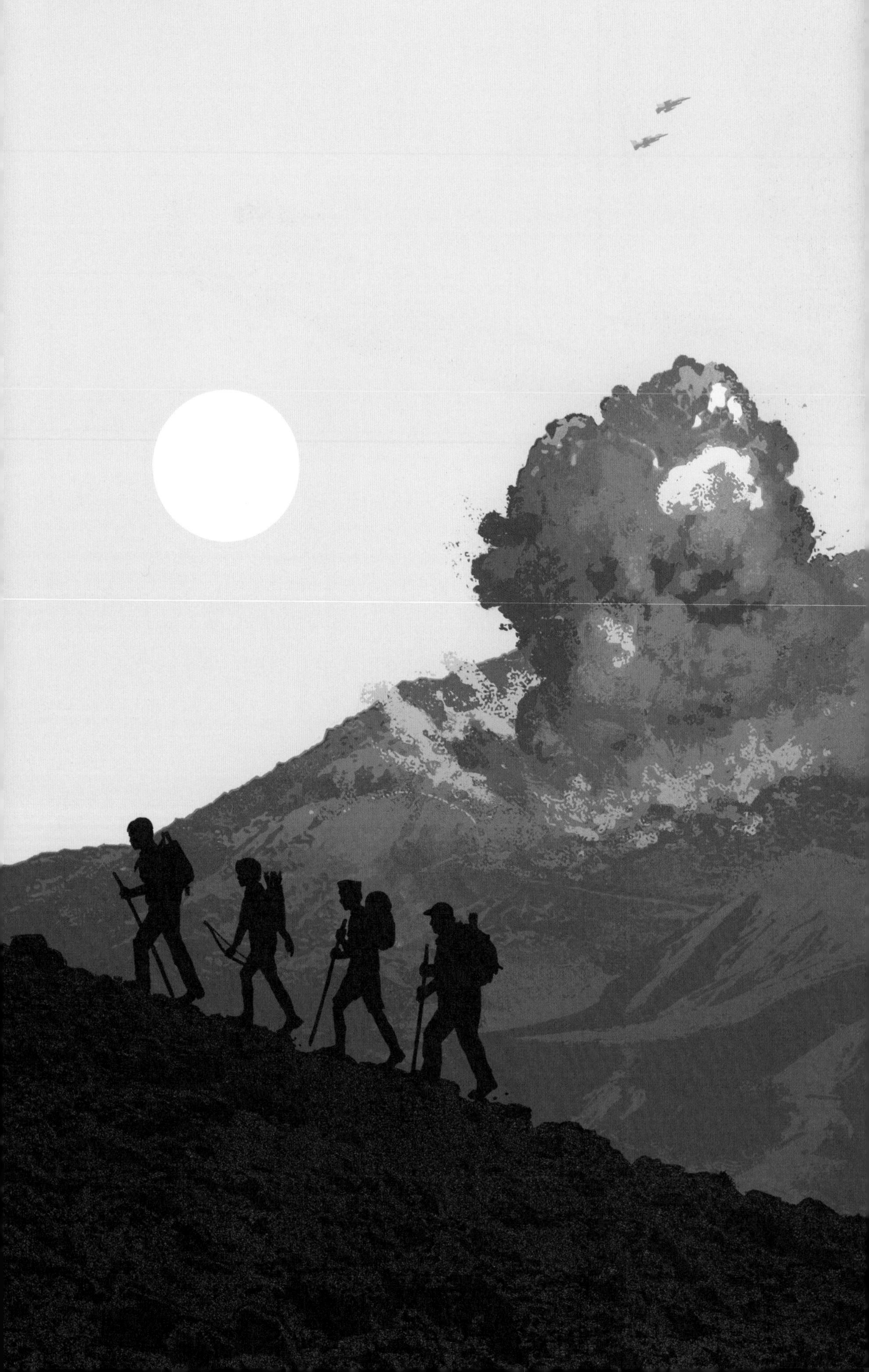

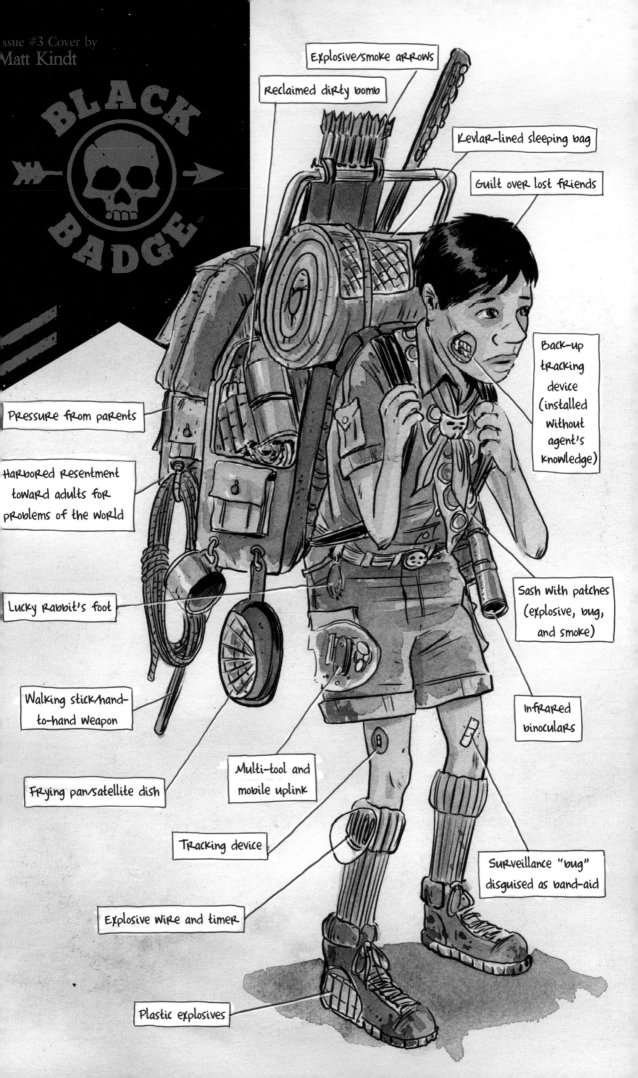

ssue #3 Cover by
Matt Kindt

BLACK BADGE™

Explosive/smoke arrows

Reclaimed dirty bomb

Kevlar-lined sleeping bag

Guilt over lost friends

Back-up tracking device (installed without agent's knowledge)

Pressure from parents

Harbored resentment toward adults for problems of the world

Lucky rabbit's foot

Walking stick/hand-to-hand weapon

Frying pan/satellite dish

Multi-tool and mobile uplink

Tracking device

Explosive wire and timer

Sash with patches (explosive, bug, and smoke)

Infrared binoculars

Surveillance "bug" disguised as band-aid

Plastic explosives

Issue #3 Cover by
Tyler Jenkins
+ Hilary Jenkins

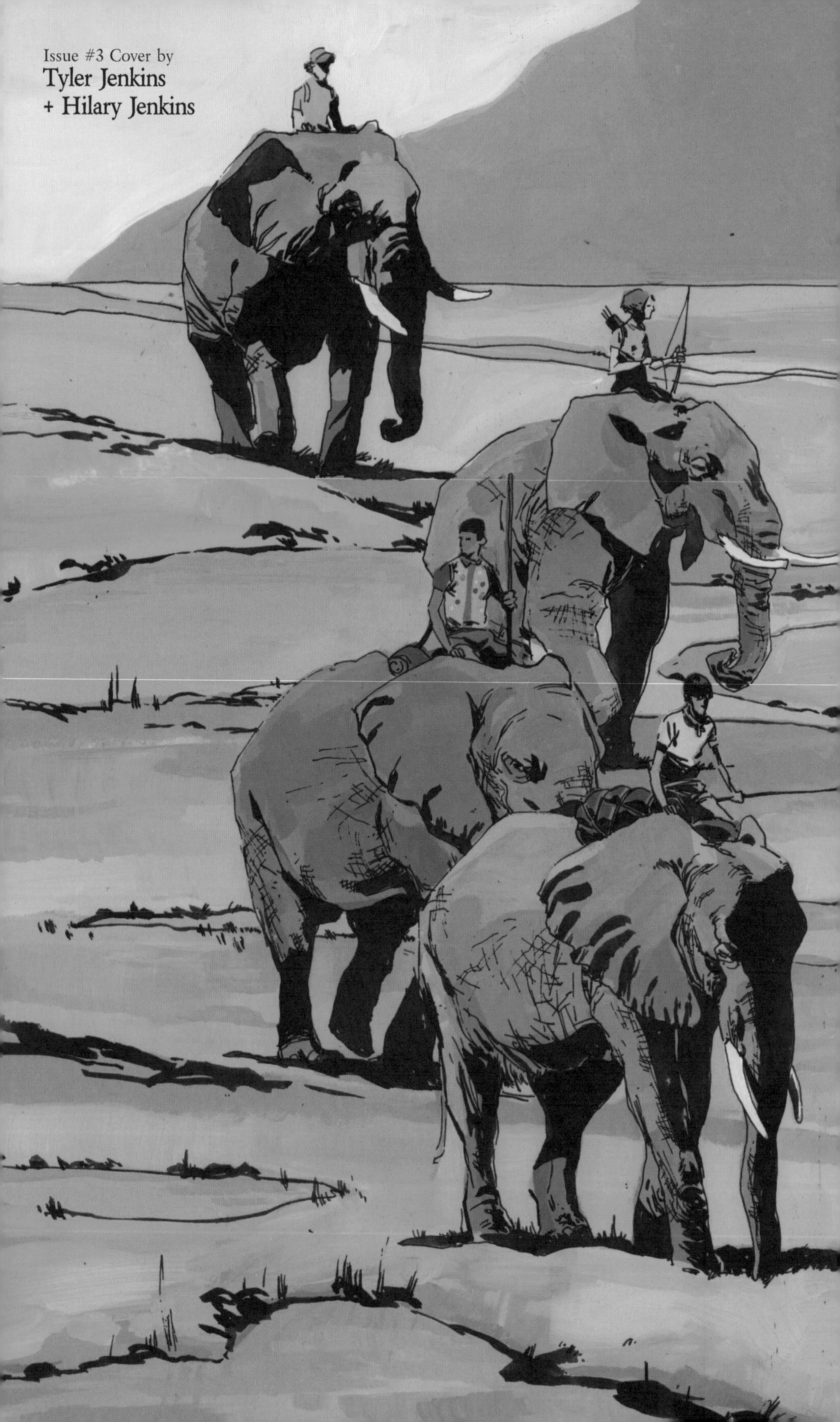

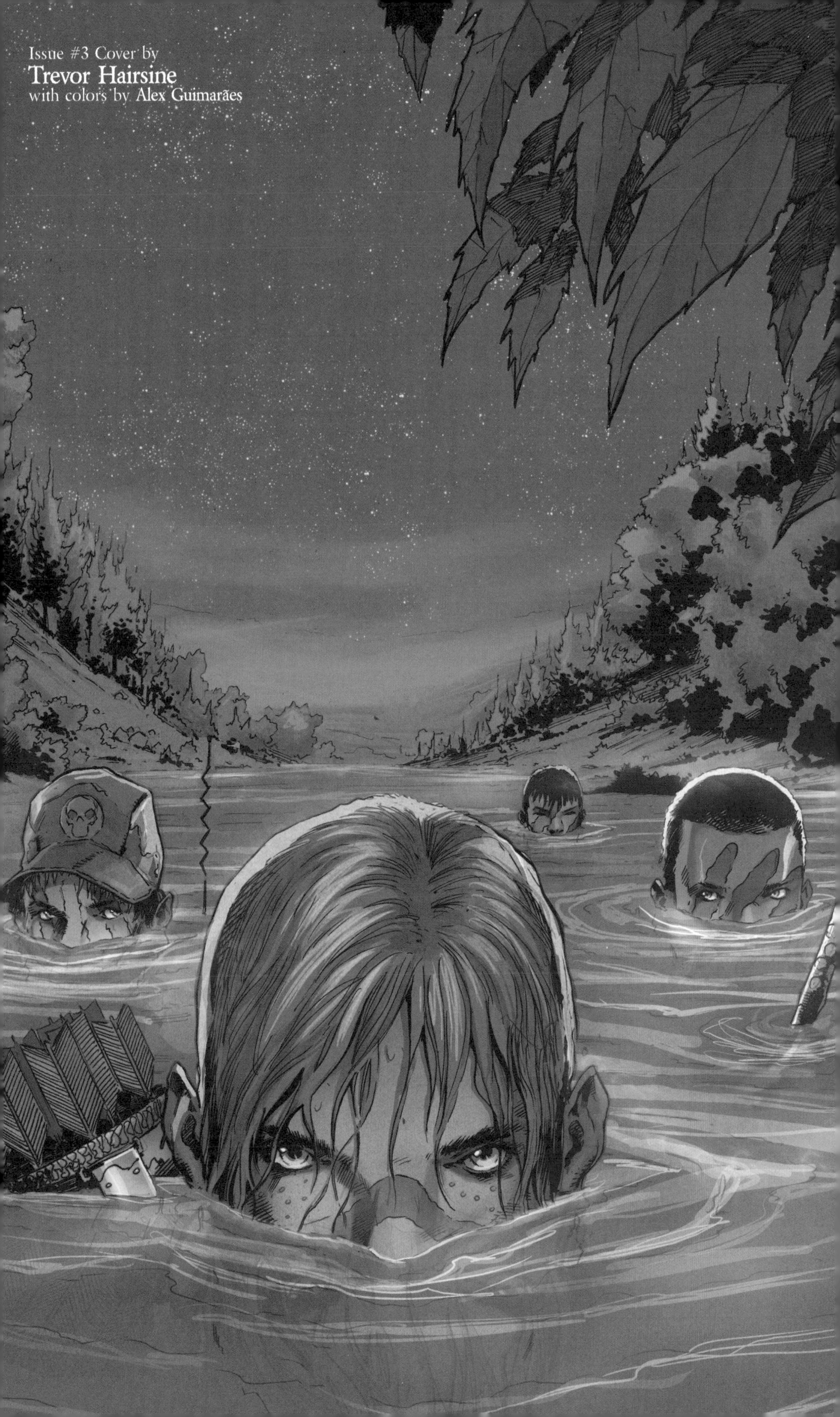

Issue #3 Cover by
Trevor Hairsine
with colors by Alex Guimarães

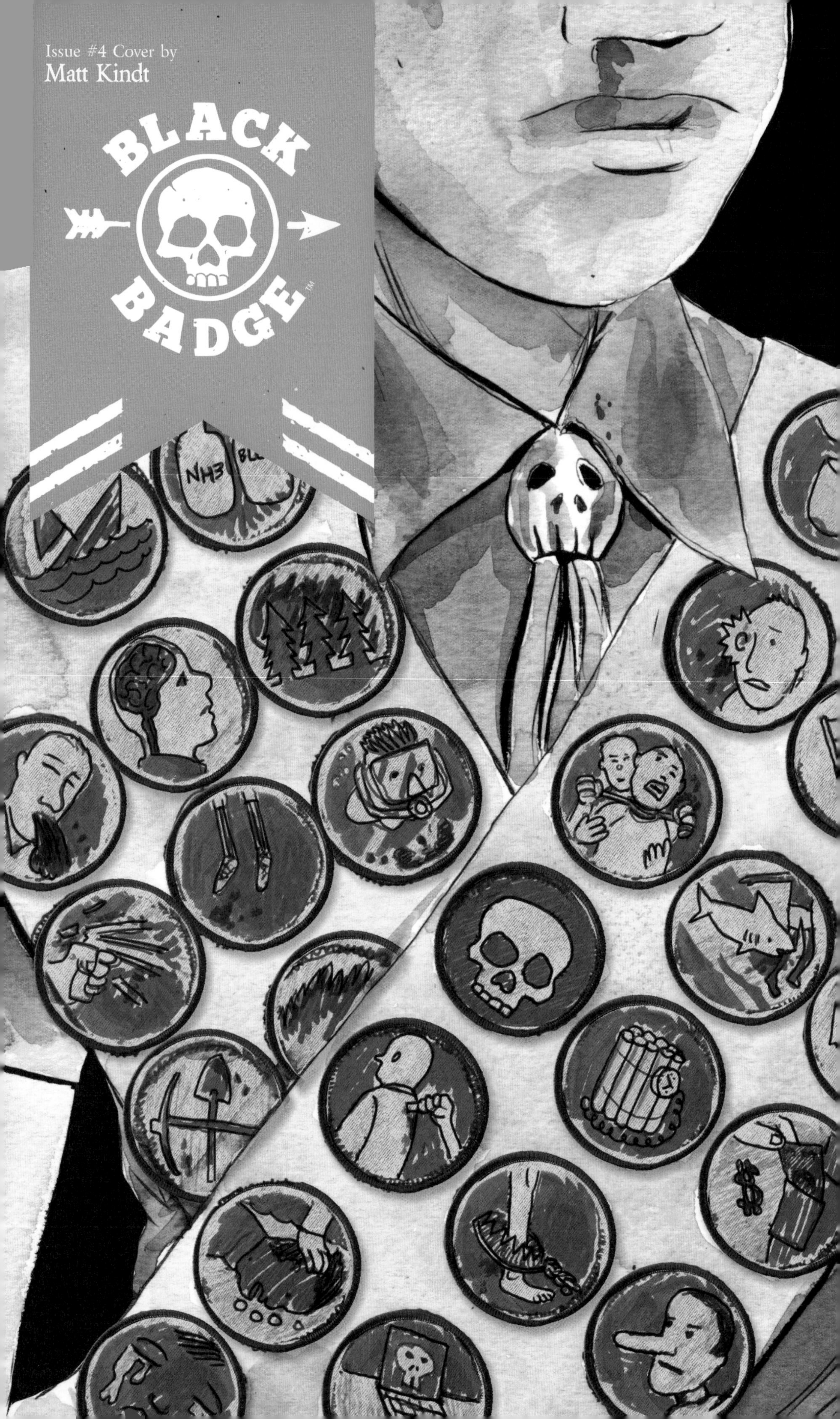
BLACK
BADGE™
NH3
Issue #4 Cover by
Matt Kindt

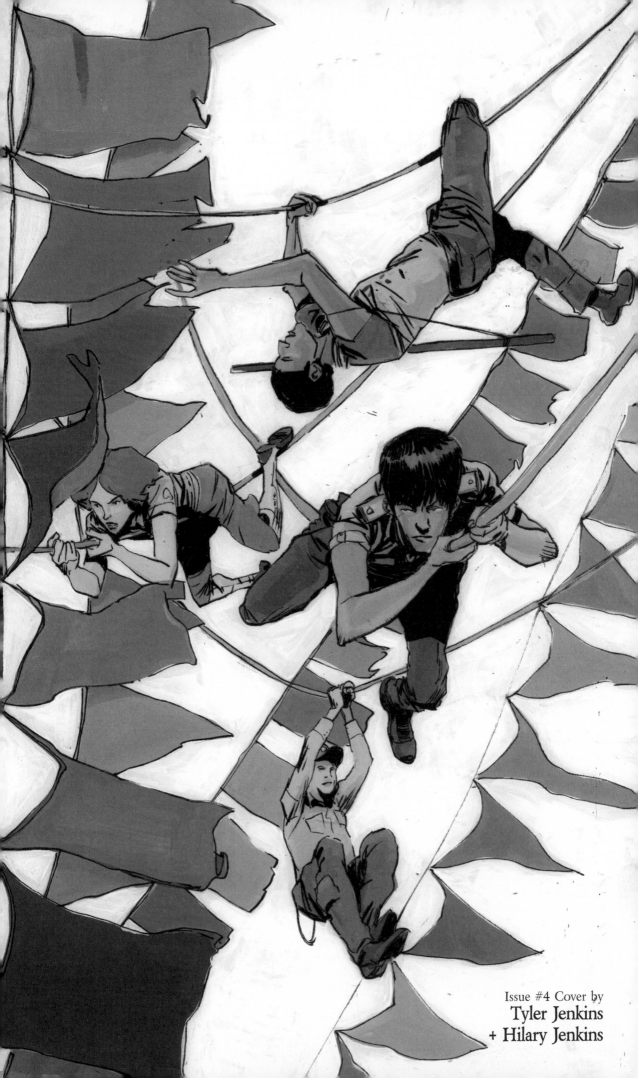

Issue #4 Cover by
Tyler Jenkins
+ Hilary Jenkins

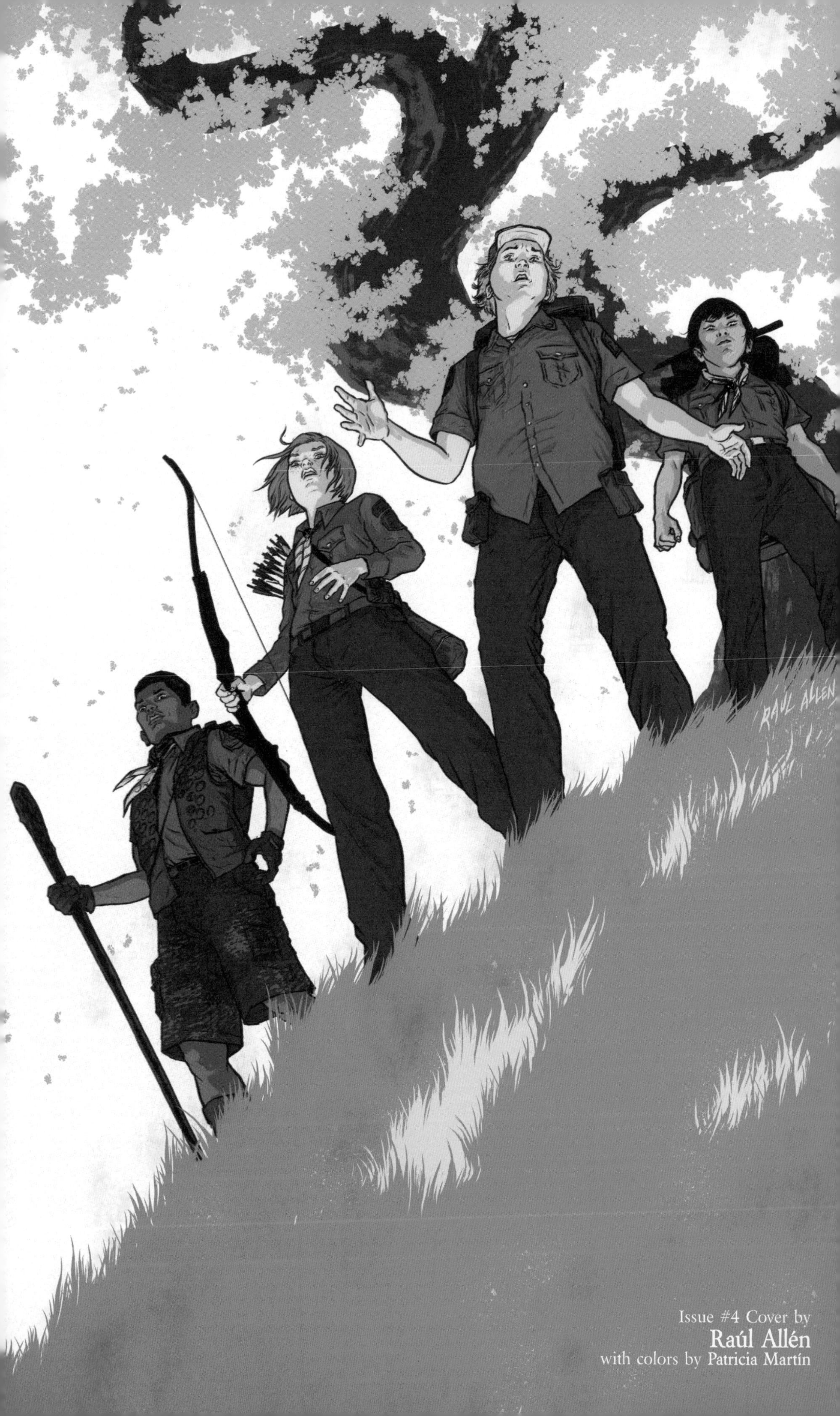
RAUL ALLEN

Issue #4 Cover by
Raúl Allén
with colors by Patricia Martín

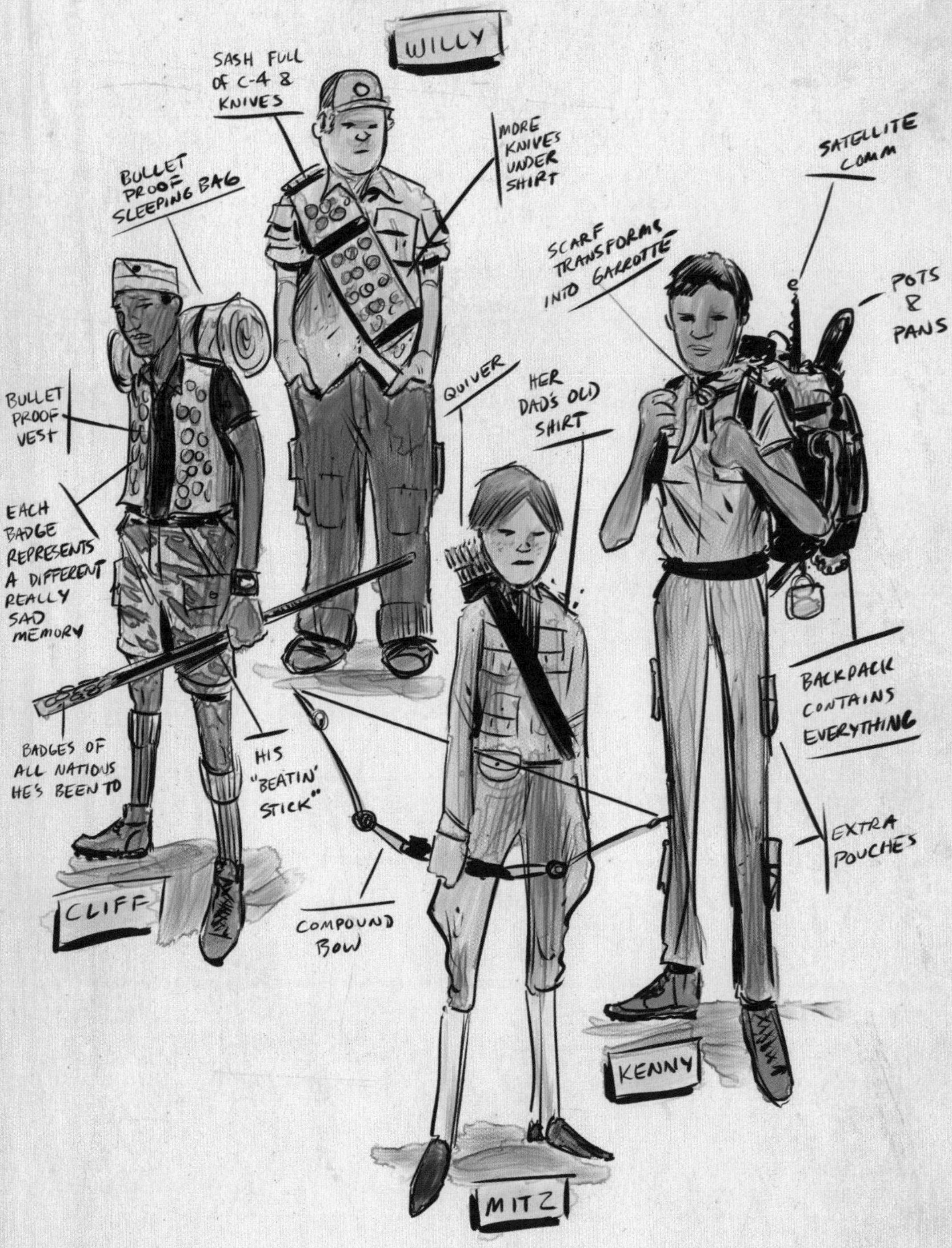
WILLY
SASH FULL OF C-4 & KNIVES
MORE KNIVES UNDER SHIRT
BULLET PROOF SLEEPING BAG
SATELLITE COMM
SCARF TRANSFORMS INTO GARROTTE
POTS & PANS
BULLET PROOF VEST
EACH BADGE REPRESENTS A DIFFERENT REALLY SAD MEMORY
QUIVER
HER DAD'S OLD SHIRT
BACKPACK CONTAINS EVERYTHING
BADGES OF ALL NATIONS HE'S BEEN TO
HIS "BEATIN' STICK"
EXTRA POUCHES
CLIFF
COMPOUND BOW
KENNY
MITZ

Character Designs by
Matt Kindt

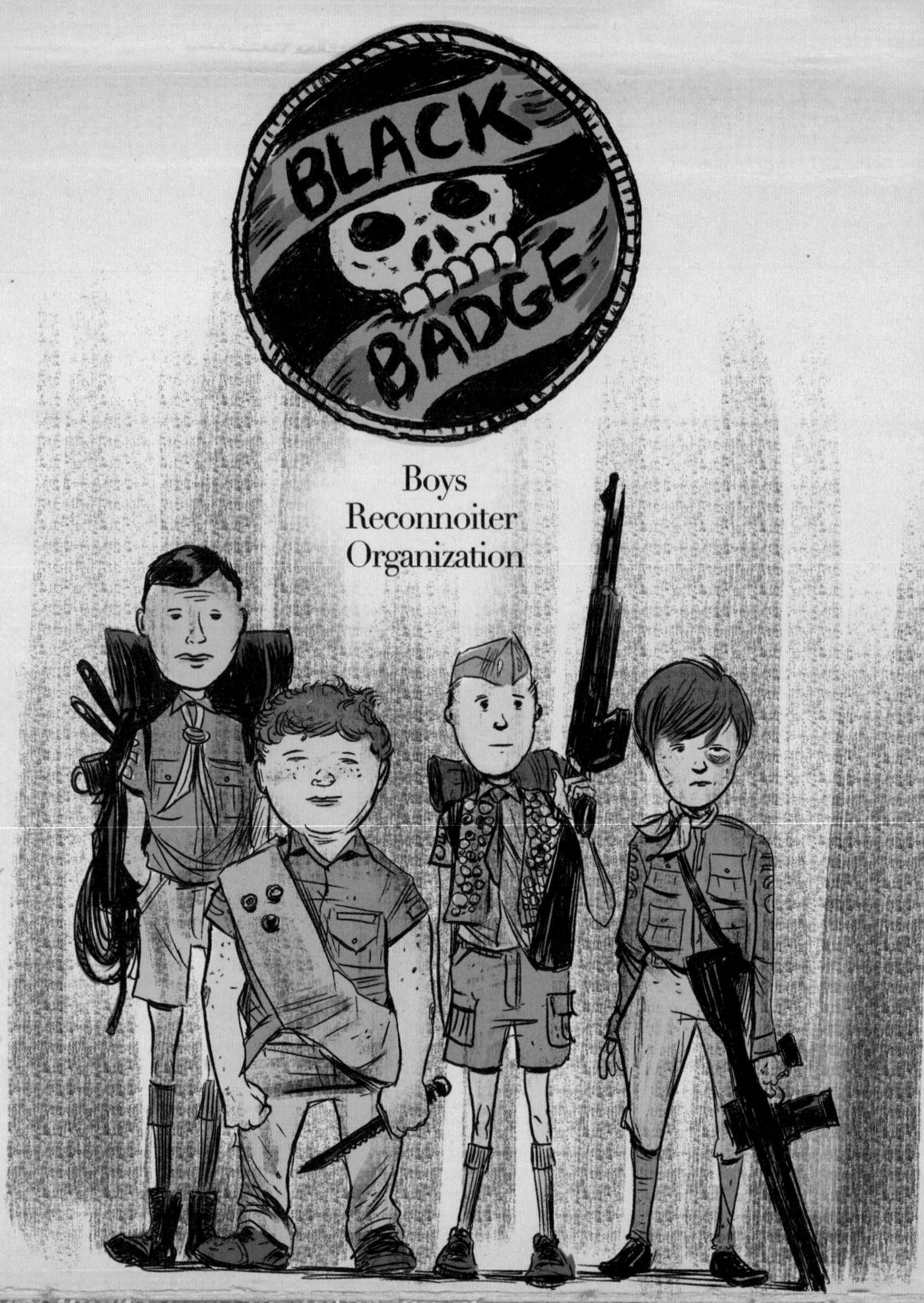
BLACK
BADGE
Boys
Reconnoiter
Organization

Always prepared.*

* for sabotage, demolitions, assassinations, and global upheaval.

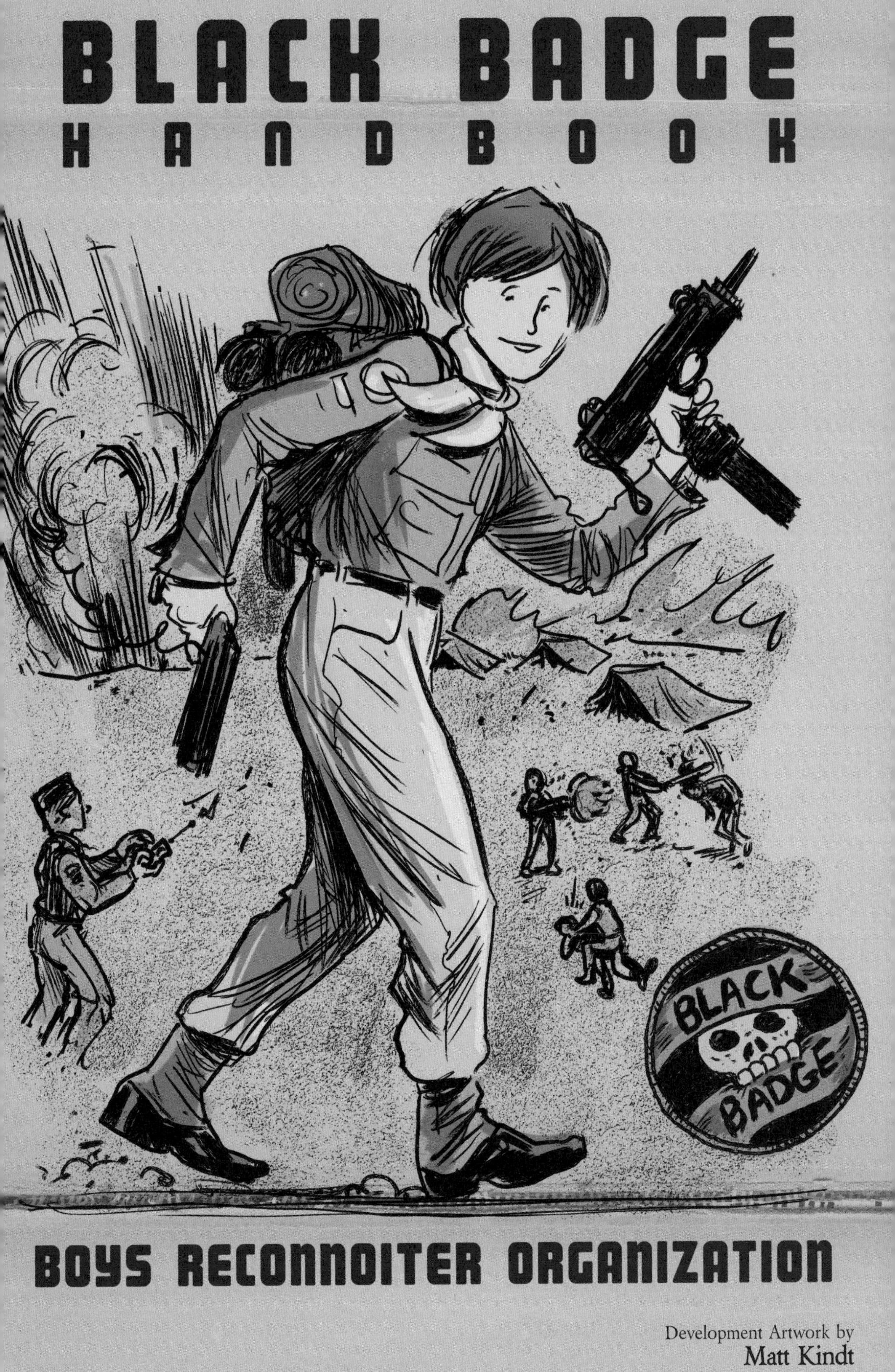
BLACK BADGE
HANDBOOK
BLACK
BADGE
BOYS RECONNOITER ORGANIZATION

Development Artwork by
Matt Kindt

Making of the Badge

Evolution of the *Black Badge* logo by
Matt Kindt and **Scott Newman**

[redacted] primary mission [redacted]
enemy lines [redacted]
Your Black Badge doubles as an explosive throwing sta

BLACK BADGE
est. 1910
No. 1

BLACK BADGE
est. 1910
No. 1

BLACK BADGE
est. 1910
Matt Kindt
Tyler Jenkins
No. 1

Matt Kindt
Tyler Jenkins
BLACK BADGE
No. 1

Matt Kindt
Tyler Jenkins
BLACK BADGE
No. 1

BLACK BADGE

Black Badge was founded in 1910 by William Rando
sub-branch of the American Boy Scouts. After the

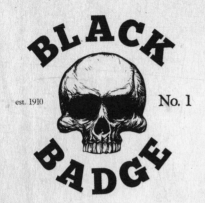

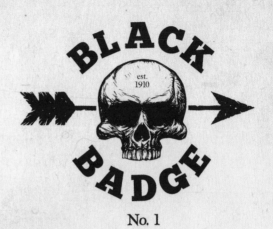

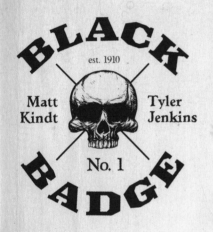

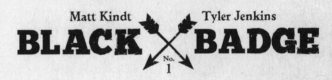

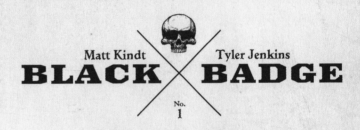

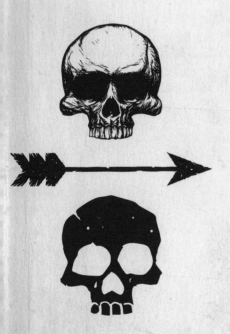

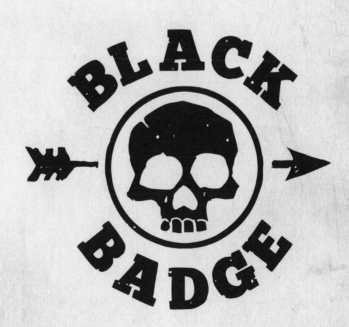

From Script to Page

Issue One Page Twenty-Four

Splash page.

The kids all walking towards us - looking super cool - but also miserable, dirty, and exhausted. Not happy.

We'll diagram and detail the kids here - echoing the opening scene with that douche Max - but now we see how cool these kids are.

KENNY: Let's go.

CAPTION: Willy. Comms expert. Equipped with the latest satellite and digital hacking equipment. Pants: Husky-sized.

primary mission

enemy lines

Your Black Badge doubles as an explosive throwing st

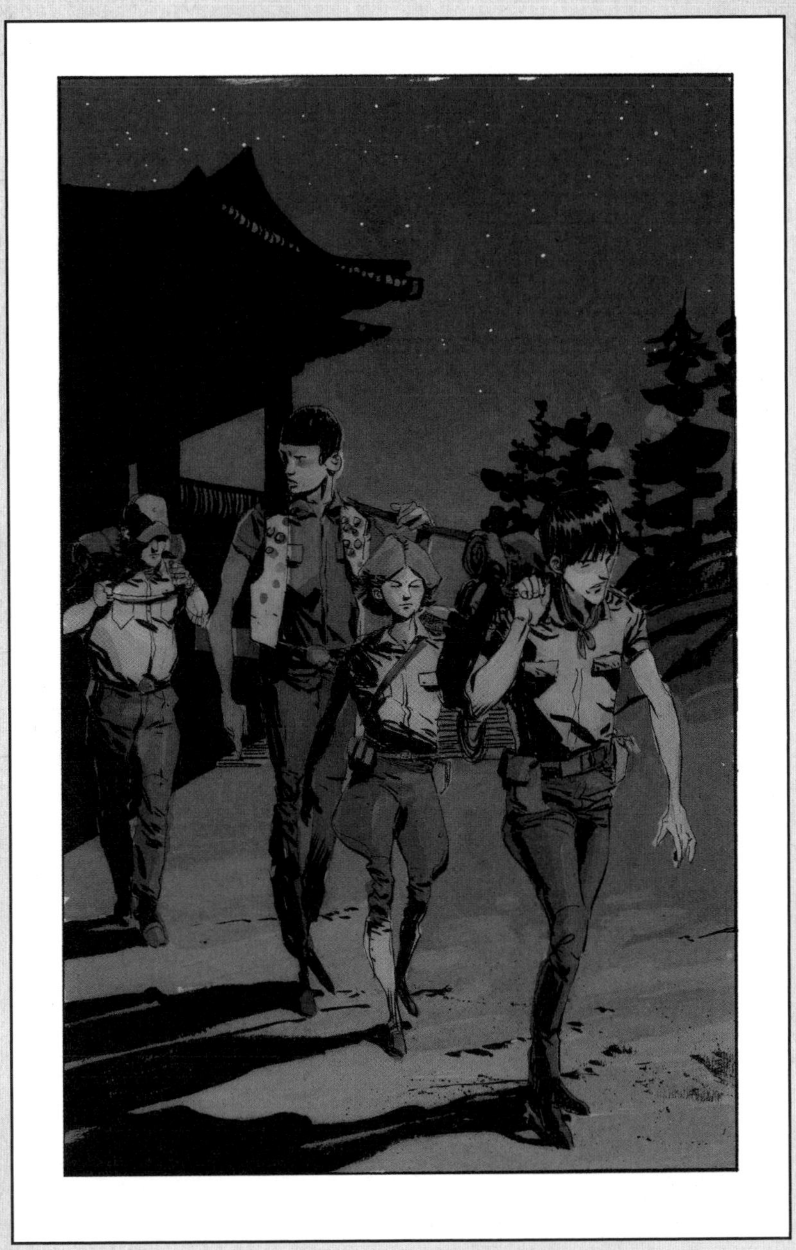

CAPTION: Cliff. Security specialist and hand-to-hand combat expert. "Walking stick" equipped with an array of trip-wire devices. His Mom is proud of him.

CAPTION: Mitz. Expert bowman and master of disguise. Belt-satchel contains specialty arrowheads, ideal for any situation. Hates marching bands.

CAPTION: Kenny. Group leader. Scarf transforms into garrote and backpack contains nearly everything (including frying pan).

TO BE CONTINUED.

Black Badge was founded in 1910 by William Rand
sub-branch of the American Boy Scouts. After the

ACK

DGE

uit Aptitude
ty Questionnaire

William Randolph Hearst as
ts. After the Boy Scouts of
name, the ABS was disbanded
ng active during both World
ng club in present day.

[redacted] locations [redacted] traction [redacted] threats [redacted] attack [redacted] scouts [redacted] impossible [redacted] enemy locations [redacted] threats [redacted] burn bags [redacted] combat zone [redacted]

BLACK BADGE
New Recruit Aptitude and Personality Questionnaire

This test is designed to judge your potential as a Black Badge recruit by systematically eliciting information regarding your personal interests, motivations, emotional stability, and decision-making. Complete the questionnaire to the best of your abilities and return the form to your assigned Black Badge handler before the time limit has expired.

CHEATING WILL RESULT IN IMMEDIATE EXPULSION AND ███████████████.

----

1. You see a turtle lying helpless on its back in the sun. Do you...

A. Eat it raw.
B. Cook it and then eat it.
C. Let the meat go rancid, serve it to your enemy, and then use the sharpened turtle shell to cut your enemy's jugular while they're suffering from food poisoning.

2. There is a trolley coming down the tracks. Ahead of the trolley there are five people tied to the tracks. The trolley will kill the five people. The only way to save the five people is to pull a lever. The lever will direct the train to another track where one person is tied. Do you...

A. Break the lever so no one ever has to make this decision again.
B. Remotely activate the C-4 you planted on the trolley beforehand, taking out the person on the trolley who is responsible for this situation in the first place.
C. You pre-arranged to have the five human targets tied to the tracks, so you simply turn and walk away. Job well done.

3. You and a teammate are caught behind enemy lines. Both of you are confined away from each other. They agree to let you go if you rat out your teammate, who will be imprisoned for three years. If you remain silent, you will both be tortured. If both you and your teammate remain silent, you will be imprisoned for one year. You are in isolation, so you have no way of knowing what your teammate is going to decide. What do you do?

A. Eat your cyanide tooth.
B. Use the C-4 hidden in your ████████ to take out yourself and the guards.
C. Feed your cyanide capsule to your teammate and then keep your mouth shut. It's the only way to be sure.

4. Your teammate dispatches an enemy target. Later, an innocent person is convicted of killing the enemy target and is sentenced to life in prison. Do you...

A. Applaud as your teammate accepts the Black Badge award for Successful Diversionary Tactics.
B. Recruit the innocent person with the promise of freedom if they will only complete a few prison missions.
C. Burn down the prison.

(TURN SHEET OVER TO CONTINUE)

Attention potential new recruit,

Congratulations! From among all of your peers, you have been selected to participate in an advanced program designed to develop your skills and worldview beyond what is normally expected of young adults.

By signing and returning this letter you are officially swearing the oath below:

I will follow orders without question.
I will keep my mouth shut.
I will show emotion only in cases where there is something to gain.
I will handle high-explosives with care.
I will not let the sight of blood affect me.

And finally:

I will faithfully read the newsletter and informational packet disguised as the comic book "Black Badge" every month.

Signed_____ Date_____

This message was approved by **BOOM!** Studios
(a Black Badge parent company)

sub-branch of the American Boy Scouts. After the Boy Scouts o
America sued Hearst for use of the name, the ABS was disbande
but Black Badge remained* - becoming active during both Wor
Wars and as a sort of elite scouting club in present day.

About the Authors

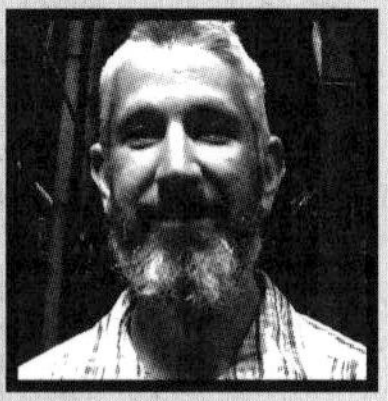

Matt Kindt is the *New York Times* best-selling writer and artist of the comics and graphic novels *Dept. H*, *Mind MGMT*, *Revolver*, *3 Story*, *Super Spy*, *2 Sisters*, and *Pistolwhip*, as well as the writer of *Grass Kings*, *Ether*, *Justice League of America* (DC), *Spider-Man* (Marvel), *Unity*, *Ninjak*, *Rai*, and *Divinity* (Valiant). He has been nominated for six Eisner and six Harvey Awards (and won once). His work has been published in French, Spanish, Italian, German and Korean.

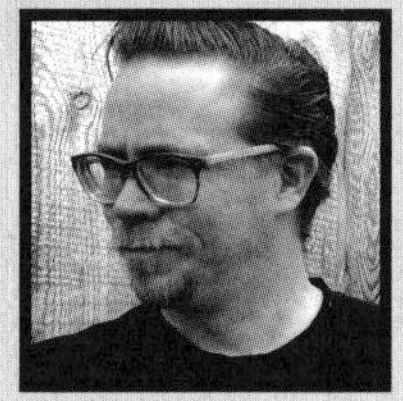

Tyler Jenkins is a dude who draws comics, makes art and music, and on occasion barbecues a mean back of ribs. Notable accomplishments include the multiple Eisner Award-nominated series *Grass Kings* with Matt Kindt and BOOM! Studios, as well as their follow-up series *Black Badge*. Tyler is also known for creating *Peter Panzerfaust* with Kurtis Wiebe and handling art duties on *Snow Blind* with Ollie Masters and *Neverboy* with Shaun Simon. Tyler lives in rural Alberta, Canada, with his wife, three small child-like creatures, and more gophers than you can shove in a tin pail. Find him at tylerjenkinsprojects on Instagram.

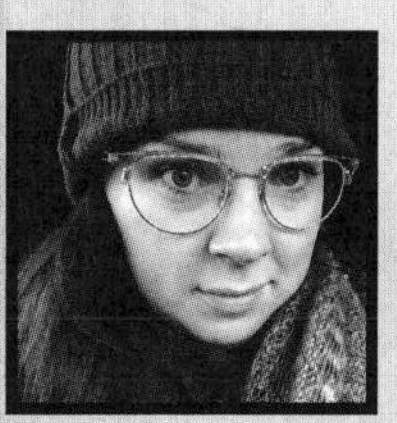

Hilary Jenkins' love for painting has helped create the unconventional process which she uses to color comics. After having used watercolor in the BOOM! series *Grass Kings*, she was ready to challenge herself with gouache. The highly opaque medium has allowed for the painterly style found in this book. Raised on a tiny little island off the coast of Vancouver, she was mentored by artist David Barker. Most everything she knows about painting can be attributed to his guidance and her own unshakable wonder of the world.

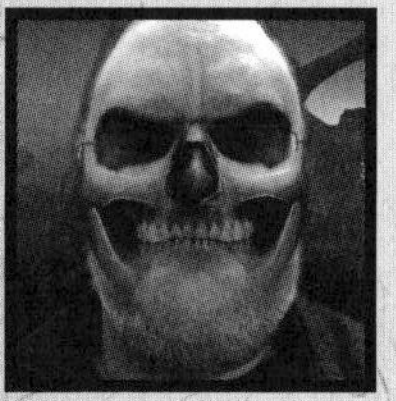

Jim Campbell has been lettering comics professionally for almost a decade, before which he worked in newspaper and magazine publishing for even longer. He knows more about print production than mortal man was meant to know and has also scanned more images than you've had hot dinners. Unless you're ninety years old. If you're very unlucky, he might start talking to you about ligatures.

GRASS KINGS™

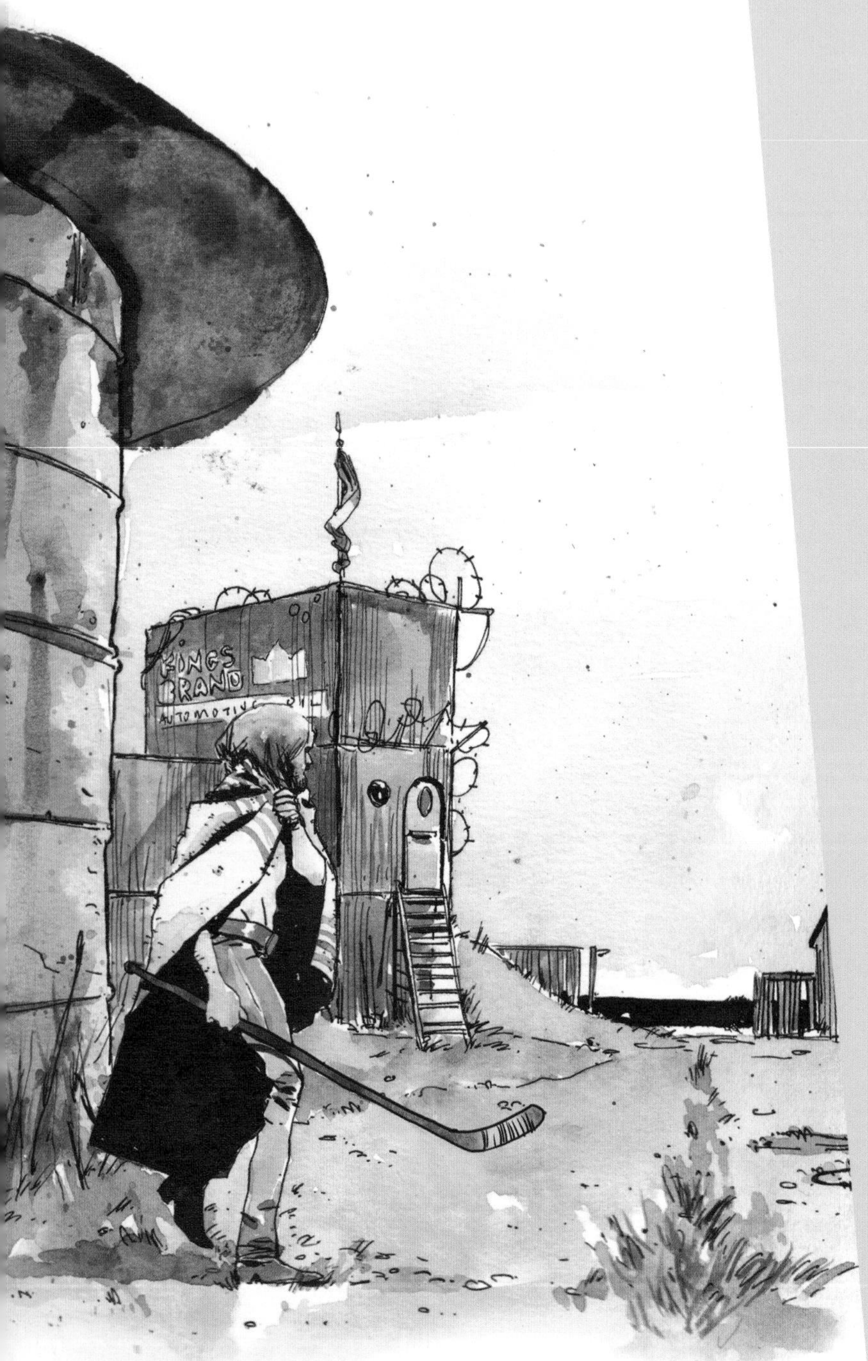

FROM *NEW YORK TIMES* BESTSELLING AUTHOR
MATT KINDT
(MIND MGMT)
AND ILLUSTRATORS
TYLER JENKINS & HILARY JENKINS
(BLACK BADGE)

"It is...amazing. GET IT."
—Patton Oswalt
(Star of Syfy's *Happy!*)

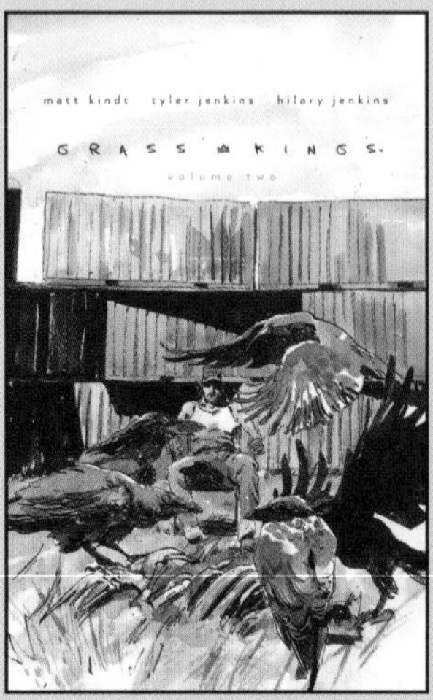
matt kindt tyler jenkins hilary jenkins
GRASS KINGS
volume two

VOLUME 2
ON SALE NOW!

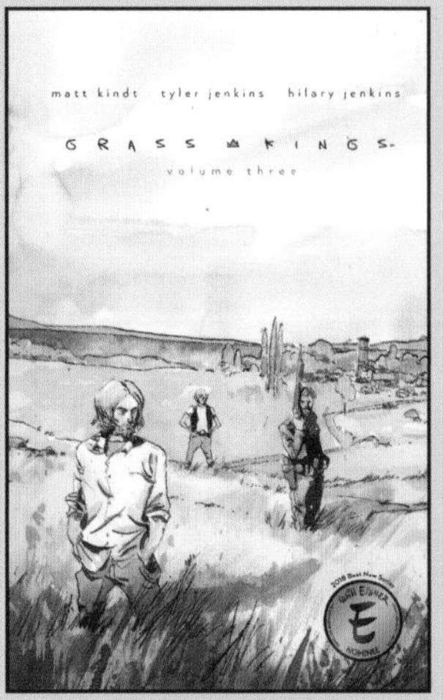
matt kindt tyler jenkins hilary jenkins
GRASS KINGS
volume three

VOLUME 3
ON SALE NOW!

VOLUME 1 **ON SALE NOW!**

BOOM! STUDIOS **DISCOVER** YOURS

/BOOMStudiosComics /boomstudios
/boom_studios boomstudios.
WWW.**BOOM-STUDIOS**.COM